The New
Role of Women

Social Inequality Series
Marta Tienda and David B. Grusky, Series Editors

The New
Role of Women

Family Formation in
Modern Societies

EDITED BY

Hans-Peter Blossfeld

Westview Press

BOULDER • SAN FRANCISCO • OXFORD

Social Inequality Series

Copyright © 1995 by Westview Press, Inc.

Published in 1995 in the United States of America by Westview Press, Inc., 5500 Central Avenue, Boulder, Colorado 80301-2877, and in the United Kingdom by Westview Press, 12 Hid's Copse Road, Cumnor Hill, Oxford OX2 9JJ

Library of Congress Cataloging-in-Publication Data
Blossfeld, Hans-Peter
   The new role of women : family formation in modern societies / edited by Hans-Peter Blossfeld.
      p.   cm. — (Social inequality series)
   Includes bibliographical references.
   ISBN 0-8133-2306-1
   1. Family—Longitudinal method.   2. Women—Employment—Longitudinal method.   I. Title.   II. Series.
HQ518.B6335   1995
306.85—dc20   94-46250
                                                                          CIP

Printed and bound in the United States of America

⊗   The paper used in this publication meets the requirements
     of the American National Standard for Permanence of Paper
     for Printed Library Materials Z39.48-1984.

10   9   8   7   6   5   4   3   2   1

Contents

Foreword

The second "demographic transition" has taken the form of secular declines in rates of entry into marriage and motherhood coupled with rising rates of unmarried cohabitation. These trends have been interpreted variously, but the prevailing view seems to be that the family and its associated institutions have become less attractive to women as they accumulate increasing amounts of work-related human capital and enter the formal labor force in record numbers. As Gary Becker argues in *A Treatise on the Family*, the opportunity costs of marriage and motherhood are often prohibitively high for educated women, since their (potential) earnings are foregone in the context of families with a traditional sex-based division of labor. The "independence hypothesis" of Becker has attracted much scholarly fanfare, but until now it has not been subjected to rigorous cross-national and longitudinal analysis.

In this pathbreaking volume, Hans-Peter Blossfeld and his colleagues provide a long-awaited test of the independence hypothesis. The simple premise underlying their analyses is that educational investments may not always depress rates of family formation because there is much variability within the modern world in the extent to which these investments have an economic payoff *within the family* and are therefore attractive to women intending to marry and have children. Although highly educated women in all countries will likely postpone marriage while still in school, it is only in "traditional" countries (in which work and family cannot be readily combined) that Blossfeld expects such women to continue to delay marriage and motherhood even during the post-schooling period. The analyses presented here are largely consistent with the foregoing revision and elaboration of the independence hypothesis. The publication of this volume therefore marks the coming of age of a distinctively sociological approach to the second demographic transition; that is, the analyses featured here suggest that trends in family formation cannot be understood exclusively in terms of individual-level investments, if only because the institutional context in which these investments may be realized is cross-nationally quite variable.

The strength of this effort owes much to its hybrid methodology that combines the benefits of scholarly collaboration with the sharply focused intellectual agenda typically found only in authored research monographs. As Blossfeld outlines in the preface to this volume, the collaborators were all asked to abide by a shared analytic template, yet they were also permitted and encouraged to deviate from this template whenever a rigid insistence on standardization would conceal distinctive national features and thus come at too high a price. This approach makes it possible, then, to compare and contrast a large number of cases while still incorporating national idiosyncrasies into the analysis. The further advantage of such an approach is that the inevitable diversity of opinion among expert scholars can be fairly represented; indeed, whereas the tendency among authors of conventional research monographs is to attempt to fashion a coherent and seamless story, such pretense is abandoned here in favor of an open and explicit airing of differences in interpretation (see Chapter 3).

This volume should be required reading for all sociologists who are losing faith in the discipline and its many achievements. If there is indeed a disciplinary malaise, it may be partly attributable to the wide terrain of subjects that sociologists cover and the relatively slow progress that can therefore be anticipated on any single front. In this regard, the great virtue of the research model fashioned here is that it galvanizes some of the top scholars in the field around a single intellectual problem, thereby making rapid and immediate progress possible. We are most pleased to welcome the resulting volume into the Social Inequality Series.

David B. Grusky
Stanford University

Marta Tienda
University of Chicago

Preface

This is an international comparative study on changes in the process of family formation and the new role of women in modern industrial societies. We used longitudinal data to examine the validity of the common view that women's growing economic independence has had a critical and presumably irreversible impact on the family system in modern societies.

The notion that the sexual division of labor in the family and in the labor market produces interdependence and organic solidarity was first presented by Emile Durkheim. It was further advanced by William J. Goode, Robert F. Bales, and Talcott Parsons in their structural-functionalist approach, in which they assumed that the traditional sex-role differentiation is important for the stability of the family and even for modern society itself. Parsons in particular believed that men specialize in gainful employment and women in work within the family to prevent disruptive competition between the spouses. More recently, the importance of sex-specific roles for the stability of the family system was also stressed in the "new home economics." Gary S. Becker, its main proponent, argued that growth in the earning power of women in modern societies is the most important factor in the long-term decline of marriage and fertility. According to Becker, women's growing earning power not only reduces the appeal marriage has held for men and women (because the sexual division of labor is less advantageous for both sexes), it also increases the value of the mother's time, raising the relative costs of children and thereby reducing the demand for children.

Indeed, the family in modern industrialized societies has been changing more rapidly since the end of World War II than during any equivalent earlier period. Nevertheless, it can still be contested whether women's rising earning power is one of the most critical factors in this process. By focusing on changes in the process of family formation in several modern industrialized countries, we empirically attempt to explore the extent to which women's rising human capital investments have indeed been responsible for the change in the rates of entry into marriage and motherhood.

The idea for this international comparative project was stimulated by a surprising finding Johannes Huinink and I made during an event history study carried out in West Germany.[1] This research showed that (1) the entry of West German women into marriage and motherhood was not influenced by their level of educational attainment, and (2) their level of career resources had virtually no effect on the rate of first marriage and only slightly affected the timing of first motherhood. Instead, the study revealed that extended schooling of successive birth cohorts of women was the most important factor responsible for change in the process of family formation in West Germany. An increasing number of better-educated women only temporarily postponed their entry into marriage and the birth of a first child. Thus, it was not the *level* of labor market–related human capital investments of women but *the time it took to acquire qualifications* that seemed to be the driving force behind change in the process of family formation in West Germany.

These findings indicated that the common view, which holds that women's rising earning power is the most critical factor in changing family formation of modern societies, is theoretically and empirically unwarranted. In theoretical terms, educational expansion in connection with normative expectations that young people who attend school are "not ready" to enter marriage and parenthood seems to be far more important for changes in the process of family formation than women's growing economic independence. In empirical terms, support for the hypotheses of the economic theory of the family, which has been claimed on the basis of cross-sectional and aggregated time-series data, is likely to be a product of the specific methods and type of data used. This data cannot differentiate between the effect of accumulation of human capital over the life course and the effect of school enrollment in keeping women out of the marriage market.

The primary interest in our nine-nation comparison was therefore to test the generality of our earlier findings and interpretations. To maintain sufficient similarity and to prevent our comparison from being too complex, we limited our study to modern Western industrial societies. In order to maximize variations in family systems and take into consideration the inevitable constraints of data availability and expertise, we chose to compare the United States, Great Britain, Sweden, the Netherlands, France, West Germany, Hungary, Italy, and Spain.

Our agenda was both theoretical and empirical. From a theoretical point of view, we wanted to know whether our earlier substantive conclusions with respect to women's growing economic independence and school enrollment would hold true in the other countries or would indicate the existence of nation-specific institutions and traditions particular to West Germany. The impact of institutions is hard to discern in a single country analysis. Perhaps this is why most family and demographic theories fail to recognize them. In the economic theory of the family, the prediction that women's growing economic independence is the major determinant of recent demographic shifts is derived from a quite specific family model. It is the "conventional" or "traditional" conjugal family, with rigid role segregation of husband and wife. Although it is hard to imagine that any real family system has ever satisfied all of the strong model assumptions made by this formalized theory, existing family systems do at least to a varying degree conform to this model. The societies studied in this book vary widely in terms of distribution of household types (single, married, divorced), age when children leave the parental home, proportion and significance of consensual unions, fertility rate, stability of marriage, and rate of entry into remarriage. Thus, there is another important question we chose to examine; we wanted to know whether the impact of women's growing economic independence was stronger in those countries having a more "conventional" or "traditional" family system. Our premise here is that the influence of women's economic independence on family formation had been decreasing within the course of development and differentiation of modern family systems.

From an empirical point of view, the purpose of our cross-societal analysis was to utilize longitudinal data and methods to study the dynamic relationship between the changes in the role of women and the development in family formation. In pursuing this goal, we reviewed the most recent developments and long-term trends, studied the change across successive birth cohorts of women in various countries, and included the most important factors influencing changes in family formation over time in the statistical models. Due to the complexity of data for every country involved, it was important to engage at least one resourceful demographer or sociologist living in the respective society to conduct those studies. This intimate knowledge on the specifics of different societies was then fused to our collective effort to make this cross-societal research project as coherent and consolidated as possible. It was for this purpose that I organized a workshop in Florence in 1991 to discuss the first drafts of the research group and make the country-specific analyses comparable.

The book is divided into four sections. In the introductory chapter, I develop the theoretical framework of the cross-national comparative project, describe the common methodology, summarize the main results of the country-specific analyses, and draw some more general conclusions. Part Two presents nine country-specific studies on women's rising educational attainment and changes in the process of family formation. Part Three discusses the findings of the country-specific studies from two quite different perspectives. These two chapters are written by authors from whom I have learned a great deal with respect to the relationship between the new role of women and the changes in the family system in modern industrial societies. Annemette Sørensen is quite supportive of the independence argument. She concludes that the results of the country-specific studies do not seem to contradict the economic theory of the family. Valerie K. Oppenheimer is skeptical of the independence hypothesis. She questions Sørensen's conclusion and argues that Sørensen "saves" the independence argument by being incapable of explaining the enormous changes in family formation already observed. Finally, in Part Four, Johannes Huinink examines whether the process of family formation in West Germany is different for men and women and to what extent it is dependent upon patterns of sex-role segregation in modern societies.

As organizer of the cross-national research project and editor of the book, I want to thank the individual contributors for their fruitful cooperation and for the enormous amount of work they put into their manuscripts. All the chapters in the book were peer-reviewed by the members of the project and revised several times. They were then evaluated by an anonymous Westview

Press reviewer; I am grateful for his/her thoughtful and helpful comments. I also wish to give my heartfelt thanks to David Grusky and Marta Tienda, who encouraged me to publish this volume in their Social Inequality Series.

Special thanks go to Clare Tame at the European University Institute in Florence, who served as the production editor of this volume. She helped me organize the workshop, coordinate the review process of the book chapters, and improve the linguistic quality of the book by extensive stylistic editing. After my move to Bremen University in summer 1992, Julie Winkler-Vinjukova took care of the book manuscript. She coordinated the final revisions of the volume and provided valuable assistance during the last stage of the editing process, for which I am very grateful.

Finally, I would like to express my appreciation to the Research Council of the European University Institute in Florence and the University of Bremen for their financial support, which enabled me to facilitate the editing of this volume. I also thank the Commission of the European Communities, Directory General for Employment, Industrial Relations and Social Affairs (DG V/C/1) in Brussels for their grant supporting the workshop in Florence in November 1991.

Hans-Peter Blossfeld

Notes

1. Blossfeld, H.-P., and J. Huinink (1991), "Human Capital Investments or Norms of Role Transition? How Women's Schooling and Career Affect the Process of Family Formation," *American Journal of Sociology*, 97, 143–68.

PART ONE

Introduction

1

Changes in the Process of Family Formation and Women's Growing Economic Independence: A Comparison of Nine Countries

HANS-PETER BLOSSFELD

Over the past three decades the process of family formation and structure of households has changed dramatically in all European countries and the United States.[1] The trend toward early and universal marriage observed for the first two-thirds of the century has been reversed, with age at first marriage now rising much faster than it fell during the previous period. Most countries are faced with low levels of fertility and an increasing age at entry into first motherhood across birth cohorts, and previously rare family types such as single-parent families, female-headed families and *de facto* unions have become increasingly common.[2]

These changes have not occurred in isolation, and are part of major transformations of the family and household relationships in modern societies (Moen 1992). They point to the role of changing societal institutions which now structure the life-courses of individuals in modern societies differently (White 1990). We observe a re-evaluation of the role of women in society, together with increasing female labor-force participation and better career opportunities for women.[3] The occupational structure of the labor force is being transformed, and the number of women in higher education has risen (Blossfeld 1985, 1987, 1990; Tölke 1989).

Trends in marriage and fertility have been charted for many industrial societies, but empirical work has relied overwhelmingly on the analysis of cross-sectional data (Prioux 1990; Murphy 1991). Although there have recently been several important exceptions, most of what we know about changes in the family system and its relationship to developments in the educational system and the labor market comes from census reports or surveys, each referring to distributions at a single point in time. Yet comparative-static analysis cannot easily reveal the causal processes at work (Aalen 1988). We think that it is important to embed macrosociological arguments about the relationship of socioeconomic trends and changes in the family system in a microsociological dynamic framework, so that the various dimensions of this process can be disentangled at the level of the life course of individuals. In a seminal article Glenn Elder described this approach as follows:

> The life course refers to pathways through the age-differentiated life span, to so-cial patterns in the timing, duration, spacing, and order of events; the timing of an event may be as consequential for life experience as whether the event occurs and the degree or type of change. ... Such differentiation is based in part on the social meaning of age and the biological facts of birth, sexual maturity and death. These meanings have varied through social history and across cultures at points in time, as documented by evidence on socially recognized age categories, grades and classes. ... Over the life course, age differentiation also occurs through the inter-play of demographic and economic processes, as in the relation between eco-nomic swings and the timing of family events. Sociocultural, demographic and material factors are essential elements in a theory of life-course variation. (Elder 1978:21–22)

Previous research has shown that structural changes in the educational sys-tem and the labor market are particularly connected with changes in the fam-ily system (Rindfuss and Hirschman 1984; Cooney and Hogan 1991; Kiernan 1992; Vannoy 1991). They engender attitude and value changes, which in turn affect the family (Alwin, Converse and Martin 1985; Trent and South 1989). As a consequence, in many modern countries the distinctions between marital and non-marital childbearing, marriage and consensual unions are losing their normative force, and marriage is becoming more of an option—espe-cially in highly developed welfare-state countries such as Sweden (Hoem and Rennermalm 1985; Hoem and Hoem 1987a, 1987b, 1992).

These arguments suggest a close relationship between family formation and modernization in all industrialized countries (Hareven 1976; Lesthaeghe 1983; Trovato 1986), but there are also great differences in the timing and tempo of changes in family formation between countries with similar levels of economic development (Muñoz-Pérez 1989; Prioux 1990, Kiernan 1993). This variation attests to the strength of dominant country-specific cultures, differ-ences in family traditions, and family policies in various industrialized coun-tries interacting with the process of modernization and producing different tempos and levels of nuptiality and fertility.

Much of the research in this volume concentrates on one specific aspect of this complex interrelationship between the modernization process and coun-try-specific family contexts: that is, the degree to which the impressive in-crease in women's educational attainment experienced by all industrialized countries (Blossfeld and Shavit 1993) affects the process of family formation within various country-specific family contexts. Our emphasis on women's educational attainment reflects our recognition of its importance in the re-search literature, together with the fact that it is an indirect indicator of labor-force participation and women's socioeconomic status (Mincer 1974; Kalleberg and Rosenfeld 1990).

Our collective research builds on previous analyses of determinants of the timing of entry into marriage and motherhood,[4] but goes beyond it in several respects. First, a theoretical framework is presented within which effects of important influences on the timing of entry into marriage and motherhood can be interpreted. In particular, it allows the identification of several dimensions of changes in women's educational attainment on the process of family formation. Second, a wider range of influences is included in most of the country-specific analyses than has been the case for much research to date. These include measures of age-dependencies of entry into marriage and motherhood, social class, participation in the educational system, level of education or cohort membership. Third, the process of family formation is studied on the basis of a continuous succession of birth cohorts. Thus, cohort comparisons not only reflect the most recent changes in the process of family formation in Europe, but can also be used to examine the long-term impact of educational expansion across a very broad range of birth cohorts. The latter aspect is theoretically interesting because the persistent rise in the proportion of women with better education across birth cohorts occurred during both the fall and rise in the age at marriage and first motherhood. Finally, this research presents the results of comparable studies of family formation for nine different countries, offering a range of variations in important variables such as industrial development and culture, political systems and history, and family traditions.

The countries examined in Part Two are Sweden, Italy, Great Britain, West Germany, Spain, the Netherlands, France, Hungary and the United States. Each study was conducted by researchers, who have an intimate understanding of the country in question, and most employed relatively recent nationally representative data, covering cohorts of women educated over a broad historical period. In particular, they studied changes in family formation for cohorts of women who entered marriage and motherhood over the past forty years. We also employed very similar statistical analyses, but preferred to avoid complete standardization of method because both the institutional structure of the educational system and family systems themselves varied from one country to another. However, we did attempt to maintain sufficient standardization to enable a systematic comparison of the results. Thus, almost all studies follow a common set of guidelines. The theoretical implication of their results is evaluated in Part Three.

In Part Four, the nine studies on changes in *women's* family formation are complemented by an analysis that focuses on *men*. It addresses the question of whether the life events in the process of transition to adulthood in West Germany are different for men and women, and to which extent this depends on patterns of sex-role segregation.

This introductory chapter is an attempt to synthesize the main results of the country-specific analyses, and is organized as follows: (1) a discussion of the effects of influences on the timing of entry into marriage and motherhood, and a summarization of the major changes in the process of family formation in modern industrialized countries is presented; (2) the three main hypotheses examined in this volume are developed; (3) a description of the data is given, with a discussion of the variables and models used; (4) the results of the country-specific studies are summarized; and finally, (5) some more general conclusions about the relationship between women's educational expansion and the process of family formation in Europe and the United States are drawn.

Hypotheses and Summary of Changes in Family Formation

Although much has been written on changes in family systems, explanations for changes in family formation are rare. Most theoretical frameworks point to the influence of changes in the larger social structure on the family system, and only indirectly, on the process of family formation. Women's timing of entry into consensual unions, marriage and motherhood can, however, be viewed as a function of several time-constant and time-dependent influences.

Age Dependence of Family Formation

A first, 'law-like' time-varying influence is the age-dependence of both entry processes. Empirical estimates of the rate of entry into marriage and motherhood reveal a non-monotonic age pattern for different countries, cohorts and social classes.[5] With increasing age, the rate of entry into marriage and motherhood initially increases up to a maximum and then decreases. There are at least three explanations for this bell-shaped relationship (Diekmann 1989).

A first explanation conceives age at marriage as the result of durations in two different states: 'not ready for marriage or motherhood' and 'ready for marriage or motherhood.' Coale and McNeil (1972), argued that the duration until entering the 'ready state for marriage' can be considered as normally distributed and that the search time prior to entry into marriage may be thought of as the sum of exponentially distributed durations. A combination of both durations over age then leads to the observed bell-shaped pattern over age. The second explanation is based on a search model (Diekmann 1987) where the readiness for marriage and motherhood increases linearly with age, and the degree of this increase varies in the population according to characteristics of the individuals. As a result, a bell-shaped aggregated population rate of entry into marriage and motherhood is observed. The third explanation considers entry into marriage and motherhood as a process of social diffusion. Hernes (1972) holds that there is some kind of social pressure exerted by people who are married or who have children, on those who are unmarried or childless within each cohort. He argues that with increasing age, there is an increasing social pressure, inducing imitation and a decreasing chance to find a partner, together leading to the observed bell-shaped age-dependence.

All three explanatory models refer to influences on the rate of entry into marriage and motherhood which are conceptually important, but hard—or even impossible—to measure. Another interesting example of such a variable, especially important for the analysis of younger birth cohorts, was recently mentioned by Hoem (1983, 1984), who describes distortions caused by non-observation of periods of cohabitation.

Given the empirical regularity of the bell-shaped age dependence in different countries, cohorts and social classes, it is reasonable to control for such types of unobserved heterogeneity in our country-specific analyses of entry into marriage and motherhood on the basis of measures of a non-monotonic age dependence.[6]

Class-Specific Orientations

Apart from unobserved heterogeneity, there are theoretically important influences which can be included in most of our country-specific models at least on the basis of proxy measures. Among these influences we count women's class-specific orientations towards marriage and motherhood, as it is well-known from the literature that socioeconomic background has a strong effect on ages at entry into marriage and motherhood (Mayer 1977; Kiernan and Diamond 1983; Michael and Tuma 1985; Marini 1985; Huinink 1987).

Three different components have been distinguished here (Haller 1981). The first concerns women's class-specific expectations regarding love and a marriage relationship, which influence the time when women consider themselves ready for marriage. The second involves the socioeconomic resources of a woman's family of origin. Thus, class differences in educational attainment and career are very important because it is most common for a woman to be out of school before entry into marriage and motherhood. And the third component is the class-structured mate-selection process itself. Here, class-specific differences in duration and types of schooling as well as in employment careers are important insofar as they structure women's life courses and marriage markets, especially during youth and early adulthood.

Historical Context

In addition to influences of social class, variations in ages at marriage and motherhood are dependent upon the historical context of when a woman reaches the age when mate-selection takes place. Caldwell et al. (1988) show that for a number of industrialized countries ages at marriage and motherhood fell from the beginning of the century until the 1960s and have since been increasing. Several explanations have been put forward, especially with respect to the dramatic changes after the 1960s.

Focusing on the Netherlands, van de Kaa (1987) considers the recent development as a series of successive events driven largely by social change. He argues that with increasing economic prosperity there has been a transition to 'postmaterialism' which can be characterized by substantial changes in attitudes to marriage, the family and sexuality.

Caldwell and Ruzicka (1978) state that the perfection of birth control through contraception and abortion allows young people to separate sexual relations from marriage and leads to an increase in age at marriage in a society where most people still regard it as the preliminary to parenthood but not to sexual relations.

Analyzing West Germany, Blossfeld and Huinink (1991) argue that the change in the 1960s could be explained by the lag of societal norms behind economic development (the so-called 'cultural lag' hypothesis): until the late 1960s, the opportunity for children to leave the parental home had increased remarkably because of the improvement of economic conditions, but at the same time, the social norm that they had to marry before living with a partner of the opposite sex still applied. The result was that until the end of the 1960s, the age at entry into marriage was decreasing because young adults living in consensual unions were normally subject to social disapproval and encountered problems, for instance, in finding housing, until they married. This norm became much weaker at the end of the 1960s, partly as a result of the student movement. However, in recent years, cohabitation appears to have been taken up to a similar extent by young people across classes—irrespective of where this form of behavior was originally located, socially and educationally (Bernhardt and Hoem 1985; Kiernan 1989; Oppenheimer/Blossfeld/Wackerow in this volume).

Oppenheimer (1988) explains the increasing prevalence of consensual unions among young people by the increasing socioeconomic uncertainties at an earlier age during the last twenty years.

> Cohabitation gets young people out of high-cost search activities during a period of social immaturity but without incurring what are, for many, the penalties of either heterosexual isolation or promiscuity, and it often offers many of the benefits of marriage, including the pooling of resources and the economies of scale that living together provide. (Oppenheimer 1988:71)

For many people cohabitation is not the same as marriage either in promised permanence or in likely parenthood (Caldwell et al. 1988). Thus, cohabitation seems not to be merely another name for marriage, and thus the rising age at marriage is a real rather than an apparent change. McDonald (1975) has argued that despite a rise in the incidence of consensual unions most people do marry eventually, but that given the ease with which births can now be planned, marriage has become a less significant life-cycle event than the birth of the first child. In the words of Bracher:

> In this view, the present decline in marriage, rather than reflecting more liberal attitudes toward marriage, represents a return to a more conservative ethic in which the timing of marriage is determined by a couple's ability to accumulate sufficient savings to establish themselves in a home before the birth of their first child or, if they plan to delay the first birth after marriage, by their assessment of having reached the 'psychologically proper time' to marry. (Bracher 1988)

Although we cannot empirically assess all of these different hypotheses regarding the interplay of economic development, changes in values and demographic behavior in this volume, we can control for the long-term historical shifts in ages at entry into marriage and motherhood on the basis of a detailed set of birth-cohort variables in most of the country-studies. Given these factors, we now focus on the question of how the increasing educational attainment of women affects their ages at entry into marriage and motherhood.

The Impact of Women's Education on
Family Formation: Educational Attainment

Economists in particular have been prominent in offering explanations for the relationship between women's growing economic independence (as a result of better education and improved career opportunities) and the rise in delayed marriage and fertility. According to Becker (1981), the main exponent of the economic theory of the family, unmarried men and women can be viewed as trading partners who decide to marry if each partner has more to gain by marrying than by remaining single. As in all trading relationships, the gains from marriage are based on the fact that each partner has something different to offer. Traditionally, women rely on men for the provision of food and shelter, and for protection; and men rely on women for the bearing and rearing of children and the maintenance of the home. This means that the socialization process traditionally induces a comparative advantage of women over men in the household because women invest mainly in human capital that raises household efficiency, and a comparative advantage of men over women in the labor market because men invest mainly in capital that raises market efficiency. According to Becker, it is this sex-specific specialization of labor in our society, and the mutual dependence it produces between the sexes, that provides the major incentive for partners to marry. Becker concludes that: "the gain from marriage is reduced by a rise in the earnings and labor force participation of women ... because a sexual division of labor becomes less advantageous" (Becker 1981:248)

The result is that women with higher education and better career opportunities increasingly delay or avoid marriage. Becker has not only drawn conclusions from his economic approach to the family with respect to entry into marriage, but also in relation to the decision to have children. He argues that the bearing and rearing of their own children is one of the main purposes of the family, which use market goods, services and parental time to achieve this goal. Because of the sex-specific differentiation of labor within the family, it is particularly the mother's time that is the major part of the total costs of bearing and rearing children. Increases in the value of women's time as a result of increases in investments in education and career opportunities will therefore immediately affect the relative costs of children. Thus Becker argues that, "a growth in the earning power of women raises ... the relative cost of children and thereby reduces the demand for children ..." (Becker 1981:245–47). We should thus expect a negative relationship between women's increasing level of education and the rates of entry into marriage and motherhood.

The Impact of Women's Education on
Family Formation: Educational Enrollment

Apart from the pure quantity of women's human capital investments influencing their time of entry into marriage and motherhood, there may also be a delaying effect generated by women's increasing enrollment in the educational system itself (Hoem 1985; Marini 1984, 1985; Etzler 1987; Blossfeld and Huinink 1991). One reason is that some activities, such as acquiring education, tend to be incompatible with adult family role activities (Marini 1985). Moreover, attending school, university, or vocational training programs is associated with a high degree of economic dependence on parents (Blossfeld and Nuthmann 1989). Women enrolled in school or vocational training programs may therefore consider themselves to be not sufficiently 'mature' for entry into marriage and motherhood. Thus, finishing education is expected to count as one of the important prerequisites for entering into adulthood status, and thereby entering into marriage and parenthood. This is true not only for men, but also for women, as over the last four decades their education has become more important, and their opportunity costs of 'dropping-out' before completion have risen sharply (Oppenheimer 1988).

Although previous research indicates that both age at first marriage and first birth also have an impact on the educational enrollment of women (Hofferth and Moore 1979; Marini 1978, 1984), the dominant direction of influence is from educational enrollment to the timing of entry into marriage and parenthood (Marini 1985).

Why Separate the Effects of Level of Education and Educational Enrollment?

The separation of the effects of the level of women's educational investments and women's educational enrollment is important for theory and family policy. The effect of educational enrollment is confined to the period of transition from youth to adulthood and therefore means only a temporary postponement of family events such as marriage and childbirth. On the other hand, the effect of the level of educational investments, also initiated during this transition period, will continue throughout much of adult life and therefore reflects a persistent role conflict between women's growing economic independence and their traditional family roles.

The Role of Country-Specific Differences

The 'liberating effect' of women's educational attainment on women's entry into marriage and motherhood according to the economic theory of the family is based on the assumption that the 'conventional' or 'traditional' family-type, with a strict gender-specific division of labor, is the typical and dominant model of living together in modern societies. Although it is hard to imagine that any family system has ever satisfied *all* of the strong model assumptions made by the economic theory of the family, family systems *do* at least to widely varying degrees conform to the family model assumed by economists. There are marked differences among Western European countries with respect to this conformity in terms of the distribution of household types (single, married, divorced), the age when children leave the parental home, the proportion and significance of consensual unions, the fertility rate, the stability of marriage and the rate of entry into remarriage.

Given relatively similar levels of economic modernization in most Western European countries, these differences must be explained by the countries' dominant cultural values, family and religious traditions, and family policies (Lesthaeghe and Surkyn 1988). They will mainly be exemplified here for the countries representing the two extremes among the Western European countries under consideration: Sweden and Italy.

In terms of dominant cultural values, Swedes emphasize the principle of egalitarianism in public life, while most other Europeans try to find a balance between the concept of egalitarianism and the principle of individual freedom. In addition, religion also continues to be an important element in the lives of men and women today—especially in Italy and Spain—even if there have been important changes in the relationship between the Roman Catholic Church and individuals in the post-war period. It is well-known from historical studies of the family that changes in family and fertility in several Western European countries—including Sweden, the Netherlands, Great Britain, France, Germany, and even Italy—occurred earliest and most rapidly in areas where the influence of organized religion was weakest and secularization strongest (Lesthaeghe 1980; Lesthaeghe and Meekers 1986; Thornton 1985). Although the authority of the Roman Catholic Church over the behavior of individuals has declined in Italy over recent decades, it still influences attitudes to family formation and family stability (Menniti, Palomba and Sabbadini 1987).

The weight placed on egalitarianism in Sweden helps to explain that country's more coherent policies in promoting the integration of work and the family (Kalleberg and Rosenfeld 1990). In most other European countries and the United States, policies that influence the family have been developed in a piecemeal fashion, and have often been designed to reach goals other than those concerning the family. In the words of Hoem: "In Sweden, perhaps more than in other countries, priority is given to ensuring a decent level of living for everyone rather than letting market forces provide a wide range of choices only to those who can afford it." (Hoem in this volume). These policies also affect the labor-market conditions and unemployment rates of young people and women, thus influencing entry into marriage as well as married women's labor-force participation, which is higher in Sweden than in any other European country or the United States (Blossfeld and Huinink 1991).

Compared to other European countries, Sweden also provides very generous parental leave, and has invested far more in public child-care facilities, although demand still outstrips supply (Hoem and Hoem 1987a, 1987b). Many countries such as Germany have no general daycare policy at all, and in Italy, Great Britain or the United States the supply of daycare is well below the level of demand (Kalleberg and Rosenfeld 1990).

Many European countries have some form of children's allowance, but these payments are often viewed as incentives to increase population. Sweden has an explicit income-tax policy by which partners in a couple are taxed separately, thus encouraging women's employment. In other European countries, such as the Federal Republic of Germany, the income of the couple is taxed together, penalizing married couples with relatively equal earnings.

Thus, even if in Sweden there is still a gap between the ideology of equality of sex-specific opportunities and everyday life, regulations promoting women's right to equality with men must be considered as by far the most egalitarian among the countries considered in this volume—if not in the world (Hoem and Hoem 1987a, 1987b).

Because of these dominant cultural and religious values as well as different family policies, a new style of living arrangements emerged earlier and developed at a faster rate in Sweden than in any other European country. The Swedes, who have a tradition of non-marital cohabitation that goes back more than a century, were among the first to show an increase in the number of young people living in consensual unions and to develop cohabitation as a separate, yet equally stable way of living together (Hoem and Hoem 1987a, 1987b). Others such as the West Germans, French, Dutch or English followed about ten years later in the rise of consensual unions, reaching however only a far lower percentage today and still using cohabitation to a large extent as a relatively short prelude to marriage.[7] In Hungary, Italy and Spain, consensual unions are still almost unknown among young people (see Blossfeld and De Rose, 1992). In former socialist Hungary, this was a result of housing allocation policy and shortages; it was hard for unmarried couples to find housing—and even many married couples were forced to live with their parents for long periods before moving into their own apartments (Robert and Blossfeld in this volume). In Italy and Spain, young people still tend to live either with their parents, or if they live with a partner of the opposite sex, then they are usually married. This confirms the persistence of a behavioral norm in Italy and Spain that leaving the parental home is marked by marriage, and rarely takes place for other reasons.

Many Swedes who marry have lived in a consensual union for quite some time, and it has become relatively common to have at least one child before marriage (Hoem and Hoem 1987a, 1987b). This underlines the fact that there is very little conventional pressure to marry in Sweden, and shows that the composition of the Swedish group that does get married has changed completely during the last twenty years. Marriage formation in Sweden has also become progressively more selective towards groups that traditionally have had relatively low divorce risks: fewer teenagers, fewer 'forced' marriages due to unplanned pregnancies, more couples with children (Hoem and Hoem 1987a, 1987b). Given these changes, it is easy to understand that the (in terms of international standards) very high total divorce rate in Sweden dropped slightly in the 1980s—while in it was still on the rise in many other Western European countries (Blossfeld et al. 1993).

Although the percentage of young men and women who live for a short period in consensual unions before marriage has been quickly increasing in Great Britain, France or West Germany during the last decade or so, the Dutch, French, British and German studies of transition into marriage show that being pregnant is still the most important influence for entry into marriage. This means that even if the proportion of children born outside marriage is rising among young Dutch, French, British and West German women, the arrival of a child is closely connected with a desire to legalize the union. In

Italy and Spain, the percentage of children born to young unmarried women is by far the lowest among the considered countries, but shows a moderate tendency to increase.

Finally, there are great differences between European countries in the incidence of divorce (and separation) today. In Sweden more than in the Netherlands, France, Britain or West Germany, and in those countries more than in Italy or Spain, people view divorce as a normal and acceptable alternative to an unsatisfying marriage (Amato 1987). This also means that in Sweden more than in France, Britain or West Germany, and in those countries more than in Italy or Spain, divorce has become less dependent on women's bargaining power and earning capacity and thus less selective with respect to educational attainment.

On the other hand, divorce is still considered a stressful experience by most people in Sweden, and Swedes enter marriage more consciously and carefully than in France, Britain, the Netherlands or West Germany (and even more carefully than in Italy or Spain), where marriage is still a more effective norm for those wanting to live together (Emery 1988). If marriage becomes less traditional, it is plausible that the effect of women's education on entry into marriage will decline. This means that with respect to women's educational investments, marriage will be less selective in Sweden than in France, the Netherlands, Great Britain or West Germany and in those countries less selective than in Italy or Spain. Thus, in the course of the development and differentiation of family systems in modern societies, we expect a decreasing influence of women's educational level on entry into marriage and motherhood.

Summary of Main Hypotheses

To summarize, we have suggested the following three hypotheses regarding the effects of educational attainment on family formation.

First, the *effect of human capital investments*. If other important factors such as cohort membership, duration dependence, children and age at marriage are statistically controlled, increases in the level of women's educational attainment (as a global indicator of women's earning capacity or bargaining power) will reduce the rate of entry into marriage and motherhood.

Second, the *differential impact of human capital investment*. We expect, however, that this 'liberating effect' of women's educational attainment on entry into marriage and motherhood will differ among countries with different family systems. In particular, we hypothesize that the impact of women's educational attainment will be stronger the more 'conventional' or 'traditional' the family system is. In other words, we hypothesize that the delaying impact of women's educational attainment on entry into marriage and motherhood should be highest in Italy and Spain, lower in France, the Netherlands, Great Britain, and West Germany, and lowest (or even reversed) in the United States and Sweden.

Third, *the institutional effect of education*. In addition to the effect of the quantity of women's human capital investments influencing the time of entry into marriage and motherhood, we expect also that there will be a delaying or, statistically speaking, negative effect of women's extended enrollment in the educational system on the rate of entry into marriage and motherhood.

The Comparative Project:
Countries, Data, and Methods

The Countries

The countries included in this study (Italy, Spain, Sweden, Great Britain, West Germany, the Netherlands, France, Hungary, and the United States) constitute an interesting sample of industrialized societies and show considerable variations in the following characteristics: the level and timing of industrialization (compare Great Britain with Spain and Sweden); the political system (democracies, former socialist states as regards Hungary); the structure of the distributive system (market-based versus bureaucratically determined); the organization of the education system (centralized, decentralized or regional); the influence of religion (compare Southern and Northern Europe); and the goals of family policy (integration of work and family in Sweden versus pronatalist France and other goals). Thus the array of countries enables an evaluation of the hypothesis listed earlier in a variety of societies.

Data and Methods: Partial Standardization

All the studies employ nationally representative data for successive cohorts born between the second decade of the twentieth century and the 1960s:

(1) Italy: The analyses utilized the Italian Family Structure and Behavior Study (FSBS) from 1983. In this study, family events of women between the ages of 15 and 64 at the time of the interview were retrospectively collected.

(2) Spain: For the analysis of births, data were taken from the Spanish vital statistics (M.N.P.). The data on living arrangements, which also allow approximating the importance of consensual unions, are taken from an unpublished survey carried out by the Centro de Investigaciones Sociologicas (1991) covering people older that 18 years at the time of the interview.

(3) Sweden: The 1981 Swedish Fertility Survey and the 1991 Swedish Labor Force Survey were used.

(4) Great Britain: The analysis on Great Britain is based on the British General Household Surveys (annual sample surveys of private households, which have been carried out by the Office of Population Censuses and Surveys since 1971).

(5) West Germany: The study on West German women is based on the German Socio-Economic Panel. Since 1984 there has been a panel wave every year. The analyses in this volume used retrospective data on women of selected birth cohorts who participated in the panel waves between 1984 and 1988. The study on West German men by Johannes

Huinink is based on the 1981 German Life History Study. In this study, life histories of 2,171 German respondents from cohorts born 1929–31, 1939–41, and 1949–51, collected between 1981 and 1983, were used.

(6) France: The study on France is based on the 1988 INED Fertility Survey and the 1985-1986 INED Survey on Family History.

(7) The Netherlands: For the Netherlands, the Netherlands Fertility Survey, conducted every five years by the Netherlands' Central Bureau of Statistics and including women born between 1945 and 1964, as well as the survey on Social Integration of Young Adults, conducted by the Vrije Universiteit of Amsterdam, were used.

(8) Hungary: The study on Hungary is based on the 1983 Hungarian Mobility Survey (located at the TARKI Data Archive, Budapest). This dataset contains retrospective information on individuals as well as on families and households.

(9) United States of America: For the analyses in the United States of the 1987–1988 National Survey of Families and Households (NSFH) was utilzed. These data contain retrospective life-history information covering major marital, educational, and employment events.

Earlier, we indicated that the country-specific studies share very similar methods, but that unique features of some societies, as well as limitations of available data, compelled some researchers to deviate from the common model. Most studies employ nationally representative data for successive cohorts born between about 1935 and the 1960s (France, Hungary, the Netherlands, Great Britain, and Sweden), and in some studies data are available for even older cohorts (Italy, Spain, US, and Germany).

All nine studies describe cohort differences in women's educational attainment, consensual unions, entry into first marriage and first motherhood. In most studies (with the exception of Spain and Great Britain) the relationship between women's increasing educational attainment across cohort and family formation are analyzed using longitudinal models. The dependent variable in these models is the rate of women's entry into marriage or motherhood (see Blossfeld, Hamerle and Mayer 1989; Tuma and Hannan 1984).

Using continuous event history models (or discrete time models in the case of France, the Netherlands and Sweden), we have attempted to specify the rates of entry into marriage and motherhood as a function of time-constant and time-dependent covariates (see Blossfeld and Huinink 1991).

In most models, observation begins at age sixteen and ends with the event of first marriage or the birth of the first child, or, for right censored cases, with the date of the interview or age forty-six, whichever occurs first.[8]

Variables

Most studies include measures of age-dependence, social class, and cohort, in addition to the level of education and educational enrollment as independent variables.

In order to model women's accumulation of general and vocational qualifications in school, the vocational training system and the university, we used dummy variables for different levels as well as the average number of years required to obtain them. To model changes in the accumulation of these qualifications over the life-course, the studies have updated the level of education for each woman at the age when the respondent normally obtains each higher level.

However, as indicated above, there may also be another aspect of education on the timing of family formation. Enrollment in the educational system is time-consuming and affects a woman's propensity to marry and have a first child. Thus, the country-specific models also included a time-dependent dummy variable, indicating whether or not a woman is attending the educational system at a specific age.

As background variables, most of the studies include father's social class. Most of the studies analyze the process of entry into marriage and motherhood during a historical period of about forty to fifty years. In some analyses, the oldest cohorts studied were born between 1919 and 1923 and entered into marriage and motherhood during the period stretching from the late 1930s to the late 1940s. Thus, they began family formation during the unrest generated by World War II. The youngest cohorts analyzed in some of the studies were born between 1964 and 1968 and started to enter marriage and motherhood during the 1980s, that is, during a period of high educational expansion and economic uncertainty. To control for cohort effects generated by historical events and changes in values as well as economic development, the country-specific models used a set of dummy variables, each representing specific birth groups.

Results of the International Comparison

Women's Increasing Educational Attainment

Important changes in the timing of entry into marriage and fertility are frequently attributed to changes in women's educational attainments. Accordingly, we start our international comparison by posing the question: "What are the effects of educational expansion on the levels of women's educational attainment across successive cohorts in the countries under study?"

If we look at the changes in women's educational attainment across cohorts in each of the countries, then the improvement in educational opportunities for each younger cohort of women is clear: educational expansion is strong and universal in all nine countries—whether socialist or capitalist, Northern or Southern European or the United States. Women's average level of educational attainment has risen across cohorts. In all nine societies, primary, and even some types of lower secondary education have become almost universal for women during the period under study, and the proportion of women in tertiary education has also increased in most of them. All countries experienced a substantial reduction in the differences between the mean educational attainment of men and women. Although gender differences persist, the gap is even narrowing at the tertiary level, and in some societies (Germany and Hungary), women's mean educational attainment in recent cohorts has even surpassed those of men at the upper-secondary level. These developments indicate that women in particular have profited from educational expansion in modern industrial countries (Shavit and Blossfeld 1993).

The central point of this observation is that there has been a uniform, long-term trend across successive birth cohorts in all nine countries: not only have women's average levels of educational attainment steadily risen from one birth cohort to another, but women's enrollment in the educational system over the life-course has similarly extended in duration, especially between the ages of eighteen and twenty-eight, when family formation traditionally takes place.

Coupled with the fact that women are increasingly better educated is the rising share of women's total employment—even if these levels for the countries of the European Community are still well below those in Eastern Europe (Kiernan 1992) and the United States. From one cohort to the next, however, women in the European Community have gained more access to career-oriented positions, especially in the service sector (Blossfeld and Mayer 1991). Women's work is, however, still strongly dominated by part-time employment (Kiernan 1992; Blossfeld 1994).

Changes in Women's Ages at Entry into Marriage and Motherhood

As shown in the country chapters for Sweden, West Germany, France, the Netherlands and Great Britain, age at first marriage fell from the older cohorts to the cohorts around 1945, and have since been rising again until the youngest birth cohorts. The greatest movements occurred amongst women aged twenty to twenty-four. As far as the youngest cohorts can be followed, they have a similar high age at entry into marriage as for the oldest cohorts, or even exceed this age.

In the United States this U-shaped pattern of age at entry into marriage across cohorts started about fifteen years earlier, with the cohort born around 1930. In the Southern European countries such as Italy, and Spain, we find, however, a delay of about ten birth cohorts. In these countries age at marriage starts to rise around the cohort born in 1955. Finally, in Hungary, we observe basically no significant change at all in the age pattern across cohorts—despite a slight tendency among the younger birth cohorts for age at entry into marriage to rise; this stability across cohorts is explained by the specific housing policy in former socialist Hungary (Robert and Blossfeld in this volume).

Looking at ages of entry into first motherhood, we observe basically the same trends as for entry into marriage. Again, in Sweden, West Germany, France, the Netherlands and in Great Britain, it is the cohort around 1945 which entered motherhood at the youngest ages, with not only marriages but also entries into motherhood being highly concentrated. And again, in these countries we find similar age patterns of entry into motherhood for the youngest cohorts as for the oldest cohorts.

In the United States, the U-shaped pattern of age at entry into motherhood across cohorts again started about fifteen years earlier, and in the Southern European countries, we observe again a delay of about ten birth cohorts. In these countries age at first motherhood starts to rise around the birth cohorts of 1955. Finally, in Hungary, we observe basically no change in the age pattern for motherhood across cohorts, which may again be explained by the specific housing situation of young couples in Hungary.

Several points are important for our argument. First, in most of the Northern European countries and the United States up to now, we find an entrance pattern for ages into marriage and motherhood which is very similar to that observed forty or fifty years ago. It is only relative to the cohorts of around 1945 (or 1930 in the United States) that the increase in marriage and motherhood age patterns appear so dramatic. However, as Kiernan (1989) points out, in Britain the generation around 1945 became brides at the earliest average age ever recorded since the start of civil registration. This change took place about fifteen years earlier in the United States and ten years later in Southern Europe. But the U-shaped pattern of the timing of marriage and motherhood in non-socialist countries and the unchanged pattern for former socialist Hungary is not in synchrony with the monotonic upward trend in women's educational attainment across cohorts. At this point in our discussion, it is therefore questionable whether changes in marriage and motherhood can be attributed mainly to women's growing economic independence (as a result of better education and improved career opportunities), as Becker (1981) has argued.

The Role of Consensual Unions

It is interesting to examine the changing role of consensual unions in the process of family formation in the nine countries under study, especially since marriage may be increasingly delayed because of the increase in the number of couples forming non-marital unions prior to marriage (Bumpass and Sweet 1989).

As far as we know, cohabitation was not very common during the decades before 1960, and when non-marital cohabitation then suddenly started to grow in popularity, it received very little initial public attention even in Sweden. Compared to marriage and fertility, there is therefore a lack of statistics on the long-term development of consensual unions in all of the countries under study.[9] This analysis therefore can only build on more recent data sources in evaluating the role of consensual unions in different European countries in the 1970s and 1980s.

In theoretical terms, there are different perspectives on the relationship between marriage and consensual unions (Manting 1991a, 1991b). Some authors argue that for the process of family formation it is only important that a man and a woman establish a joint household with an intimate sexual relationship. Thus, the *difference* between marriage and consensual union may *not be important* (Bumpass and Sweet 1989). Other authors emphasize that consensual unions and marriage are two *alternative* living arrangements, and that marriage is a form of living arrangement with additional legal barriers and a higher level of commitment. Most authors, however, admit that there is some kind of a *sequential process* of non-marital cohabitation and marriage, in which non-marital cohabitation can be seen as a prelude to, or a probationary period for marriage (see Oppenheimer 1988).

The results of our international comparison with respect to non-marital unions are summarized in Table 1.1 and clearly show that Sweden led the way in the growth in non-marital cohabitation. In 1965, 44 percent of childless Swedish women under the age of twenty-five had lived in a non-marital union. In 1977, the respective figure had risen to 96 percent (Hoem and Hoem 1987a). This means that in the late 1960s and 1970s, non-marital unions became more or less universal in Sweden. With a delay of about fifteen years, the other Northern European countries and the United States follow Sweden's route: in the period 1984–1989, 33 percent of German men and women aged twenty-one to thirty-five lived in consensual unions; in France the proportion of men and women who entered marriage in 1985 cohabited before at a level of about 75 percent; in the Netherlands, 51 percent of women from the 1961 birth cohort had cohabited before the age of twenty-six (Liefbroer 1991); and in the United States, 44 percent of persons who entered first marriages in the late 1980s had cohabited prior to marriage (Bumpass and Sweet 1989). In Italy, Spain and Hungary, however, consensual unions are still virtually unknown and have little quantitative importance, but even in these countries the proportions of non-marital unions are continuously rising, especially within the age group between twenty and twenty-five. This can be interpreted as a sign that the South will experience a similar structural transformation of the family system as the North—but with a delay of one or two decades.

In all countries where consensual unions are quantitatively important, cohabiting living arrangements did not last particularly long (Table 1.1), with the exception of Sweden: depending on country and birth cohort, more than 50 percent of cohabiting couples either married or separated between two to four years. More of these unions ended in marriage than in separation. Thus, in the 1970s and 1980s, consensual unions could still be considered as a prelude or probationary period for marriage.

Non-marital cohabitation is however most uncommon among those still enrolled in school. However, if, in the United States, students live in non-marital unions and leave school, the probability that they will enter into marriage is very high. This is in line with Oppenheimer's view that cohabitation is a socially and psychologically acceptable alternative to singlehood or risky partner-search.

However, during the 1980s in all countries consensual unions lasted for increasingly longer periods (Table 1.1). This could mean that younger couples are less motivated to legalize their union quickly by marrying because consensual unions have become a relatively normal and widespread phenomenon. Nevertheless, even in Sweden, where the law treats unmarried and married couples equally in most respects, modern consensual unions cannot be considered as interchangeable with marriage:

TABLE 1.1   Non-Marital Cohabitation in Different European Countries and the United States of America

Country	Relevance	Cohort/ Period	Characteristics of Non-Marital Consensual Unions				
			Proportion	Duration	Prelude to Marriage	Difference to Marriage	Transition to Marriage
S	Great	1965	44% (ever)	Short, some years	Mostly	Yes	Pregnancy (+)
	Universal	1977	96% (ever)	Increasingly longer	Decreasingly	Yes	Pregnancy (+)
FRG	Great	1984-89	33% (at ages 21-30)	Some years (median: 3y.)	Mostly, but decreasingly	Yes	Pregnancy (+)
F	Moderate	1970	20% (ever)	Short	Mostly	Yes	Pregnancy (+)
	Great	1985	75% (ever)	(median: 2y.)	Decreasingly	Yes	Pregnancy (+)
NL	Moderate	1945-49	10% (ever)	Short	Mostly	Yes	Pregnancy (+)
	Great	1960	51% (ever)	Increasingly	Decreasingly less	Yes	Pregnancy (+)
GB	Moderate	1971-73	7% (ever)	Short	Mostly	Yes	Pregnancy (+)
	Great	1987	48% (ever)	Some Years	Decreasingly less	Yes	Pregnancy (+)
USA	Moderate	1970	11% (ever)	Short	Mostly	Yes	Pregnancy (+)
	Great	1984	44% (ever)	Some years	Decreasingly	Yes	Pregnancy (+)
I	Low	1980s	about 5%	-	-	-	-
E	Low	1980s	about 4%	-	-	-	-
H	Low	1980s	about 3%	-	-	-	-

A modern consensual union does not have *all* the characteristics of a formally sanctioned marriage. The behavior of cohabitants is sufficiently different from that of married people to merit regarding consensual union as a separate civil status, in particular because people live in such unions *for quite long segments of their lives.* (Hoem, in this volume)

As far as estimates for the transition from consensual union to marital union are available, one can say that each younger birth cohort lives in consensual unions significantly longer, and that there is a very strong effect of pregnancy on the rate of entry into marriage (Table 1.1). This indicates that the birth of a child is closely connected with the desire to legalize the union. Moreover, enrollment in the educational system delays entry into marriage, and makes finishing education an important precondition for entry into marriage.

Effects of Education on the Rate of Entry into First Marriage and First Motherhood

Let us now turn to the question of how the improvement of educational attainment of women across cohorts has affected their entry into first marriage and motherhood. Table 1.2 summarizes the effects for the different countries. In seven of the nine countries (exceptions: Great Britain and Spain), authors were able to estimate continuous or discrete event history models and controlled for several important influences before they included the variables of interest here, namely, the time-dependent measure of educational level and the time-dependent measure of enrollment in the educational system. We should mention here that by far the most important influence in the 'marriage model' was whether a woman was pregnant before entry into marriage. In the model 'entry into motherhood' the most important influence was whether a women had entered marriage. These events are closely related to each other in all the models, and this is true across all social classes.

The results of the influences of women's educational attainment on *entry into marriage* are summarized in the first part of Table 1.2. As discussed above, the theoretical importance of education may be viewed from two different perspectives. For the 'new home economists,' the accumulation of human capital in terms of an increasing level of marketable qualifications raises women's labor-market attachment and thereby leads to greater marriage delays (Mincer 1974; Becker 1981); and from a sociological point of view there is the normative societal expectation that young people enrolled in education are 'not ready' for marriage, and that the completion of education is an important step towards becoming ready for marriage (Marini 1985; Oppenheimer 1988; Blossfeld and Nuthmann 1989). The seven country-specific studies have constructed time-dependent measures for both aspects of the effects of education and included them in a continuous or discrete event history model. Table 1.2 shows that enrollment in the educational system in all seven countries has a strong and significant negative effect on the rate of entry into marriage. Thus, the major delaying effect of educational expansion on the timing of first

TABLE 1.2 Effects of Women's Increasing Education on the Rate of Entry into Marriage and Motherhood in Different European Countries and the United States of America

Country	Effect on Entry into Marriage		Effect on Entry into Motherhood	
	School Enrollment	Level of Education	School Enrollment	Level of Education
S	Strong (-)	No effect	Strong (-)	Weak (-)
FRG	Strong (-)	No effect	Strong (-)	No effect
F	Strong (-)	Weak (-)	Strong (-)	Weak (-)
NL	Strong (-)	Weak (-)	Strong (-)	Weak (-)
I	Strong (-)	Strong (-)	No effect	Strong
H	Strong (-)	No effect	Strong (-)	Weak (-)
USA	Strong (-)	Weak (+)	Strong (-)	No effect

marriage is connected with educational enrollment and is therefore limited to the transition from youth to adulthood.

Nevertheless, the effect of the level of education on entry into marriage differs among the various countries (Table 1.2). In Sweden, West Germany and Hungary, there is no significant effect of women's level of education on the rate of entry into marriage. In France and the Netherlands, this effect is significant and negative, but weak in size. This means that in all of these countries, women's marriage timing is more or less independent or only slightly influenced by the amount of women's human capital investments—which runs counter to the hypothesis of the economic theory of the family which predicts a strong negative impact of women's level of education on entry into marriage. The result for the United States is the opposite of what one would expect based on this thesis because each successively higher educated group of women enters marriage to an even higher rate (positive effect of women's educational level) after it has left the educational system. In assessing the consequences of educational expansion for family formation in all of these countries, we may therefore conclude that more highly educated women tend to postpone marriage because they postpone the transition from youth to adulthood and not because they have accumulated a greater stock of human capital. The longer women remain in the educational system, the longer they delay entry into marriage. After leaving the educational system, most women who have delayed entering into marriage catch up with their lesser-educated contemporaries. In terms of the economic theory of the family, the conflict between women's increasing educational attainment and marriage is therefore confined to the period of transition from youth to adulthood and does not appear to continue throughout much of adult life. In this sense, we cannot attribute the decline in marriage in Northern Europe and the United States to the improvement in women's educational attainment.

Italy, however, is an exception. The Italian study reports a strong delaying effect of educational level on entry into marriage as predicted by Becker (1981). This exception is highly significant for our study, and it seems that the 'liberating effect' of women's educational attainment on entry into marriage is only important in a more traditional family system. Indeed, if we compare the effect of women's educational level across countries, the delaying influence of women's educational investments on entry into marriage differs with the differentiation in the family system. It is strong in Italy, lower in France and the Netherlands, and non-existent in Sweden, Germany, Hungary or the United States.

Finally, let us consider the impact of women's educational level on the age at *first motherhood* across countries (Table 1.2). With the exception of Italy, attending school strongly delays women's propensity to have a first child. There are normative societal expectations that young women enrolled in education are 'not ready' to have a child. Finishing education, as one of the important steps towards adult status, thus leads to a steep rise in the rate of entry into parenthood (see Blossfeld and Nuthmann 1989).

The result for Italy may be explained by the fact that being married is a strong precondition for conception and childbirth. So, if in the event history model 'being married' is included into the model, then the effect of women's educational enrollment disappears. The educational enrollment effect in the model of entry into motherhood is therefore completely mediated via entry into marriage.

Support for the economic theory of the family, however, may be seen in the negative effect of the level of education on the rate of entry into motherhood in most countries, where the accumulation of human capital investments conflicts with societal expectations regarding a woman's role as mother. Women still take primary responsibility for childcare, even in developed family systems such as Sweden, and are still disadvantaged in their careers when they interrupt their work lives for the birth of a child. Women who have accumulated a high stock of human capital, therefore, try to postpone or avoid the birth of a first child, and the more traditional the family system, the stronger this effect. This means that the economically based conflict between a woman's accumulation of human capital and societal expectations regarding her role as mother is especially pronounced in traditional family systems.

Summary and Conclusions

The main purpose of this book is to study the question of whether women's growing economic independence, resulting from better education, is one of the major factors in the decline of marriage and fertility. Using representative data from different European countries and the United States, we describe women's long-term educational attainment and women's ages at entry into marriage and motherhood across cohorts. We also model women's educational investments and their enrollment in the educational system as a changing process over the life course, and estimate the effects on the rate of entry into first marriage and first motherhood. There are several results of substantive importance in this volume.

First, in describing the effects of educational expansion on the levels of women's educational attainment in successive birth cohorts, we find a uniform long-term trend in all modern industrialized countries: not only have women's average levels of educational attainment steadily risen from one birth cohort to another, but their duration of enrollment in the educational system over the life course was also increasingly extended. This process was connected with a rising share of women's total employment and women's increasing access to career-oriented positions, especially in the service sector, although women's work is still strongly dominated by part-time employment (Blossfeld 1994).

Second, in charting changes in the process of women's entry into marriage and motherhood across cohorts, we observe that the long-term trend in ages at entry into marriage and motherhood is not in line with the long-term trend in women's educational attainment in all countries. In Sweden, West Germany, the Netherlands and Great Britain, age at first marriage fell from the older cohorts to the cohorts around 1945, and have since been rising again until the youngest birth cohorts. The greatest movements occurred amongst women aged twenty to twenty-four. The result is that as far as the youngest cohorts can be followed, they have a similarly high age at entry into marriage and motherhood as the oldest cohorts. In the United States this U-shaped pattern of age at entry into marriage across cohorts started about fifteen years earlier, with the cohort born around 1930. In the Southern European countries of Italy and Spain, however, there is a delay of about ten birth cohorts. In these countries age at marriage starts to rise around the cohort born in 1955. Finally, in former socialist Hungary, we observed basically no significant change in the age pattern across cohorts, despite the slight tendency for the age of entry into marriage to rise for the younger birth cohorts. On the basis of these observations, it is not warranted that women's growing economic independence (derived from better education and improved career opportunities) is a major factor for the non-monotonic changes in ages at marriage and motherhood.

Third, the recent rise in ages at entry into marriage in all European countries and the United States appears to be less dramatic than has been suggested in the scientific and social-policy debates. Among the younger birth cohorts, we have observed similar patterns for ages of entry into marriage as was the case for cohorts of women some fifty years ago. It is only relative to the 1944–1948 cohort (or the 1930 cohort in the United States) that the recent marriage patterns appear so dramatic. It is therefore important to analyze the effects of women's improvement in educational attainment on the timing of marriage and motherhood over a very long period.

Fourth, the results of our international comparison with respect to non-marital unions clearly show that Sweden has led the way in the growth of non-marital cohabitation, with the great majority of unions formed during the 1980s (about 90 percent) being non-marital; the other Northern European countries and the United States appear to follow suit with a delay of about fifteen years. In Italy, Spain and in Hungary, consensual unions are still relatively unknown and of little quantitative significance, but even in these countries the proportions of non-marital unions are continuously rising, especially within the twenty to twenty-five age-group, and this may be read as an indication that Southern Europe will experience a similar structural transformation of the family system to that seen in the North—albeit with a delay of one or two decades.

In all countries in which consensual unions are of quantitative importance, cohabitating living arrangements did not last very long. More than 50 percent of cohabiting couples either married or separated within two to four years, and more of these unions ended in marriage than in separation. So, in the 1970s and 1980s (perhaps with the exception of Sweden), consensual unions can still be considered a prelude to or probationary period for marriage.

Non-marital cohabitation is still most unlikely among those who are still enrolled in school. However, if students live in non-marital unions and then leave education, the probability that they will enter into marriage is very high. During the 1980s in all countries, consensual unions lasted for increasingly longer periods, which could indicate that it is now less important for younger couples to legalize such unions quickly by marrying, given that consensual unions have become a normal and widespread phenomenon. Even in

Sweden, where the law treats unmarried and married couples equally in most respects, consensual unions and marriage cannot be considered as an equal living arrangement. As far as the transition from consensual unions to marital unions is concerned, one can say that each younger birth cohort lives in consensual unions longer and that there is a strong effect of pregnancy on the rate of entry into marriage.

Fifth, although our understanding of the causes of this change from marriage-and-birth-boom to marriage-and-birth bust in Europe and the United States is not perfect, we can at least say that on the basis of the present international comparative study, women's increasing educational attainment is partly responsible for the changes in the process of family formation. In analyzing the processes of first marriage and first motherhood, we showed that the delaying effect of educational expansion on the timing of first marriage is mostly limited to the phase of transition from youth to adulthood only; more highly-educated women simply marry and have their first child later.

The effect of the level of education on entry into marriage is, however, different in the various countries. In Sweden, West Germany and in Hungary, there is no significant effect of women's level of education on the rate of entry into marriage. In France and the Netherlands this effect is significant and negative, but weak in size. This means that in all of these countries, women's marriage timing is more or less independent or only slightly influenced by the amount of women's human capital investments—which is in contradiction to the hypothesis of the economic theory of the family that predicted a strong negative impact of women's level of education on entry into marriage. The result for the United States is the opposite of what one would expect according to this thesis because a higher level of education leads to a higher marriage intensity after leaving school. In assessing the consequences of educational expansion for family formation in all of these countries, we may therefore conclude that more highly educated women mainly postpone marriage because they postpone their transition from youth to adulthood and not because they have accumulated a greater stock of human capital. The longer women remain in the educational system, the longer they delay their entry into marriage. Hence, it seems not to be justified to attribute the decline in marriage in the Northern European countries and the United States to the improvement in women's educational attainment.

The only exception is Italy, where there is a negative effect of educational level on entry into marriage as predicted by Becker. This exception is theoretically important, as it would appear that the 'liberating effect' of women's educational attainment on entry into marriage only functions in a more traditional family system. Indeed, if we compare the effect of women's educational level across countries, the delaying influence of women's educational investments on entry into marriage differs according to the differentiation in the family system. Thus, it is strong in Italy, lower in France and the Netherlands, and non-existent in Sweden, West Germany, Hungary and the United States.

The economic theory of the family is only supported by the delaying effect of the level of education on rates of entry into motherhood in most countries. The accumulation of human capital investments conflicts with societal expectations regarding a woman's role as mother. Women still take primary responsibility for childcare, even in developed family systems such as Sweden, and are still disadvantaged in their careers when they interrupt them due to the birth of a child. Women who have accumulated a high stock of human capital, therefore, tend to postpone or avoid the birth of a first child. This effect, and hence the economically based conflict between a woman's accumulation of human capital and society's expectations of her role as mother, is especially pronounced in traditional family systems such as in Italy. Thus, with further improvement of educational opportunities of younger cohorts of women, resolving this conflict will turn out to be increasingly important for all modern industrialized societies, and will be particularly important for the more traditional family systems in Southern Europe.

Notes

1. Höpflinger 1987; Sweet and Bumpass 1987; Nave-Herz 1988; Muñoz-Pérez 1989; Caldwell et al. 1988; Prioux 1990.

2. For low fertility and an increasing age at first birth see Rindfuss and St. John 1983; Roussel 1975; Santow 1989. For atypical family-types see, Prioux (1990) and Kiernan (1993).

3. Bernhard 1988, 1989; Sorensen 1990; Huinink 1990, Handl 1988, 1989; Müller, Handl and Willms 1983; Ott and Rolf 1987; Kiernan 1992; Blossfeld 1986, 1989.

4. See Elder and Rockwell 1976; Hogan 1978; Cherlin 1980; Kiernan and Diamond 1983; England and Farkas 1986; Etzler 1987; Hoem and Rennermalm 1985; Hoem 1985; Marini 1985; Hoem and Hoem 1987a; Diekmann 1987, 1989; Kiernan and Eldridge 1987; Huinink 1987; Bracher 1988; Blossfeld and Huinink 1991; Klein 1989.

5. See Espenshade 1983; Sørensen and Sørensen 1985; Papastefanou 1987; Diekmann 1989.

6. See Blossfeld, Hamerle and Mayer 1989; Blossfeld and Hamerle 1989; Blossfeld and Huinink 1991.

7. See Leridon 1989; Hobcraft and Joshi 1989; Bozon and Heran 1989.

8. With the exception of France (seventeen to twenty-four) and the Netherlands (eighteen to twenty-seven).

9. Because of the informal nature of consensual unions, it is also methodologically problematic to collect the data retrospectively (Hoem 1983).

References

Aalen, O. (1988). "Dynamic Modelling and Causality," *Scandinavian Actuarial Journal* 12:177–90.

Alwin, D. F., Ph. E. Converse and S. S. Martin (1985). "Living Arrangements and Social Integration," *Journal of Marriage and the Family*, 47:319–4.

Amato, P.R. (1987). *Children in Australian Families: The Growth of Competence*, Sydney: Prentice-Hall.

Becker, G. (1981). *A Treatise on the Family*, Cambridge, Mass.: Harvard University Press.

Bernhardt, E. M. (1988). "Changing Family Ties, Women's Position and Low Fertility," *Stockholm Research Reports in Demography*, No. 46, University of Stockholm.

Bernhardt, E. M. (1989). "Fertility and Employment," *Stockholm Research Reports in Demography*, No. 55, University of Stockholm.

Bernhardt, E. M. and B. Hoem (1985). "Cohabitation and Social Background: Trends Observed for Swedish Women Born between 1936 and 1960," *European Journal of Population*, 1:375–95.

Bloom, D. E. (1982). "What's Happening to the Age at First Birth in the United States? A Study of Recent Cohorts," *Demography*, 19:351–70.

Blossfeld, H.-P. (1985). *Bildungsexpansion und Berufschancen*, Frankfurt and New York: Campus.

Blossfeld, H.-P. (1986). "Career Opportunities in the Federal Republic of Germany: A Dynamic Approach to the Study of Life-Course, Cohort, and Period Effects," *European Sociological Review*, 2:208–25.

Blossfeld, H.-P. (1987). "Labor Market Entry and the Sexual Segregation of Careers in the Federal Republic of Germany," *American Journal of Sociology*, 93:89–118.

Blossfeld, H.-P. (1989). *Kohortendifferenzierung und Karriereprozeß* Frankfurt and New York: Campus.

Blossfeld, H.-P. (1990). "Changes in Educational Careers in the Federal Republic of Germany," *Sociology of Education*, 63:165–77.

Blossfeld, H.-P. (1994). "Family Cycle and Growth in Women's Part-Time Employment in Western European Countries," *Final Project Report*, Bremen University.

Blossfeld, H.-P. and A. Hamerle (1989). "Unobserved Heterogeneity in Hazard Rate Models: A Test and an Illustration from a Study of Career Mobility," *Quality and Quantity*, 23:129–41.

Blossfeld, H.-P., A. Hamerle, and K. U. Mayer (1989). *Event History Analysis*, Hillsdale (NJ), Erlbaum.

Blossfeld, H.-P. and J. Huinink (1991). "Human Capital Investments or Norms of Role Transition? How Women's Schooling and Career Affect the Process of Family Formation," *American Journal of Sociology*, 97:143–68.

Blossfeld, H.-P. and A. De Rose (1992). "Educational Expansion and Changes in Entry into Marriage and Motherhood. The Experience of Italian Women," *Genus*, 3–4: 73–91.

Blossfeld, H.P., A. De Rose, J.M. Hoem and Götz Rohwer. "Education, Modernization, and the Risk of Marriage Disruption: Differences in the Effect of Women's Educational Attainment in Sweden, West Germany and Italy," *Stockholm Research Reports in Demography*, No. 76, University of Stockholm.

Blossfeld, H.-P. and R. Nuthmann (1989). "Strukturelle Veränderungen der Jugendphase als Kohortenprozeß," *Zeitschrift für Pädagogik*, 35:845–67.

Blossfeld, H.-P. and Y. Shavit (1993): "Persisting Barriers: Changes in Educational Opportunities in Thirteen Countries," in Shavit and Blossfeld (eds), *Persistent Inequality*, Boulder, Westview.

Bozon, M. and F. Heran (1989). "Finding a Spouse: A Survey of How French Couples Meet," *Population* (English Section No. 1) 44:91-121.

Bracher, M. (1988). "A Reconsideration of First Marriage—Trends in Australia," Working Paper No. 7 of the Australian Family Project, Research School of Social Sciences, Australian National University, Canberra, ACT 2601.

Bumpass, L. and J. Sweet (1989). "National Estimates of Cohabitation," NSFH Working Paper No. 2, Center for Demography and Ecology, University of Wisconsin.

Caldwell, J. C., P. Caldwell, M. D. Bracher, and G. Santow (1988). "The Contemporary Marriage and Fertility Revolutions in the West," Working Paper No. 3, the Australian Family Project, Research School of Social Sciences, Australian National University, Canberra, ACT 2601.

Caldwell, J. C., and L.T. Ruzicka (1978). "The Australian Fertility Transition: An Analysis," *Population and Development Review*, 4:94–6.

Cherlin, A. (1980). "Postponing Marriage: The Influence of Young Women's Work Expectations," *Journal of Marriage and the Family,* 42:355–65.

Coale, A. J. (1971). "Age Patterns of Marriage," *Population Studies,* 25:193–214.

Coale, A. J. and D. R. McNeil (1972). "The Distribution by Age of the Frequency of First Marriage in a Female Cohort," *Journal of the American Statistical Association,* 67:743–49.

Cooney, T. and D. P. Hogan (1991). "Marriage in an Institutionalized Life Course: First Marriage among American Men in the Twentieth Century," *Journal of Marriage and the Family,* 53:178–90.

Diekmann, A. (1987). "Determinanten des Heiratsalters und Schei- dungsrisiko," habilitation thesis, Institute for Sociology, University of Munich.

Diekmann, A. (1989). "Diffusion and Survival Models for the Process of Entry into Marriage," *Journal of Mathematical Sociology,* 14:31–44.

Elder, G.H., Jr. (1978). "Family History and the Life Course," in T.K. Hareven (ed.), *Transitions: The Family and the Life Course in Historical Perspective,* New York.

Elder, G. H., Jr., and R. C. Rockwell (1976). "Marital Timing in Women's Life Patterns," *Journal of Family History,* 1:34–53.

Emery, R. E. (1988). *Marriage, Divorce and Children's Adjustment,* Beverly Hills, Sage.

England, P. and G. Farkas (1986). *Households, Employment, and Gender—A Social, Economic, and Demographic View,* New York, Aldine.

Espenshade, Th. J. (1983). "Marriage, Divorce, and Remarriage from Retrospective Data: A Multiregional Approach," *Environment and Planning,* 15:1633–52.

Etzler, C. (1987). "Education, Cohabitation and the First Child: Some Empirical Findings from Sweden," *Stockholm Research Reports in Demography,* No. 34, University of Stockholm.

Haller, M. (1981). "Marriage, Women, and Social Stratification: A Theoretical Critique," *American Journal of Sociology,* 86:766–95.

Handl, J. (1988). "Der langfristige Geburtenrückgang in Deutschland—Heiratskohorten 1920–1960," *Zeitschrift für Bevölkerungswissenschaft,* 14:295–322.

Handl, J. (1989). *Berufschancen und Heiratsmuster,* Frankfurt and New York: Campus.

Hareven, T. K. (1976). "Modernization and Family History: Perspectives on Social Change," *Signs,* 2:190–206.

Hernes, G. (1972). "The Process of Entry into First Marriage," *American Sociological Review,* 37: 173–82.

Hobcraft, J. and H. Joshi (1989). "Population Matters," in H. Joshi (ed.), *The Changing Population of Britain,* Oxford, Basil Blackwell.

Hoem, B. (1992). "Early Phases of Family Formation in Contemporary Sweden," in M. Rosenheim and M. Testa (eds.), *Early Adulthood,* Rutgers University Press.

Hoem, B. and J. Hoem (1987a). "Patterns of Deferment of First Birth in Modern Sweden," *Stockholm Research Reports in Demography,* No. 42, University of Stockholm.

Hoem, B. and J. Hoem (1987b). "The Swedish Family: Aspects of Contemporary Developments," *Journal of Family Issues,* Vol. 9 (3), 397–424.

Hoem, J. (1983). "Distortions Caused by Non-Observation of Periods of Cohabitation Before the Latest," *Demography,* 20: 491–506.

Hoem, J. (1984). "Marriages Connected with First Births Among Cohabiting Women in the Danish Fertility Survey of 1975," *Stockholm Research Reports in Demography,* No. 19, University of Stockholm.

Hoem, J. (1986). "The Impact of Education on Modern Family Union Initiation," *European Journal of Population,* 2:113–33.

Hoem, J. and B. Rennermalm (1985). "Modern Family Initiation in Sweden: Experience of Women Born between 1936 and 1960," *European Journal of Population,* 1:81–112.

Hofferth, S. L. and K. A. Moore (1979). "Early Childbearing and Later Economic Well-Being," *American Sociological Review*, 44: 784–815.

Hogan, D. P. (1978). "The Effects of Demographic Factors, Family Background, and Early Job Achievement on Age at Marriage," *Demography*, 15: 139–60.

Höpfinger, F. (1987). *Wandel der Familienbildung in Westeuropa*, Frankfurt and New York: Campus.

Huinink, J. (1987). "Soziale Herkunft, Bildung und das Alter bei der Geburt des ersten Kindes," Zeitschrift für Soziologie 16: 367–84.

Huinink, J. (1990). "Familienbildung und Geburtenentwicklung," in K.- U. Mayer (ed.), *Lebensverläufe und gesellschaftlicher Wandel*, Sonderheft 31/1990 *Kölner Zeitschrift für Soziologie und Sozialpsychologie*.

Kaa, D. J. van de (1987). "Europe's Second Demographic Transition," *Population Bulletin*, 42.

Kalleberg, A. and R. Rosenfeld (1990). "Work in the Family and in the Labor Market: A Cross-National, Reciprocal Analysis," *Journal of Marriage and the Family*, 52:331–46.

Kiernan, K. E. (1989). "The Family: Fission or Fusion," in H. Joshi (ed.), *The Changing Population of Britain*, Basil Blackwell, Oxford.

Kiernan, K. E. (1992). "The Respective Roles of Men and Women in Tomorrow's Europe in Proceedings of Eurostat Conference on *Human Resources in Europe: At the Dawn of the 21st Century*, Eurostat, Luxembourg.

Kiernan, K.E. (1993). "The Future of Partnership and Fertility in Europe," in *The Future of Europe's Population*, Council of Europe, Strasbourg.

Kiernan, K.E. and I. Diamond (1983). "The Age at Which Childbearing Starts: A Longitudinal Study", *Population Studies*, 37 (3).

Kiernan, K.E. and S.M. Eldridge (1987). "Inter and Intra Cohort Variation in the Timing of First Marriage," *British Journal of Sociology*, 38 (1).

Kiernan, K.E. and Valerie Estaugh (1993). "Cohabitation: Extra-Marital Childbearing and Social Policy", Occasional Paper 17, Family Policy Studies Centre, London.

Klein, T. (1989). "Bildungsexpansion und Geburtenrückgang," *Kölner Zeitschrift für Soziologie und Sozialpsychologie*, 41:483–503.

Leridon, H. (1989). "Cohabitation, Marriage, Separation: An Analysis of Life Histories of French Cohorts from 1968 to 1985," *Population Studies*, 44:127–44.

Lesthaeghe, R. (1980). "On the Social Control of Human Reproduction," *Population and Development Review*, 6:527–48.

Lesthaeghe, R. (1983). "A Century of Demographic and Cultural Change in Western Europe: An Exploration of Underlying Dimensions," *Population and Development Review*, 9:411–35.

Lesthaeghe, R. and D. Meekers (1986). "Value Changes and the Dimensions of Familism in the European Community," *European Journal of Population*, 2:225–68.

Lesthaeghe, R. and J. Surkyn (1988). "Cultural Dynamics and Economic Theories of Fertility Change," *Population and Development Review*, 14:1–45.

Manting, D. (1991a). "First Union Formation in the Netherlands," PDOP Paper No. 5, Department of Physical Planning and Demography, University of Amsterdam.

Manting, D. (1991b). "The Timing of Marriage of Cohabiting Women in the Netherlands," PDOP Paper No. 7, Department of Physical Planning and Demography, University of Amsterdam.

Marini, M. M. (1978). "The Transition to Adulthood: Sex Differences in Educational Attainment and Age at Marriage," *American Sociological Review*, 43:483–507.

Marini, M. M. (1984). "Women's Educational Attainment and the Timing of Entry into Parenthood," *American Sociological Review*, 49:491– 511.

Marini, M. M. (1985). "Determinants of the Timing of Adult Role Entry," *Social Science Research,* 14:309–50.

Mayer, K.-U. (1977). "Fluktuation und Umschichtung," habilitation thesis, University of Mannheim.

McDonald, P.F. (1975). "Marriage in Australia, 1860–1971," Australian Family Formation Monograph No. 2, Canberra, The Australian National University.

Menken, J. (1985). "Age and Fertility: How Late Can You Wait?" *Demography* 22: 469–83.

Menniti, A., R. Palomba and L.L. Sabbadini (1987). "Family Models in Italy: A Traditional Catholic Country," in Istituto di Ricerche sulla Populatione (ed.), *Alternative Patterns of Family Life in Modern Societies,* Rome.

Michael, R. T. and N. B. Tuma (1985). "Entry into Marriage and Parenthood by Young Men and Women: The Influence of Family Background," *Demography* 22: 515–43.

Mincer, J. (1974). *Schooling, Experience, and Earnings,* New York: Columbia University Press.

Moen, P. (1992). *Women's Two Roles: A Contemporary Dilemma,* New York et al, Auburn House.

Müller, W., A. Willms and J. Handl (1983). *Strukturwandel der Frauenarbeit 1880–1980,* Frankfurt and New York: Campus.

Muñoz-Pérez, F. (1989). "The Decline of Fertility in Southern Europe," *Population* (English Selection No. 1), 44: 261–90.

Murphy, M. (1991). "The Collection and Comparability of Demographic and Social Data in Europe," London School of Economics (manuscript).

Nave-Herz, R. (ed.) (1988). *Wandel und Kontinuität der Familie in der Bundesrepublik Deutschland,* Stuttgart.

Oppenheimer, V. K. (1988). "A Theory of Marriage Timing," *American Journal of Sociology,* 94:563–91.

Ott, N. and G. Rolf (1987). "Zur Entwicklung von Frauenerwerbstätigkeit und Geburtenhäufigkeit," Arbeitspapier Nr. 244 des Sfb 3 der DFG "Mikroanalytische Grundlagen der Gesellschaftspolitik," Frankfurt.

Papastefanou, G. (1987). "Familienbildung und Lebensverlauf. Eine empirische Analyse sozialstruktureller Bedingungen der Familiengründung bei den Kohorten 1929–31, 1939–41 und 1949–51," Dissertation, Berlin.

Prioux, F. (1990). "Fertility and Family Size in Western Europe," *Population* (English Selection), 2:141–62.

Rindfuss, R. R. and Ch. Hirschman (1984). "The Timing of Family Formation: Structural and Societal Factors in the Asian Context," *Journal of Marriage and the Family,* 55: 205–14.

Rindfuss, R. R. and C. St. John (1983). "Social Determinants of Age at First Birth," *Journal of Marriage and the Family,* 45: 553–65.

Roussel, L. (1975). "Le mariage dans la société française contemporaine," INED, *Travaux et Documents,* 73.

Santow, G. (1989). "Work and Family in the Lives of Australian Women," paper presented at the Symposium "Life Histories and Generations," June 22–23, Netherlands Institute for Advanced Study in the Humanities and Social Sciences.

Shavit, Y. and H.-P. Blossfeld (eds) (1993). *Persistent Inequality,* Boulder, Westview.

Sørensen, A. (1990). "Unterschiede im Lebenslauf von Frauen und Männern," in K.-U. Mayer (ed.), *Lebensverläufe und gesellschaftlicher Wandel—Zwischen Sozialdemographie und Biographie,* Sonderheft 31/1990 of *Kölner Zeitschrift für Soziologie und Sozialpsychologie.*

Sørensen, A.B. and A. Sørensen (1985). "An Event History Analysis of the Process of Entry into First Marriage," *Current Perspectives on Aging and Life Cycle*, 2:53–71.

Sweet, J.A. and L.L. Bumpass (1987). *American Families and Households*, New York, Russell Sage Foundation. Thornton, A. (1985). "Reciprocal Influences of Family and Religion in a Changing World," *Journal of Marriage and the Family*, 47:381–94.

Tölke, A. (1989). *Lebensverläufe von Frauen. Familiäre Ereignisse, Ausbildungs- und Erwerbsverhalten*, Weinheim and Munich, Juventa.

Trent, K. and J.S. South (1989). "Structural Determinants of the Divorce Rate: A Cross-Societal Analysis," *Journal of Marriage and the Family*, 51:391–404.

Trovato, F. (1986). "The Relationship between Migration and the Provincial Divorce Rate in Canada, 1971 and 1978: A Reassessment," *Journal of Marriage and the Family*, 48:207–16.

Tuma, N. B. and M. T. Hannan (1984). *Social Dynamics: Models and Methods*, New York: Academic Press.

Vannoy, D. (1991). "Social Differentiation, Contemporary Marriage, and Human Development," *Journal of Family Issues*, 12:251–67.

White, L. K. (1990). "Determinants of Divorce: A Review of Research in the Eighties," *Journal of Marriage and the Family*, 52:904–12.

PART TWO

Country-Specific Studies
on the Trends in Family
Formation and the New
Role of Women

2

Sweden

BRITTA HOEM

Introduction

Although Sweden has shared the general features of recent demographic developments with most other Western nations, this country has often acted as a demographic pace-setter, as has been pointed out on many occasions, including by Popenoe (1987), and more recently by *The Economist* (13 April 1991). In the period after the mid-1960s, Sweden led the way in the decrease in marriage rates and the growth in non-marital cohabitation, and in the late 1980s its fertility went through a remarkable recovery that most other countries have yet to experience. This analysis describes features of family formation that are particular to the Swedish context and questions some conventional explanations and interpretations.

During the 1950s and early 1960s, young men and women left their parental homes at ever younger ages. Most of those who wanted to live with a partner of the opposite sex, married before or shortly after doing so. This development was reflected in a decrease in the age at marriage and a simultaneous decrease in the age at first childbearing, because at that time starting a conjugal union also involved having children for most people. The standard explanation is that young people strongly wanted to become independent of their parents and that improvements in economic conditions gave them increasing opportunities for leaving their parental home (Caldwell 1982).

During the late 1960s and the 1970s, young Swedes continued to start living with a partner at increasingly younger ages, but now many of them decided to live in a consensual union *instead* of marrying. Marriage rates fell dramatically. Initially the decline in marriage rates was more than compensated by an increase in entries into non-marital unions. Almost 50 percent of women born in the late 1950s started a union as teenagers compared to slightly less than 20 percent of women born twenty years earlier (Hoem and Rennermalm 1985). Even if young men and women continued to live together at ever younger ages, the age at which they had their first child moved in the opposite direction. The near-perfection of birth control by modern contraception allowed young people to separate sexual relations and union formation from childbearing.

These changes in the process of family initiation have often been explained as consequences of women's changing life roles facilitated by their improving educational attainment and increasing labor-force participation rates (Blossfeld and Huinink 1991; Martinelle, Qvist and Hoem 1992; de Beer 1990).

Such explanations certainly have some merit, but in our opinion, the Swedish experience suggests that they need modification. It is true that women's enrollment in the educational system is an important determinant of the age at entry into motherhood, simply because most women leave school before they marry and before they have children. Improved education also definitely means better chances in the labor market. Most Swedish women still leave school before they are twenty, however, and thus have ample time to find a job and start a career long before they begin to have children in their mid-to-late twenties, thus the argument is an incomplete explanation. Indeed, there has only been a very limited—if any—increase in education above the age of twenty in Sweden since the cohorts born around 1950, while the median age at first birth has increased by three years between women born around 1950 and 1963 and is now a little more than 27.5 years. At the same time, the postponing effect of being a student lost some of its importance. While students initially entered conjugal unions at much lower rates than other groups, they partially compensated for this during the 1970s, particularly because cohabitational unions became progressively more common among them (Hoem 1986).

Instead of a simplistic theory to the effect that the postponement of family formation has mostly been driven by the improvement in educational achievement and consequent developments in the labor market, an alternative explanation is that recent family trends in Sweden can also be seen as the outcome of a series of successive adjustments induced by general social and attitudinal change. The transformation of gender roles is thus only one (albeit important) factor along with many others that affect young people's plans and hopes for the future. This analysis describes some of the facts involved and argues the case for a more complex explanation.

Developments in Educational Attainment

During the 1960s and early 1970s, there was a marked increase in the educational level of young people. In line with developments in most Western nations, more and more young Swedes continued their education beyond compulsory school.[1] In the mid-1970s, however, there was a reversal in this trend. Most women aged eighteen and over, that is those born 1956–1960, actually spent a smaller fraction of the time in education than those born just five years earlier, for instance (Table 2.1). Swedish educational expansion did not continue in the late 1970s and the 1980s, and it is in fact those Swedes born around 1950 who have the highest educational level among all cohorts.

The most important change during the last fifteen to twenty years has been the great increase in the percentage of young people studying up to age eighteen, that is, beyond the compulsory school-leaving age. To a great extent, even this development is 'merely' a consequence of formal changes in the

TABLE 2.1   Percentage of Total Exposure-Time Spent in
            Full-Time Studies, by Cohort and Age (women)

Age	Birth Cohort				
	1936-1940	1941-1945	1946-1950	1951-1955	1956-1960
17	27	34	42	56	60
18	23	29	33	41	34
19	20	25	27	28	21
20	17	20	24	25	20
21	15	18	21	22	19
22	12	14	16	17	17

Source: 1981 Swedish Fertility Survey.

school system, as more and more vocational training has been incorporated into the regular school program. As a consequence, most of today's Swedes go to school until they are eighteen or nineteen years old. After that age, at least three out of four young people leave school and enter the labor market.[2] According to the 1991 Labor Force Survey, for instance, women aged thirty-eight to forty (that is, those born in the early 1950s) had the highest share of post-secondary education, while the youngest cohorts (born around 1970) had the highest share of secondary-school education (*gymnasium*) (Table 2.2). Since it has become quite common in Sweden to enroll in adult education and to alternate periods of paid work with going to school, we cannot yet calculate the final percentages for those with higher education in the younger cohorts. Nevertheless, we can safely say that there has been no further increase in the mean educational level, in contrast to what is observed in many other countries.

Family Policy

In Sweden, perhaps more than in other countries, priority is given to ensuring a decent level of living for everyone rather than letting market forces provide a wide range of choices only to those who can afford it. Family policy is one of the cornerstones of the Swedish welfare system and has attracted considerable attention in other countries, especially in recent years when Sweden has had one of the highest fertility rates in Europe *and* labor-force participation rates for women have been at a record high.

Sweden does not have an official pro-natalist family policy. Instead, as has been pointed out by Söderström (1992), Swedish family policy has been designed with three objectives in mind, namely: to promote equality between men and women; that all childbirths should be wanted childbirths; and to guarantee all children a reasonable standard of living.

Since Swedish family policy is so strongly concerned with equality between men and women, a number of measures have been implemented in order to

TABLE 2.2   Distribution of Women by Educational Level for Each Age Group in 1991 (%)

Age	Compulsory School	Secondary School			Post-secondary Education			Unknown
		At Most 2 yrs	More Than 2 yrs	Total	At Most 2 yrs	More Than 2 yrs	Total	
20-22	12	43	35	78	8	1	9	2
23-25	10	42	25	67	15	6	21	2
26-28	13	43	17	60	15	11	26	2
29-31	15	42	13	55	16	12	28	2
32-34	17	40	12	52	17	13	30	1
35-37	16	38	13	51	18	13	31	1
38-40	19	36	11	47	17	15	32	2
41-43	25	33	10	43	15	16	31	1
44-46	30	33	9	42	12	14	26	2
47-49	36	29	8	37	12	13	25	3
50 +	47	25	5	30	8	8	16	7

Source: 1991 Swedish Labor Force Survey.

promote this. Moen (1989) has emphasized the fact that the dilemma of employed parents is a public rather than a private issue in Sweden, and argues that this has led to the adoption of institutional support for working parents that are unmatched throughout the world.

In Sweden, the beginning of maternity leave rights for employed women dates back to 1938. Since that time, rights have been extended successively and there is now (since 1989) paid maternity leave for as much as fifteen months. An amount of income compensation has been introduced along the way. At present, the compensation is income-related and amounts to 90 percent of pre-tax earnings during the first twelve months of leave (up to a high ceiling), and is SEK 60 (the equivalent of circa U.S. $8.00) per day for the last three months. (Wage agreements give some groups up to 100 percent compensation for some of the leave.) In order to promote gender equality both in the labor market and at home, in 1974 Sweden was the first country in the world to introduce a system that enables both the father and mother to share the parental leave essentially in any manner that they choose. Working women can take out pregnancy pay for a maximum of fifty days if they are unable to work during the last months of pregnancy. There are also ten 'daddy-days' of leave for fathers at childbirth. Parents who have an employer, have a right to return to their job after parental leave and may 'bank' some of their leave for later use instead of taking it all at once. In fact, the law specifically states that *no* employer may penalize the career of a working parent because he or she has used parental rights.

Parents are also entitled to compensation for the occasional care of children. Today parents have a legal right to stay at home and take care of a sick child for as much as ninety days a year per child. Parents with children aged from four to twelve years are entitled to two-days' leave a year per child for parental participation in day-care or school activities. Furthermore, employed parents with a child under the age of eight have the right to reduce their working time by 25 percent, though this is without income compensation. In addition, Sweden has a comprehensive system of heavily subsidized public child-care, including high-quality day-care centers, family day-care, and after-school facilities. In 1987, 69 percent of all children from the ages of one to six years had access to public child-care and today the figure is even higher (Sundström 1991a).

Families with children also receive direct public economic support, the most important component of which is the child allowance. Low-income families are entitled to a housing allowance, and there is a system of public child-support advances for lone parents who have difficulties collecting child-support payments from the non-custodial parent.

Cohabitation: An Old Practice Revived

Sweden is a secularized society with open-minded norms concerning the way men and women choose to live together. The choice between a formal marriage and informal cohabitation has long since been an essentially private matter.

There is no premium attached to any particular family form, and not even Swedish family law (last revised in 1987) is confined to married couples. The law treats unmarried and married couples equally in most aspects. For instance, no distinction is made between married and unmarried couples with respect to tax assessment or when housing allowances or child benefits are granted.[3] This liberal view may help explain why non-marital cohabitation was so rapidly accepted in Sweden compared to many other countries, being soon regarded as a social institution rather than as deviant behavior.

Non-marital cohabitation has old roots in Sweden, in particular in the capital and in the (inland) northern parts of the country. According to Trost (1988), there were two different types of cohabitation at the beginning of this century. One very visible type was called *samvets-äktenskap* (marriage of conscience) and was practiced by a group of intellectuals as a protest against the fact that only religious marriage existed in Sweden at the time. Their protest was successful, in that civil marriage was introduced in 1909. The other form of consensual union was called *Stockholms-äktenskap* (Stockholm marriage) and was endemic among poor people who could not afford to marry.

As time went on, this practice appears to have almost disappeared, however. As far as we know, cohabitation was not very common during the decades before 1960. When informal cohabitation then suddenly started to grow in popularity, it received almost no public attention initially. When marriage rates fell dramatically, it became clear that the number of marriages was no longer a reliable measure of family formation, and consensual unions were recognized as a recordable living arrangement in the 1975 census. Nevertheless, it came as a real surprise when the 1981 Swedish Fertility Survey revealed that as many as every third woman born in the period 1936–1940 (the oldest birth cohort in the survey) had started her first union without marriage (Hoem and Rennermalm 1985). The survey also showed that these cohabitants, who most often came from the working class, married soon afterwards, and that durable consensual unions were relatively rare (Bernhardt and Hoem 1985). In subsequent cohorts, non-marital unions progressively became even more common and such unions stayed consensual for increasingly longer periods of time.

Lack of adequate statistics makes it hard to study the details of how cohabitation in its new guise spread in the Swedish population. Given the old traditions that we have mentioned, it is easy to jump to the conclusion that an old-standing basis for consensual unions existed, therefore, and that the modern increase came about simply because new groups imitated 'old' behavior. This seems too simple, however, given that traditional cohabitation was confined to certain regions and certain population groups, and the practice was probably not initially well known to the general public. The new increase can alternatively be seen as a largely independent phenomenon, much like a classical innovation process, although its rapid acceptance may have been facilitated by media attention given to the 'old tradition' when it became clear that new developments were underway. This interpretation is prompted by what we know about the geographical pattern of the new upsurge of consensual unions. If this were a process of a new imitation of old mores, we would ex-

TABLE 2.3 Time Spent Going Steady before Starting a Conjugal Union.
Women Born in 1936--1960 Who Lived in a Union at Interview
in 1981

Time spent going steady	Birth Cohort				
	1936-1940	1941-1945	1946-1950	1951-1955	1956-1960
0 - 5 months	6	10	14	19	25
6 - 12 months	19	18	21	24	25
13 - 24 months	26	26	27	25	22
25 months and over	49	46	38	32	27
Total	100	100	100	100	100

Source: 1981 Swedish Fertility Survey.

pect the extension to start where this living arrangement was best known beforehand, namely in northern Sweden, and to then spread to other population
groups that had most contact with the initiators, but this was not the case. The
early growth in cohabitation was especially pronounced in the Stockholm
area, where 'direct marriage' (that is, marriage not preceded by unmarried cohabitation) almost disappeared between the cohorts born in 1941–1945 and
1946–1950 (Hoem 1984). Young people in the northern regions did not change
their behavior as fast as people in the middle parts of the country, and the
changes that did occur may well have been inspired in part by the publicity
given to what was happening in the capital. In the typical manner of an innovation process, the real late-comers to non-marital unions were people in regions where they had been practically unheard of before, namely in parts of
Western and Southern Sweden that are often called the 'bible belt.'

A modern consensual union does not have all the characteristics of a formally sanctioned marriage. The behavior of cohabitants is sufficiently different from that of married people to merit regarding consensual union as a separate civil status, in particular because people live in such unions for
relatively long periods of their lives. Childbearing behavior in consensual
unions most resembles that in marital unions in the working class, while
young women from the bourgeoisie rapidly adopted cohabitation as a practical living arrangement but were much less willing to have children before
converting the union into a marriage (Bernhardt 1984). Students adopted this
new behavior more quickly than most other groups, but it would be wrong to
say that students initiated modern cohabitation in Sweden. This group simply
adopted this practice with enthusiasm because it gave them a type of union
that suited their needs. Rates of consensual-union formation among female
students more than doubled between the cohorts born in 1936–1940 and
1946–1950 (Hoem 1986). Like other groups for whom marriage was not a real-
istic current option, students were quick to take the opportunity to live together, possibly as an alternative to 'going steady,' and many young people
took this step after having known each other for quite a short while (Table

TABLE 2.4   First-Marriage Rates per 1000 Single Women,
by Age, 1966-1990

Age	1966	1973	1980	1987	1990
15-19	39	11	5	4	4
20-24	194	90	53	37	39
25-29	173	97	81	73	73
30-34	78	53	53	55	51
35-39	38	27	30	31	28
40-44	20	12	14	17	15

Source: Published Swedish population statistics.

2.3). Surely, starting a consensual union is not seen as much of a definitive move, while marrying is. In fact, two young partners do not always agree on whether they are living together or not when interviewed (Trost and Levin 1978).

The Prevalence of Marriage

Even if entering a conjugal union without marrying was already increasingly common in the early and mid-1960s, it was not until 1967 that the number of marriages started to decline dramatically. In five years they decreased from 60,000 to 40,000, and the decline was greatest among the youngest age groups. While almost 200 out of 1000 single women aged twenty to twenty-four married in 1966, the corresponding figure was only about forty in the late 1980s (Table 2.4). The median age at marriage has increased more than five years since the mid-1960s and is now thirty-one years for men and twenty-eight for women (Table 2.5).

The impact of the changes in marriage patterns on the proportion of women who have never married is illustrated in Table 2.6. There is an evident shift towards marriage at earlier ages between the cohorts born in the 1920s and those from the mid-1940s. Almost half the women born in 1921 were still unmarried at age twenty-four, compared to about 35 percent of women born between the early 1930s and the mid-1940s. However, in the subsequent years, the proportion increased rapidly to over 50 percent for women born in 1949. Seven out of ten women born in the mid-1950s were still unmarried then, and today almost 80 percent have never been married at age twenty-four (women born in 1965). At age thirty-two, every third woman has never been married. By comparison, only one in four is still childless at that age, a relation that is an inversion of what one would traditionally expect to be the case.

TABLE 2.5   Median Age at Marriage, 1950-1990

Year	Women	Men
1950	24.6	27.6
1960	23.3	26.4
1966	22.6	24.9
1970	23.5	25.5
1980	26.8	29.6
1985	28.1	30.9
1988	28.5	31.4
1989	31.8	34.8
1990	27.8	30.7

Note: A change as of 1 January 1990 in women's rights to a public widow's pension strongly influenced marriage patterns in 1989. See section dealing with this topic.

Source: Published Swedish population statistics.

TABLE 2.6   Never-Married Women by Age and Year of Birth (%)

Year of Birth	Age					
	20	24	28	32	36	40
1969	95.8					
1965	96.6	78.8				
1961	95.1	79.5	54.4			
1957	92.2	72.5	53.7	35.9		
1953	90.5	62.4	44.3	33.9	24.5	
1949	82.1	52.5	33.3	25.6	21.7	17.4
1945	77.0	36.0	23.3	17.2	14.7	13.3
1941	77.7	34.0	17.5	13.1	10.9	9.9
1937	77.1	33.9	15.6	10.8	9.1	8.1
1933	78.7	36.1	16.3	10.5	8.7	7.9
1929	80.1	40.4	18.9	11.5	8.9	8.0
1925	82.7	42.4	21.1	12.9	9.8	8.4
1921	87.4	47.1	23.3	14.8	11.1	9.4

Source: Published Swedish population statistics.

TABLE 2.7   Percentage of First Marriages Not Preceeded
              by Cohabitation, by Religious Activity Level
              (women born 1936-1950)

| Year of Birth | Religiously Active? | | All Women |
	No	Yes	
1936-40	57	85	59
1941-45	42	78	45
1946-50	18	69	22
1951-55	6	69	10

Source: Hoem and Hoem 1992, Table 2.

Factors Influencing the Propensity to
Marry Among Cohabiting Women

Modern cohabitation is one of the more important social innovations of recent decades. It has changed the pattern of family formation radically. Nevertheless, we still know too little about why some people subsequently marry and others do not.

Since the mid-1970s, almost all Swedish women who have married have been cohabitants first, and it is of special interest to investigate factors that influence the decision to continue to live in a consensual union or to marry. As can be seen in Table 2.7, among women born after 1960 it was especially the relatively few religiously active women who married directly.

Table 2.8 gives results from an intensity regression analysis concerning marriage among childless cohabiting women in their first union (Hoem 1987). The first three factors in Table 2.8 (the woman's year of birth, her social background, the age at which she started to cohabit) are fixed covariates, that is, their value does not change during the period of observation (which begins when the woman started her first non-marital union). Her current occupation in a month of observation, her current level of education, and whether she is pregnant or not are time-varying covariates, that is, their values are updated each time one of these factors changes value. This may happen once or several times during observation. We followed the respondents until they marry, have their first child, terminate the consensual union, or are interviewed, whichever occurs first. Union duration is our time factor.

It is not surprising that there is a great decline over our cohorts in the tendency to marry among childless cohabitants. Social background has little specific influence and there is also a relatively small effect of the woman's educational level, though the marriage 'risk' does rise somewhat as educational level improves.

In addition to the cohort factor, whether the woman is pregnant or not has the most important impact on marriage formation; its effect has a value just

TABLE 2.8   Relative "Risk" of Marriage Among
             Cohabiting, Childless Women (%)

Woman's year of birth:

1936-40	2.9
1941-45	1.8
1946-50	1
1951-55	0.6
1956-60	0.3

Her father's occupation:

Unskilled work	1
Skilled or clerical work	1.1
Managerial	1.1
Farming & self-employed	1.1

Age at start of cohabitation:

16-19 yrs	0.8
20-25	1
26-35	0.8

Respondent's current
employment status:

Wage earner	1
Student	0.8
Housewife	1.1
Other	1.1

Educational level:

Low	0.8
Medium	1
High	1.2

Pregnant?

No	1
Yes	4.2

Notes:

1. Effect of union duration not shown.
2. First unions only.
3. Model without interactions.

Source: Hoem 1987, Table 4.1.

TABLE 2.9   Interaction Between a Woman's Year of Birth and Her Pregnancy Status

Cohort	Pregnant? No (1)	Yes (2)	Yes/No (2) : (1)
1936-40	3.3	8.6	2.6
1941-45	1.6	8.0	5.0
1946-50	1	3.9	3.9
1951-55	0.5	2.4	4.6
1956-60	0.3	1.4	5.3

Source: Hoem 1987, Table 4.3.

over 4. This shows that it is still very common for people to marry in the advent of a first birth even though this is by no means necessary by social norms in Sweden. Today, every second Swedish child is born to a woman who is not married. This is true for as many as two out of three first-order births. Only about 5 percent of children born to unmarried women do not have parents who cohabit, however (Landgren Möller 1989). In some countries, a child born to an unmarried woman may mean an illegitimate child born to a single woman, and be indicative of social deprivation and lack of choice etc., whereas, by contrast, in Sweden in most cases it simply means that the parents have chosen not to marry legally.

It is of special interest to see whether the impact of a pregnancy differs between groups of women, that is, to what extent this factor is involved in interactions with other factors. One would like to know whether some special groups of women are particularly prone to enter motherhood in a consensual union. It turns out that two interactions are significant at the five-percent level, namely the one between pregnancy status and the woman's year of birth, and that with her current employment status.

Table 2.9 indicates that the effect of a pregnancy has not become any less important over our cohorts, as one might have thought. (See the third column in the table.) A pregnancy clearly increases the marriage rate among childless women who cohabit in their first union, did not change over our cohorts. For both pregnant and non-pregnant cohabiting women alike, however, the incidence of marriage has diminished strongly. Even though a declining fraction married during the first few years of cohabitation, they remained highly influenced by the imminent arrival of a child. This in turn implies that marital fertility has remained relatively constant over our cohorts. It has also remained relatively independent of cohabitational duration before marriage (Etzler 1986).

**TABLE 2.10   Interaction Between the Pregnancy Factor
and the Woman's Current Employment Status**

Employment Status	Pregnant? No (1)	Pregnant? Yes (2)	Yes/No (2):(1)
Wage-earner	1	4.2	4.2
Student	0.7	4.8	7.2
Housewife	1.6	3.8	2.4
Other	1.2	3.9	3.4

Source: Hoem 1987, Table 4.4.

The interaction between the pregnancy factor and the woman's current employment status is significant at the one percent level. A possible pregnancy influenced the tendency to marry most strongly among students (Table 2.10, third column). In this group, pregnant women who were studying had a seven-times-greater 'risk' of marrying than their non-pregnant counterparts, almost as if pregnancy were a 'precondition' of marriage for a female student.

During the period covered by these data, cohabitation has become an accepted living arrangement. It is now preferred by the overwhelming majority of couples at union formation. Nevertheless, pregnancy clearly increases the incidence of marriage among childless women cohabiting with a male partner and this pattern did not change as far as our data go (until the early 1980s).

Marital and Non-Marital Unions in the 1980s

Until data become available from the 1992 Family Survey, we have very limited information about family formation in Sweden during the 1980s, and must rely on cross-sectional data to a great extent. The great majority of unions formed during the 1980s (circa nine out of ten) were non-marital. This means that at the younger ages, most couples were not married. Of women aged twenty to twenty-four who lived in a conjugal union in 1991, as many as 78 percent cohabited. The proportion who marry increases strongly with the woman's age, however, and by age thirty to thirty-five, the pattern is almost reversed (Table 2.11). Of all women who lived in a union at that age, 28 percent were cohabitants and the rest (72 percent) were married. Table 2.11 also shows the differences between childless women and women with at least one child in the proportion married.

The behavior of people in non-marital unions, however, does not exactly mirror that of married people, even in Sweden. Couples who live in an informal union have lower first-birth rates than married couples (mainly because

TABLE 2.11   Percentage Married Among Swedish Women in
              Conjugal Unions, by Age Group, 1991

Age	Among All Women in Unions	Women at Parity 0	Women at Positive Parities
18-19	10	8	
20-24	22	12	41
25-29	50	26	62
30-34	72	40	76
35-39	79	50	83

Source: 1991 Swedish Labor Force Survey.

many people marry in connection with the first pregnancy). Union disruption is also more common among cohabiting couples than among the married, and this remains true even when we control for compositional effects, such as the effects of the number of children (Hoem and Hoem 1992, Meisaari-Polsa 1990). In the mid-1980s, the risk of dissolution was an estimated two to three times higher for unmarried than for married couples.

Taken together, these trends mean that the proportion of each age group who live in a marital or non-marital union has declined during the 1980s. The first signs of this development were already evident in the data from the 1981 Fertility Survey. According to Hoem (1986), students in particular appeared to defer union formation as early as the late 1970s. Other analyses (Hoem 1984) suggest that such deferral was particularly prevalent in the Stockholm area. In other words, the groups that changed their behavior most rapidly in the late 1960s, have again been forerunners in the 1980s. Initially, this decrease was interpreted as an outcome of a more difficult labor market situation faced at the beginning of the 1980s by young people in particular, in conjunction with a worsening housing market. Subsequent developments have demonstrated, however, that such behavior did not change when youth unemployment decreased and that a similar deferral of adult independence has occurred in other countries as well.

According to results from the population censuses, the total proportion of women who lived in a marital or non-marital union declined steadily from 1975 to 1990 (Table 2.12). A decline in the proportion married in each age group is no longer compensated by an increase in the proportion cohabiting. Due to the strict rules concerning registered residence, censuses always record lower numbers of cohabiting persons than do surveys (most surveys rely on self-reported status), but despite this there has been a clear decline during the last fifteen years or so irrespective of which source is used.

TABLE 2.12   Women Living in a Conjugal Union,
             by Age, 1975-1990 (%)

Age	1975	1980	1985	1990
18-19	19	13	11	10
20-24	52	47	41	42
25-29	76	72	67	64
30-34	82	80	77	74
35-39	83	81	79	78

Source: Swedish census data, adjusted for
        the census undercount.

Marriages in December 1989

During the 1970s and 1980s, about 40,000 couples married each year in Sweden. In 1989, the number of marriages suddenly jumped to 109,000. Before November, there had been no sign of any new and different marriage pattern, but in November the number of marriages doubled compared to the same month one year before, and in December the figure leapt to 64,000. In a normal December there are 2,500 to 3,000 marriages.

The direct cause of this sudden increase was the transitional provisions included in a reform of the National Widow's Pension Scheme that came into force at the beginning of 1990. The main purpose of the reform was to abolish women's rights to a public widow's pension. Generous transition rules ensured, however, that women born in 1944 and before could come under the old provisions, provided they were married by the end of 1989. This feature influenced the median age at marriage, which increased by more than three years in 1989 compared to in 1988 (cfr Table 2.5). For more information, see Hoem (1991).

One can ask why the widow's pension reform triggered such a strong reaction. After all, even before the law was changed, many women would have received a better widow's pension if they were married than if they lived in a consensual union when their partner died. The 1989 reform did not introduce any new rights, but simply gave some groups a last chance to obtain old rights that they had not made use of previously. Furthermore, the reaction to the change of rules did not come about when the new legislation was introduced, or in the period that followed, but at the very last moment after it had received a great deal of attention in the press. It would appear that many couples who then married had made little effort to compute any potential gain to themselves in beating the deadline before the new law came into force. There must have been a strong bandwagon effect—also due to the publicity that the

TABLE 2.13   Fraction of Women Who Became Pregnant Before
             Entering a Conjugal Union, by Cohort (%)

	Birth Cohort				
	1936-1940	1941-1945	1946-1950	1951-1955	1956-1960
Proportion pregnant	28	28	23	13	4

Source: Hoem 1987, Table 3.6.

sudden increase in marriages received—with many couples simply deciding that the time had come to marry.

This example indicates two things. First of all, many people live as cohabitants without seriously informing themselves about the consequences of not marrying. A further indication of this is the fact that it has *not* been common to eliminate the remaining discrepancies in the formalities of family arrangement by contracts.

Secondly, it is obviously not so hard to persuade many Swedish cohabitants to change their legal marital status. We may conclude that for most people—in Sweden at least—the reasons for not marrying are weak and not very ideologically based. This was again reflected in the 1981 Fertility Survey when women who lived in consensual unions very commonly said they were considering getting married in the future, and very rarely said that they planned not to do so.

The Deferment of First Birth

Successively, the implications for a woman of living with a man changed after the mid-1960s. Judging from the behavior of women born in the late 1930s, most of them must have entered a union to start a family and have children quickly, and almost 30 percent of them were pregnant at the time they started marriage or cohabitation.[4] Many of these children were unplanned; two-thirds of the women who became pregnant before first union formation reported that their pregnancy came too early or was not wanted. By contrast, less than 5 percent of women born in the late 1950s were pregnant when they entered their first union, even though more than twice as many had started a union as teenagers (almost 50 percent compared to less than 20 percent among women born twenty years earlier) (see Table 2.13).

The substantial postponement of the start of childbearing since the late 1960s manifested itself as a decrease over the cohorts in age-specific first-birth rates at young ages. Among women born in the early 1940s, only about one-fourth had not entered motherhood by the age of twenty-eight. The corresponding number was as much as 45 percent for women born in the early 1960s (see Table 2.14).

TABLE 2.14   Childless Women by Age and Year of Birth (%)

Year of Birth	Age					
	20	24	28	32	36	40
1969	94					
1965	94	71				
1961	92	71	45			
1957	86	63	40	25		
1953	83	55	34	22	17	
1949	79	50	28	19	15	13
1945	78	48	26	17	14	13
1941	81	49	26	17	14	13
1935	81	51	27	18	15	14
1930	83	54	31	20	16	15

Source: Data from the Swedish fertility register.

As we noted in the introductory section, improved education for women has been a popular explanation of the postponement of first birth. Any educational impact on the age at entry into motherhood can hardly have been direct, however, for it is highly questionable whether time spent in school at the relevant ages has been sufficiently extensive to merit any prime role in the story of childbearing in Sweden. In this country, most women complete their schooling as early as at eighteen or nineteen years of age, and there has been almost no change in the educational pattern at higher ages during the last fifteen years, which is the period of first-birth postponement. To the extent that there has been an effect of improved education, it must have been indirect, for example via women's improved chances in the labor market.

In line with this, it is often argued that it is has become successively more important for women to achieve a firm foothold in the labor market before first birth since most Swedish women see themselves as members of the labor force for most of their adult lives. One reason is the regulations covering Swedish leave policy, in which the most extensive improvements in parental benefits have been limited to employed parents. These benefits are based on earnings, which is an inducement to try to achieve as a good a salary as possible before entering motherhood.[5] This will be important not only in order to improve one's income compensation during parental leave but also for later segments of life when caring for a child may hamper a woman's ability to improve her income and make progress in her job.[6]

This line of reasoning is probably most valid for more highly educated women, but as a general explanation it is weakened by the fact that most women in Sweden are not employed in jobs with a strong income gradient after the first few years of work. It is therefore hard to believe that most women will earn so much more money by postponing their first birth by two to three extra years after entering permanent employment.

On the other hand, there are other reasons beside the obvious economic ones to become established in the labor market before having children. Most women want a secure job that they enjoy and wish to return to after parental leave. Moreover, even if Swedish parents with a child under the age of eight have a legal right to reduce their working hours, it may be easier to exercise this right and to obtain flexible working hours if they are in a stable and permanent employment.

All in all, Swedish women certainly have a lot of impetus to get established in the labor force at an early stage in their adult lives. This has always been the case, however; it has not changed so much over the last twenty years. To argue that such a feature has played an prominent role in the progressive postponement of first childbearing, one must also show that it has become more important over time, and this is hard to do. Indeed, the reverse may be true. It may have been more important to have labor-force experience before childbearing at times when mothers were homemakers for several years, for any such experience could then be a key issue in a satisfactory subsequent return to work. It is probably easier to be a member of the labor force as a mother of small children in Sweden today than it was twenty years ago. For reasons of this nature, the argument that it has become successively more important to obtain seniority in the labor market before entering motherhood may have been somewhat overplayed.

It may be that the main effects of whatever educational improvement there has been for women, have been indirect, for they have gone hand-in-hand with attitudinal changes. Instead of interpreting the substantial periods that women now spend in the labor force prior to motherhood mainly as the time needed to become established in their careers, the paid work that we observe for long periods of their young adult lives may well be regarded as a *natural* activity for women before they start to have children. We have a new level of public and individual consciousness concerning the importance of really planning childbearing. Public norms stress the responsibilities of parenthood and stress that each child born should be wanted and well cared for. This may have produced an observable new age-grading of young adult roles. One piece of evidence is the finding that young male and female respondents in the 1985 Swedish Youth Survey were more interested in getting ahead in their jobs and in earning money to spend or to develop their leisure-time activities than in starting a family and having children (Roleén and Springfeldt 1987).[7] There are no direct indications that more Swedish men and women will want to remain childless in the future, even if an increasing proportion are childless in their late twenties. Childbearing is certainly seen as an important part of a full life, but for many young people it is an issue for a later stage in life.

Conclusions

Research in recent years has improved our insight into family formation processes. Nevertheless, much remains to be understood. In particular, there seem to be unexplained waves of changes in mood that sweep over nations and even over most of the Western world. The 1990 round of European Values Survey seems to have picked up signs of a stronger family orientation than they did in the corresponding round ten years before, not only in Sweden but all over Europe.[8] Only further observation and research can tell what impact any current secular reorientation in family values may bring in its wake.

During the 1970s and the first part of the 1980s, much effort was put into explaining the low and decreasing fertility level in most European countries. Sweden (for one) experienced a strong postponement of the first birth at the same time as a substantial decline for third-order and subsequent births. At that time, it was not hard to argue for the importance of women's changing roles in this development as the main explanatory factor in the intensity and timing of childbirth. With hindsight, however, I am convinced that in the case of Sweden, the standard explanations, such as improved educational level and higher labor force participation, were too simplistic and partly untrue. Indeed, women who had been members of the labor force almost continuously since first birth had about the same level of third-birth fertility, for example, as women who had not participated much in the labor market since entry into motherhood. Mothers with the higher levels of education also had the highest fertility during this period. In subsequent years, the labor-force participation and number of hours worked by women have increased further in Sweden simultaneously with a substantial rise in fertility for *all* birth orders. Such developments would simply be incomprehensible in an explanatory framework that relied exclusively on the previously standard elements.

In fact, no well-supported explanation exists today. A likely senario, however, is that many couples held back on child-bearing in the early days of growing female labor-force participation because they found parenting hard when both partners had a job or because they were uncertain about the situation, while the combination of parenting and work became (or was perceived to be) much easier later on. Despite increasingly generous family policies and labor-market regulations and despite essentially welcoming employers, much reorganization and reorientation had to occur both in the workplace and at home. By the late 1970s, this 'pioneering effect' had petered out. Policies and regulations had become sufficiently generous to turn the tide in childbearing while the increase in female labor was sustained. This interpretation fits the facts as far as we know them but more research is needed to give a really good base for firm conculsions.

Notes

I am grateful to Jan Hoem for having served as a sounding-board for my ideas and for giving me much editorial advice. I have also benefited from further editorial advice from Clare Tame.

1. Compulsory school attendance starts at age seven and lasts for nine years. Most girls and boys continue into upper-secondary school (*gymnasium*), which includes both vocational and theoretical courses.

2. According to the 1991 Labor Force Survey, the labor force participation rates for men and women aged twenty were 73.9 and 75.0 percent respectively.

3. Since 1971, husband and wife have been taxed separately in exactly the same way as a cohabiting man and woman. The only major distinction in the eyes of the law is that unmarried couples do not automatically have all property in common and do not automatically inherit each other's property, except that a surviving cohabitant inherits their common dwelling—their most valuable property for most people—when the partner dies. Normally, therefore, simplification of the legal transition of property in the case of the death of a partner is not a strong motive for commuting cohabitation to legally sanctioned marriage.

4. This was true for as many as half of those who began their first union as teenagers.

5. Eligibility for parental benefits as such cannot be a prime concern in this connection, for it takes less than a year to establish a job-holder's entitlement to parental leave and benefits (in a permanent job).

6. A temporary reduction in the number of hours worked gives a lower full-time salary in the long run (Gustafsson and Lantz 1985).

7. Similar values may be reflected in the reasons given for not yet having entered motherhood by childless respondents aged twenty-five to twenty-nine in conjugal unions who wished to have children in the 1981 Fertility Survey. The most common answer given was that they did not yet feel sufficiently mature.

8. Personal communication from Thorlief Petterson, Professor of Sociology of Religion, Uppsala University; director of the Swedish branch of the European Values Survey.

References

Bernhardt, E. (1984). "Den sociala bakgrundens betydelse för baranfödande och giftermål inom informellt samboende bland svenska kvinnor födda 1936–60," *Stockholm Research Reports in Demography*, 20.

Bernhardt, E. and B. Hoem (1985). "Cohabitation and Social Background: Trends Observed for Swedish Women Born 1936–60," *European Journal of Population* 1, 375–95.

Blossfeld, H.-P. and J. Huinink (1991). "Human Capital Investments or Norms of Role Transitions? How Women's Schooling and Career Affect the Process of Family formation," *American Journal of Sociology*, 97, 143–68.

Caldwell, J. (1982). *Theory of Fertility Decline*, New York, Academic Press.

de Beer, J. (1990). "Recent Family Trends in the Netherlands," paper presented to a meeting of the European Science Foundation, Demography Network's Working Party on Recent Family Trends, Stockholm, 13–14 December 1990.

Etzler, C. (1984). "Första steget i familjebildningen—Gifta sig, börja sambo eller få barn: Utveckling och skillnader bland svenska kvinnor med olika social bakgrund födda 1936–60," *Stockholm Research Reports in Demography*, 21.

Etzler, C. (1986). "Barnafödande inom äktenskapet: Det föräktenskapliga samboendets betydelse för förstfödslar inom äktenskapet bland svenska kvinnor födda 1936–60," *Stockholm Research Reports in Demography*, 29.

Etzler, C. (1988). "Education, Cohabitation and the First Child: Some Empirical Findings from Sweden," in H. Moors and J. Schoorl (eds), *Lifestyles, Contraception and Parenthood*, The Hague and Brussels: NiDi CBGS Publications.

Gustafsson, S. and P. Lantz (1985). *Arbete och löner*, IUI and the Centre for Working Life, Stockholm.

·Hoem, B. (1984). "Regional utveckling i det moderna samboendet, analysmetoder och resultat," *Stockholm Research Reports in Demography*, 22.

Hoem, B. (1987). "Graviditetens betydelse för barnlösa kvinnors civilstaandsförändringar," *Stockholm Research Reports in Demography*, 38.

Hoem, J. (1986). "The Impact of Education on Modern Union Initiation," *European Journal of Population* 2, 113–33.

Hoem, J. (1991). "To Marry Just in Case...: The Swedish Widow's Pension Reform and the Peak in Marriages in December 1989," *Acta Sociologica*, 34, 127–35.

Hoem, B. and J. Hoem (1992). "The Disruption of Marital and Non-marital Unions in Contemporary Sweden," in Trussel, Hankinson and Tilton (eds), *Demographic Applications of Event History Analysis*, Oxford, Clarendon Press.

Hoem, J. and B. Rennermalm (1985). "Modern Family Initiation in Sweden: Experience of Women Born between 1936 and 1960," *European Journal of Population* 1, 81–112.

Landgren Möller, E. (1989). "Barns levnadsvillkor," *Levnadsförhållanden*, Report No. 62, Statistics Sweden.

Martinelle, S., J. Qvist and J. Hoem (1992). "Fruktsamhet ur livsperspektiv," *Demografiska rapporter* 1992:1, Statistics Sweden.

Meisaari-Polsa, T. (1990). "Familjebildning och familjeupplösning under 1980–talet," *Demografiska rapporter* 1990:1, Statistics Sweden.

Moen, Ph. (1989). *Working Parents, Transformations in Gender Roles and Public Policies in Sweden*, University of Wisconsin Press, Madison, Wisconsin.

Popenoe, D. (1987). "Beyond Tradition: A Statistical Portrait of the Changing Family in Sweden," *Journal of Marriage and the Family* 49, 173–83.

Rolén, M. and P. Springfeldt (1987). "Make och far," *Statistics Sweden.*

Sundström, M. (1991a). "Sweden: Supporting Work, Family and Gender Equality," in Kamerman and Kahn (eds), *Child Care, Parental Leave and the Under-3s: Policy Innovation in Europe*, Westport (Conneticut), Auburn House.

Sundström, M. (1991b). "The Growth in Full-time Work Among Swedish Women in the 1980s," paper presented at the 3rd EALE Conference, El Escorial (Madrid).

Söderström, L. (1992). "Family Policy and Fertility in Sweden," paper presented to the 10th Nordic Demographic Symposium, Lund, 12–14 August.

Trost, J. and B. Levin (1978). *Att sambo och gifta sig: Fakta och föreställningar*, Stockholm: Statens offentliga utredningar, 55.

Trost, J. (1988). "Cohabitation and Marriage: Transitional Pattern, Different Lifestyle, or Just Another Legal Form," in H. Moors and J. Schoorl (eds), *Lifestyles, Contraception and Parenthood*, The Hague and Brussels: NiDi CBGS Publications.

3

West Germany

HANS-PETER BLOSSFELD AND GÖTZ ROHWER

In this analysis we examine the improvement in women's educational attainment across cohorts and its influence on the process of family formation in West Germany. Our aim is to assess empirically whether women's growing economic independence, resulting from better education, is one of the major factors in the rise in delayed marriage and motherhood in the former Federal Republic of Germany.

West Germany is an interesting case because of its highly international-competitive market economy combined with a welfare state providing a relatively high level of social security for all citizens. The welfare state, however, has been classified as *conservative* (Esping-Andersen 1990) because it is committed to the 'conventional' or 'traditional' conjugal family. On the one hand, the West German tax system punishes the dual full-time earner family and privileges women's non-work or part-time work, and on the other, public policy with respect to family services is underdeveloped and does not provide enough kindergardens, pre-primary schools or day care institutions (Gauthier 1992). Thus, West German women normally interrupt their employment at the time of marriage (this was mainly the case among older birth cohorts) or when the first child is born (this is the modal case among the younger birth cohorts) and, to a large extent, do not reenter the labor market again (Blossfeld 1994). However, if married women do re-enter, they normally give priorty to family-centered non-market activities and mostly prefer to work part-time (Blossfeld 1994).

Data

The empirical analysis is based on data from the German Socio-Economic Panel (GSP), which is a representative longitudinal database for the Federal Republic of Germany, suitable for use in the study of a broad range of socio-economic questions.[1] The GSP data have two main advantages for examining how women's improved educational attainment influences first marriage and first motherhood: (1) they provide longitudinal data for individuals, families

56

and households; and (2) contain not only up-to-date information from 1984 until the present day, but also a broad range of retrospective questions covering a period of over fifty years. The GSP data do not, however, allow us to reconstruct consensual unions over this extended period. This has only been possible since the first panel wave in 1984. We can also not reconstruct women's employment careers continuously over a longer period. Our analysis will therefore focus on changes in educational attainment, bearing in mind that the level of educational investments is also a good predictor of job opportunities in West Germany (Blossfeld 1989).

Methods

The dependent variable has been specified as the instantaneous rate of entry into marriage or motherhood, defined as:

$$r(t) = \lim P(t \leq T < t + \Delta t \ / \ T \geq t) \ / \ \Delta t \,,$$
$$\Delta t \to 0$$
$$\Delta t > 0$$

where P(.) is the instantaneous probability of entering into marriage or motherhood in the interval (t, t+Δt), respectively, provided that such an entry has not occurred before the beginning of this interval (see, for example, Blossfeld, Hamerle and Mayer 1989; Tuma and Hannan 1984).

Using an exponential model, our goal is to specify the rates of entry into marriage and motherhood as a function of time-constant (X_1) and time-dependent covariates (X_2 (t)) (Blossfeld and Huinink 1991):

$$r(t) = \exp[\beta_1 X_1 = \beta_2 X_2 (t)].$$

Observation begins at age sixteen and ends with the event of first marriage or the birth of the first child, or, for right censored cases, with the date of the interview or age forty-six, whichever occurs first.

To introduce the time-dependent measures into the rate equation, we used the method of episode-splitting (see Blossfeld, Hamerle and Mayer 1989), and created a separate data record for maximal half-year intervals. For each of these records four different pieces of information were provided: time at the beginning and end of the interval to which the record pertains; the values of the time-dependent covariates at the beginning of these intervals; whether the interval ended with an event or not; and the values of the other covariates relevant for the analysis.

Rate function coefficients and their t-ratios also help us to ascertain how women's educational and career investments influence first motherhood and first birth, in what direction, and at what level of significance. The magnitude of the effects and their substantive significance are, however, more easily assessed by examining survivor functions. Therefore, on the basis of the models we estimated survivor functions for different educational careers that show the probability of a woman remaining unmarried or childless at age t (Blossfeld, Hamerle and Mayer 1989:33):

$$S(t) = exp[-_{u=o}\int^t r(u)du].$$

The independent variables include measures of age-dependence, social class, cohort and education. We used a combination of two variables to control for the non-monotonic age-dependence of the rates of marriage and first birth (Coale 1971; Bloom 1982). This approach assumes that women are at risk of entering first marriage and of having a first child between the ages sixteen and forty-six (whereby i is an index for the i-th interval):

$$\log(D_i) =: \log(\text{current age} - 16),$$
$$\log(R_i) =: \log(46 - \text{current age}).$$

Including these variables in the exponential model as time-dependent covariates,

$$exp[\log(D_i) \times \beta' + \log(R_i) \times \beta''] = D_i^{\beta'} \times R_i^{\beta''},$$

models the typical bell-shaped curve of the rates of entry into first marriage and first motherhood. This curve is symmetric around the age thirty-one for $\beta' = \beta''$, right-skewed (this means marriages or births are clustered more to the left of the mean with most of the extreme values to the right) for $\beta' < \beta''$, and left-skewed (this means marriages or births are clustered to the right of the mean) for $\beta' > \beta''$.

In order to model women's accumulation of general and vocational qualifications in the general school system, the vocational training system and the university system of the Federal Republic of Germany, we use the average number of years required to obtain them (Blossfeld 1985).[2] To model changes in the accumulation of these qualifications over the life-course for each woman, we have updated the level of education at the age when individuals normally obtain each higher level. For example, for a woman who attains a lower school qualification at age fourteen, reaches the intermediate school qualification at age sixteen, leaves school with an *Abitur* at nineteen, and finishes her university studies at the age of twenty-five, we would obtain a picture of changing levels of education over the life-course as shown in the upper panel of Figure 3.1.

However, as indicated above, there may also be other effects of education which have an impact on the timing of family formation given that enrollment in the educational system takes up a woman's time and hence affects her ability to marry and to have a first child. Thus, we generated a time-dependent dummy variable, indicating whether or not a woman is attending the educational system at a specific age (see the lower panel of Figure 3.1).

As time-constant background variables we include father's social class. On the basis of the GSP we can only use a limited set of class categories: farmers,

FIGURE 3.1   Educational Career over the Life Course
in West Germany

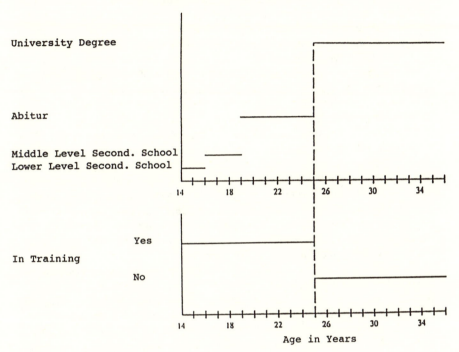

Source: German Socio-economic Panel 1988.

unskilled and skilled manual workers, unskilled and skilled administrative and service workers, professionals, and self-employed, with unskilled manual workers taken as the reference category.

This analysis studies the process of entry into marriage and motherhood for women in Germany over a period of about fifty years. The oldest cohort studied were born between 1919 and 1923, entered into marriage and motherhood from the late 1930s to the late 1940s, and thus began family formation under the Third Reich and during the turbulence generated by the World War II. The youngest cohort analyzed were born between 1964 and 1968, started to enter marriage and motherhood during the 1980s, thus beginning family formation during a period of high educational expansion and economic uncertainty. To control for cohort effects generated by historical events, changes in values and economic development, we used a set of dummy variables each representing five-year birth groups from 1919–1923 through to 1964–1968 (the reference group is the 1919–1932 cohort).

Effects of Educational Expansion

Important changes in the timing of entry into marriage and fertility are often attributed to changes in women's educational attainments, and we accordingly begin our empirical analysis by asking the question, *"What are the effects of the educational expansion on the levels of women's educational attainment in successive cohorts in West Germany?"*

Distributions of educational attainment for women from successive cohorts are shown in Table 3.1. If we compare the educational attainments of the cohort 1919–1923 with those of the 1954–1958 and 1959–1963 cohorts, the improvement in educational chances for women is clear. Women have profited from educational expansion at all levels of higher qualification. For the 1919–1923 birth cohort, the proportion of women with lower secondary school qualification without vocational training was about five times as large (51.4 percent) as for the 1959–1963 cohort (10.4 percent).[3] By contrast, compared to the 1954–1958 cohort, women of the 1919–1923 cohort were less likely to have intermediate school with vocational training (26.2 percent as against 12.9 percent), *Abitur* with vocational training (8.2 percent as against 1.7 percent), professional college qualification (2.6 percent as against 0.7 percent), or a university degree (2.1 percent as against 10.0 percent).[4]

We can say that, in a first phase, educational expansion led to a decrease in the number of women without vocational training and to a strong increase in women with vocational training (from the 1919–1923 cohort to the 1949–1953 cohort), and in a second phase, to a decrease in women with vocational training and a steep increase in women with higher formal educational qualifications, such as *Abitur* or a university degree. There appears to have been a uniform long-term trend across successive birth cohorts; not only have women's average levels of educational attainment risen steadily from one birth cohort to another, but women's educational enrollment over the life-course has also extended in time.

Changes in Women's Ages
at Entry into Marriage and Motherhood

Tables 3.2 and 3.3 show the percentages of women who have not yet entered first marriage or first birth for each birth cohort and specific ages. These percentages are based on estimates of survivor functions for each cohort for the events of entry into marriage and first birth.

As shown in Table 3.2, age at first marriage fell sharply from the 1919–1923 cohort to the 1944–1948 cohort, and has since been rising until the youngest birth cohort examined. The greatest movements occurred amongst women aged twenty to twenty-four, where the proportion unmarried dropped from 46 percent to 15 percent and subsequently increased to 40 percent. The result is that as far as the youngest cohorts (1964–1968 and 1959–1963) can be followed, they have more or less the same age pattern at entry into marriage as for the oldest cohorts (1924–1928 and 1919–1923).

TABLE 3.1   Educational Attainment of Women from Selected Cohorts in West Germany (percentages)

Educational Attainment	Birth Cohort									
	1919-23	1924-28	1929-33	1934-38	1939-43	1944-48	1949-53	1954-58	1959-63	1964-68
Lower secondary school qualification without vocational training	51.4	44.0	50.7	39.4	26.9	20.7	17.0	13.9	10.4	20.5
Intermediate school qualification without vocational training	3.5	4.4	5.3	1.7	2.2	2.2	2.7	2.8	3.5	16.9
Upper secondary school qualification (Abitur) without vocational training	0.3	0.6	0.3	0.3	0.5	0.9	0.5	1.8	7.9	13.4
Lower secondary school qualification with vocational training	27.3	34.2	24.3	38.0	43.9	44.4	44.7	34.4	26.8	17.2
Intermediate school qualificaiton with vocational training	12.9	9.8	10.9	16.5	18.2	20.7	21.1	26.2	32.3	25.2
Upper secondary school qualification (Abitur) with vocational training	1.7	3.5	3.0	1.1	2.5	1.5	4.4	8.2	10.4	6.6
Professional college qualification	0.7	2.2	2.3	0.8	2.2	3.7	2.2	2.6	2.7	0.2
University degree	2.1	1.3	3.3	2.2	3.5	5.9	7.4	10.0	6.0	-
Total	100.0	100.0	100.0	100.0	100.0	100.0	100.0	100.0	100.0	100.0
N	286	316	304	358	401	324	365	389	403	425

Source: German Socio-economic Panel, 1988.

TABLE 3.2   Changes in the Timing of Entry into Marriage
in West Germany, as Measured by Proportions
Unmarried at Specific Ages (percentages)

Birth Cohort	Proportion of Unmarried Women at Age							
	20	24	28	32	36	40	44	48
1964-68	89	-	-	-	-	-	-	-
1959-63	78	40	-	-	-	-	-	-
1954-58	73	32	19	-	-	-	-	-
1949-53	65	24	11	7	-	-	-	-
1944-48	65	15	7	4	3	-	-	-
1939-43	80	21	8	5	3	3	-	-
1934-38	76	23	9	6	5	5	4	-
1929-33	86	32	13	7	6	5	5	4
1924-28	90	40	16	11	8	6	5	5
1919-23	90	46	20	13	10	9	7	7

Source: German Socio-economic Panel, 1988.

TABLE 3.3 Changes in the Timing of Entry into Motherhood
in West Germany, as Measured by Proportions
Childless at Specific Ages (percentages)

Birth Cohort	Proportion of Childless Women at Age							
	20	24	28	32	36	40	44	48
1964-68	92	-	-	-	-	-	-	-
1959-63	90	57	-	-	-	-	-	-
1954-58	84	55	30	-	-	-	-	-
1949-53	78	47	21	15	-	-	-	-
1944-48	77	32	16	11	9	-	-	-
1939-43	87	41	18	13	10	10	-	-
1934-38	83	45	18	13	11	11	11	-
1929-33	92	54	28	19	16	16	16	16
1924-28	87	56	26	19	15	14	14	14
1919-23	91	57	30	19	15	15	15	15

Source: German Socio-economic Panel, 1988.

Looking at ages at first birth in Table 3.3, we observe a similar trend. Again, it is the 1944–1948 cohort which entered motherhood at the youngest ages. For this cohort not only marriages but also entries into motherhood were highly concentrated. Once again, we find more or less the same time pattern of entry into motherhood for the youngest and oldest cohorts, bearing in mind the curtailed period for which the former can be observed.

TABLE 3.4   Persons Married and in Consensual Unions in
             West Germany in 1984

Birth Cohort	Married		Consensual Union		Total	
	N	%	N	%	N	%
-1913	385	43.45	17	1.92	866	9.86
1914-1918	238	65.93	4	1.11	361	4.02
1919-1923	418	74.38	5	0.89	562	6.25
1924-1928	552	81.66	13	1.92	676	7.52
1929-1933	560	84.85	9	1.36	660	7.34
1934-1938	699	83.91	21	2.52	833	9.27
1939-1943	768	84.03	26	2.84	914	10.17
1944-1948	584	81.68	29	4.06	715	7.96
1949-1953	601	76.27	47	5.96	788	8.77
1954-1958	529	58.26	95	10.46	908	10.10
1959-1963	229	26.20	95	10.87	874	9.73
1964-1968	16	1.98	21	2.59	810	9.01
Total	5579		382		8987	100.00

Source: German Socio-economic Panel, 1988.

In West Germany, the delay in entry into marriage and motherhood seems to be less dramatic than that for other countries, especially Sweden (see Hoem and Hoem 1987a, and Hoem in this volume). Until the most recent birth cohorts, more or less the same entrance pattern of age at marriage and motherhood is observed as was already established fifty years ago. However, it is clear that the earlier movement toward younger and universal marriage and motherhood had also come to a halt at the end of the 1960s and the beginning of the 1970s. This reversal of the timing of marriage and motherhood is not in line however with the trend in women's educational attainment across cohorts. It is therefore questionable as to whether changes in marriage and motherhood can be attributed mainly to women's growing economic independence, as argued for example by Becker (1981).

The Role of Consensual Unions in West Germany

There is little available data on consensual unions for West Germany, and no information about the long-term development of such unions. The GSP does allow us, however, to determine the frequency of consensual unions across cohorts at the time of the first panel wave in 1984 as well as make an analysis of the dynamics of consensual unions from 1984 to 1988.

From Table 3.4, which presents *de facto* marital unions in 1984, we can see that consensual unions were more common among younger respondents. However, only about 11 percent of the people born between 1954 and 1963 had lived in consensual unions in 1984. This means that the frequency of co-habitation at the time of the first panel wave was modest.

As regards the dynamics of consensual unions between 1984 and 1988, Table 3.5, gives the distribution of entries into consensual unions across cohorts. Over 91 percent of these entries are concentrated among men and women born after 1944, and more than 76 percent of the entries can be observed between the cohorts 1954 and 1968. That is, between the ages of sixteen and thirty in 1984 and twenty-one and thirty-five in 1988. This means that the greatest dynamics of consensual unions occurs among the relatively young.

For cohorts born between 1944 and 1968, Table 3.6 reports that 31.4 percent of men and women living in consensual unions that started between 1984 and 1988 entered into marriage. Of these, 8.7 percent subsequently separated and 59.9 percent have been censored at the last examined panel wave in 1988.

Table 3.7 reports the length of cohabitation with a median of about three years (35.03 months for men and 37.60 months for women). There are marked differences in duration between consensual unions which end with entry into marriage and those that end in separation. Of men in consensual unions, 20 percent entered marriage after about one year, and 20 percent of men and women in consensual unions were separated after about three years. The median duration for a consensual union for men and women entering marriage is about four years.

Partial likelihood estimates for the transition from consensual union to marital union in the period 1984–1988 (considering the birth cohorts between 1944 and 1968) show four statistically significant effects (Table 3.8). First, the birth cohort 1964–1968 lives significantly longer in consensual unions than the older ones. This could mean there is now less pressure on younger couples to legalize a consensual union given that consensual unions have become a normal and widespread phenomenon. Second, we find a very strong effect of the influence of pregnancy on the rate of entry into marriage. This means that the birth of a child is closely connected with the desire to legalize the union. Third, former experience of marriage reduces the desire to marry again. Finally, enrollment in the educational system delays entry into marriage. This means that the increasing prevalence of consensual unions among young people must be seen in connection with increasing participation in the educational system over the life-course. Thus, finishing education is an important factor conditioning entry into marriage.

Effects of Education on
the Rate of Entry into First Marriage

Here it is useful to control for other important influences before we focus on the dynamic measure of educational level and the dynamic measure of enrollment in the educational system. All coefficients in the models are metric coefficients, but we will not compare the relative magnitude of the effects of different variables within models because they depend on the scale by which variables are measured. Instead, we rely on the significance level of each variable to decide whether or not it has an important impact. In evaluating a mod-

TABLE 3.5   Entry into Consensual Unions in
            West Germany, 1984-1989

Birth Cohort	Number of Entries	Percentage of Total
1914-1918	2	0.46
1919-1923	3	0.70
1924-1928	4	0.93
1929-1933	6	1.39
1934-1938	13	3.02
1939-1943	9	2.09
1944-1948	28	6.50
1949-1953	22	5.10
1954-1958	70	16.24
1959-1963	140	32.48
1964-1968	119	27.61
1969-	15	3.48
Total	431	100.00

Source: German Socio-economic Panel, 1988.

TABLE 3.6 Exit from Consensual Unions in West Germany
          in the Observation Period 1984-1989
          (cohorts 1944-1968)

Destination	Number of Exits	Percentage of Total
Marriage	119	31.4
Separation	33	8.7
Censored	227	59.9
Total	379	100.0

Source: German Socio-economic Panel, 1988.

TABLE 3.7 Duration of Consensual Unions in Month (Survivor Functions) in West Germany in the Observation Period (cohorts 1944-1968)*

Proportion in consensual Union	Duration			Exit: Marriage			Exit: Separation		
	Men	Women	All	Men	Women	All	Men	Women	All
0.95	4.23	4.01	4.12	4.47	4.25	4.36	18.19	21.11	19.25
0.90	7.11	6.36	6.81	7.54	6.66	7.19	25.97	29.64	28.11
0.85	8.67	10.99	9.18	10.08	11.42	10.61	31.51	37.28	35.52
0.80	11.19	14.17	12.60	13.22	15.78	14.52	36.29	40.64	39.96
0.75	15.62	18.15	16.44	18.40	20.64	20.10			
0.70	20.05	21.29	20.79	23.54	27.27	25.58			
0.65	23.40	26.33	23.96	26.99	29.97	29.56			
0.60	26.42	29.50	28.39	34.52	36.18	36.10			
0.55	29.76	34.21	31.87	43.40		50.87			
0.50	35.03	37.60	36.42	52.46					
0.45	38.76	44.66	43.89						
0.40	49.19								

* Product-limit estimates of survivor functions.

Source: German Socio-economic Panel, 1988.

TABLE 3.8 Partial Likelihood Estimates for Leaving Consensual Unions in West Germany in the Observation Period 1984-1989 (cohorts 1944-1968)

Variable	Marriage			Separation		
	Coeff	Std. Err	Signif	Coeff	Std. Err	Signif
Sex woman	0.0557	0.1910	0.2294	-0.3439	0.3619	0.6580
Cohort 1944-1948	0.0128	0.4506	0.0227	0.7191	0.7430	0.6669
Cohort 1949-1953	0.0098	0.4205	0.0186	0.9096	0.7439	0.7786
Cohort 1954-1958	0.2077	0.2472	0.5992	0.7524	0.5566	0.8235
Cohort 1959-1968	-0.5836	0.2470	0.9818	0.8415	0.4758	0.9230
Pregnancy	1.0651	0.2194	1.0000	-1.4782	1.0248	0.8508
Ever married	-0.9508	0.2901	0.9990	0.1716	0.5209	0.2581
In training	-0.6598	0.3092	0.9672	0.7552	0.4261	0.9236

Ref. group: cohort 59-63

Log likelihood: -794.57

Number of episodes: 379, splits: 406
Number of events (marriage): 119
Number of events (separation): 33

Source: German Socio-economic Panel, 1988.

el's performance we also use a likelihood ratio test, comparing the model to a baseline. The baseline for all models is the constant-rate model, Model 1. This test gives Chi-square values which are reported in Tables 3.9 and 3.10.

Model 2 in Table 3.9 includes in a first step two independent variables, Log (current age - 16) and Log (46 - current age). As discussed earlier, both measures also act as a control for unobserved heterogeneity, such as psychological readiness for marriage, and distortions caused by non-observation of periods of cohabitation. Both coefficients are significant at the 0.05 level, which means that there is indeed a non-monotonic pattern of the observed marriage rate in the data. Because the coefficient of Log (46 − current age) is greater than the coefficient of Log (current age − 16), we have a right-skewed 'bell-shaped' curve for the risk. This type of structure of the age-dependence of the marriage rate remains the same across all models.

In a second step, Model 3 in Table 3.9 introduces several dummy variables for father's social class. The estimates show that women from unskilled manual worker families (the reference group) marry much earlier than women from all other social classes. There is a continuously increasing average age at entry into marriage for women from skilled manual worker families, unskilled and skilled administrative and service worker families, and families of professionals. The mean ages of entry into marriage for women from farmer families and self-employed families are located in between the skilled administrative and service worker families and the families of professionals.

These differences in the age at entry into marriage are clearly a reflection of differences in class-specific resources determining the life chances of children. These resources comprise not only income positions, property, consumption styles and economic strategies of the families of origin, but also their social orientations, values, and beliefs—all of which influence the educational and career decisions of children (see, Blossfeld 1988; Huinink 1987). Below we shall see to what extent these effects of social origin have been transformed over the life-course into prolonged schooling, and what effect of social class on family formation remains once these influences are controlled for.

Model 4 in Table 3.9 incorporates changes in the historical background, measured on the basis of a detailed set of cohort dummy variables. The reference category is the oldest birth cohort, 1919–1923. As expected on the basis of the results in Tables 3.2 and 3.3, we observe that there is a non-monotonic relationship across cohorts. The strongest positive cohort effect is found for the 1944–1948 cohort. Although most of the younger and older cohorts have more or less the same coefficients, there is a significant negative effect for the youngest cohort (1964–1968). In the following step of the analysis we can see how much of this delaying effect can be attributed to the expansion of women's educational attainment.

But, before we do that, we have to control for the relationship between marriage and parenthood. We introduced a time-dependent covariate for 'being pregnant' before entry into marriage (Model 5, Table 3.9). We find that being pregnant has a significant positive impact on the rate of entry into marriage. This relationship is valid across all social classes, as the coefficients of father's

TABLE 3.9   Estimates for Models of Women's Rate
             of Entry into Marriage in West Germany

	Model					
Variables	1	2	3	4	5	6
Intercept	-5.02*	-28.68*	-29.67*	-29.24*	-26.66*	-25.62*
Log (current age -16)		1.97*	2.01*	2.00*	1.87*	1.76*
Log (46 - current age)		2.69*	2.71*	2.78*	2.92*	2.45*
Skilled manual workers[a]			-0.16*	-0.16*	-0.18*	-0.11*
Unskilled white-collar workers			-0.39*	-0.39*	-0.34*	-0.32*
Skilles white-collar workers			-0.41*	-0.41*	-0.33*	-0.20*
Professionals			-0.79*	-0.81*	-0.67*	-0.38*
Self employed			-0.55*	-0.58*	-0.51*	-0.43*
Farmers			-0.47*	-0.44*	-0.33*	-0.39*
Cohort 1964-68[b]				-0.65*	-0.53*	1.29
Cohort 1959-63				-0.02	0.08	0.72
Cohort 1954-58				0.15	0.25*	0.64
Cohort 1949-53				0.44*	0.50*	1.71*
Cohort 1944-48				0.64*	0.67*	0.86
Cohort 1939-43				0.37*	0.40*	0.23
Cohort 1934-38				0.30*	0.36*	-0.40
Cohort 1929-33				0.15	0.22*	-0.13
Cohort 1924-28				0.11	0.11	-0.72
Pregnant (time-dependent)					1.18*	1.12*
In school (time-dependent)[c]						-1.30*
Level of education (time-dependent)						-0.07
cohort 1964-68 * In training						-0.78
cohort 1959-63 * In training						0.44
cohort 1954-58 * In training						0.32
cohort 1949-53 * In training						0.62
cohort 1944-48 * In training						0.35
cohort 1939-43 * In training						-0.07
cohort 1934-38 * In training						0.56
cohort 1929-33 * In training						0.14
cohort 1924-28 * In training						0.25
cohort 1964-68 * Level of education						-0.14
cohort 1959-63 * Level of education						-0.05
cohort 1954-58 * Level of education						-0.03
cohort 1949-53 * Level of education						-0.10
cohort 1944-48 * Level of education						-0.01
cohort 1939-43 * Level of education						-0.02
cohort 1934-38 * Level of education						0.07
cohort 1929-33 * Level of education						0.03
cohort 1924-28 * Level of education						0.08
Number of events	2,103	2,103	2,103	2,103	2,103	2,103
Number of episodes	54,038	54,038	54,038	54,038	54,038	54,038
Chi-Square		1,577	1,685	1,819	2,219	2,370
df		2	8	17	18	38

[a] Referencegroup: Unskilled workers.
[b] Referencegroup: Cohort 1919-1923.
[c] Referencestate: Out of educational system.

* Significant at the 0.05 level.

Source: German Socio-economic Panel, 1988.

TABLE 3.10 Estimates for Models of Women's Rate of Entry into Motherhood in West Germany

Variables	Model					
	1	2	3	4	5	6
Intercept	-5.33*	-38.34*	-38.15*	-38.67*	-32.62*	-28.38*
Log (current age -16)		2.56*	2.58*	2.56*	1.45*	1.20*
Log (46 - current age)		3.85*	3.85*	3.96*	3.61*	3.22*
Skilled manual workers[a]			-0.11	-0.10	-0.06	-0.03
Unskilled white-collar workers			-0.28*	-0.29*	-0.09	-0.05
Skilles white-collar workers			-0.47*	-0.46*	-0.34*	-0.20*
Professionals			-0.91*	-0.89*	-0.59*	-0.35*
Self employed			-0.40*	-0.42*	-0.12	-0.03
Farmers			-0.31*	-0.32*	-0.06	-0.03
Cohort 1964-68[b]				-0.81*	-0.71*	2.44
Cohort 1959-63				-0.32*	-0.47*	0.08
Cohort 1954-58				-0.10	-0.29*	-0.43
Cohort 1949-53				0.16	-0.19*	-0.19
Cohort 1944-48				0.42*	0.06	-0.21
Cohort 1939-43				0.22*	-0.01	-0.70
Cohort 1934-38				0.14	-0.04	-0.64
Cohort 1929-33				-0.05	-0.17	-0.74
Cohort 1924-28				0.03	-0.04	-1.33
Married (time-dependent)[c]					2.11*	2.05*
In school (time-dependent)[d]						-1.45*
Level of education (time-dependent)						-0.08
cohort 1964-68 * In training						-0.61
cohort 1959-63 * In training						0.56
cohort 1954-58 * In training						0.15
cohort 1949-53 * In training						0.58
cohort 1944-48 * In training						0.53
cohort 1939-43 * In training						0.54
cohort 1934-38 * In training						0.65
cohort 1929-33 * In training						0.42
cohort 1924-28 * In training						0.34
cohort 1964-68 * Level of education						-0.26
cohort 1959-63 * Level of education						-0.03
cohort 1954-58 * Level of education						0.03
cohort 1949-53 * Level of education						0.01
cohort 1944-48 * Level of education						0.03
cohort 1939-43 * Level of education						0.07
cohort 1934-38 * Level of education						0.06
cohort 1929-33 * Level of education						0.06
cohort 1924-28 * Level of education						0.13
Number of events	1,862	1,862	1,862	1,862	1,862	1,862
Number of episodes	64,741	64,741	64,741	64,741	64,741	64,741
Chi-Square	1,510	1,611	1,705	3,133	3,227	
df		2	8	17	18	38

[a] Referencegroup: Unskilled workers.
[b] Referencegroup: Cohort 1919-1923.
[c] Referencestate: Not married.
[d] Referencestate: Out of educational system.
* Significant at the 0.05 level.

Source: German Socio-economic Panel, 1988.

social class stay more or less unchanged from Model 4 to Model 5. After having controlled for age-dependence, social class, cohort membership, and pregnancy, we can now try to answer the question of how important the improvement in educational opportunities has been for women's timing of marriage across cohorts.

The theoretical importance of education may be viewed from either a 'new home economy' or from a sociological perspective. In the first case, the accumulation of human capital, expressed as an increasing level of education, raises women's labor-market attachment and thereby leads to greater marriage delays (Mincer 1974; Becker 1981). In the second case, normative societal expectations induce the belief that young people who attend school are 'not ready' to marry, thus making the completion of education important for becoming ready for marriage (Marini 1985; Oppenheimer 1988; Blossfeld and Nuthmann 1989). We constructed dynamic, time-dependent measures for both aspects of the effects of education and included them (with their cohort-interaction effects) in Model 6 of Table 3.9.

This model shows that enrollment in school, vocational training or university has indeed a strong and significant negative effect on the rate of entry into marriage. However, and very interestingly, the effect of the level of education is not significant. Women's marriage timing is therefore independent of the amount of human capital investment. In assessing the consequences of educational expansion for family formation, we may therefore conclude that more highly educated women postpone marriage because they postpone the transition from youth to adulthood and not because they have accumulated a greater stock of human capital. This is illustrated in Figure 3.2 which shows estimates of the age-specific cumulative proportion unmarried (survivor function) for different levels of education.[5] The longer women are in the educational system the longer they delay their entry into marriage. After leaving the educational system, those women who have delayed entering into marriage catch up with their less-educationally qualified contemporaries who had an earlier start. The conflict between women's increasing educational attainment and marriage is therefore largely confined to the period of transition from youth to adulthood. Hence, it seems not to be justified to attribute the decline in marriage in West Germany to the improvement in women's educational attainment.

After having controlled for women's educational histories, most of the effects of father's social class still prove significant. In other words, besides class differences in educational enrollment, there seem to be important class-specific variations in expectations about marriage which influence when women regard themselves as ready for marriage.

It is also important to note that after controlling for women's educational attainment, we observe that the non-monotonic pattern of cohort effects has almost completely disappeared. This means that a great part of the differences across cohorts can be explained in terms of changes in educational participation. In particular, the significant delay of ages of entry into first marriage among younger cohorts of women can be attributed to the extension of periods of educational enrollment. However, for the cohorts 1944–1948 and

FIGURE 3.2   Estimated Proportion of Unmarried Women by
              Education in West Germany (survivor function)

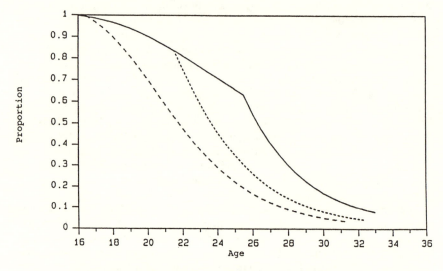

---   Lower secondary school qualification without vocational training
······   Upper secondary school qualification with vocational training
——   University degree

Source: German Socio-economic Panel 1988.

1949–1953 we still observe strong negative cohort effects. Thus, there must be also other sources of cohort-specific influences which lead to an acceleration in the ages of entry into marriage for these specific birth cohorts. One possible explanation is that these cohorts experienced very exceptional economic conditions for family formation in the late 1960s and early 1979s.

Finally, in Model 6 of Table 3.9 we observe that the interaction effects of cohort membership with level of education and enrollment in the educational system are not significant. The effect of education across cohorts of women does therefore not change across cohorts.

Effects of Education on the Rate
of Entry into First Motherhood

In considering changes in the age at which women have their first child (Table 3.10), we observe effects for age-dependence, social class and cohort membership in the first four models of Table 3.10 which are very similar to those in Table 3.9, and hence require no further substantive explanation. However, it is important to note that, compared to the cohort effects on age at marriage, the non-monotonic pattern of cohort effects of age at first birth is less pronounced and the rise in average ages of entry into marriage for the younger cohorts is steeper. This means that across the younger cohorts there is an increasing gap between ages at entry into marriage and entry into motherhood. This is easy to see if we include in Model 5 of Table 3.10 a time-dependent variable, whether or not a women is married before the birth of her first child. Then, the non-monotonic pattern across cohorts disappears completely and we only find, beginning with cohort 1949, an increasing delay of entry into motherhood. In other words, the non-monotonic pattern of ages at entry into motherhood is completely mediated by the marriage process. In the next step, we finally analyse whether the increasing delay of entry into motherhood can be explained by increasing educational expansion of women.

In Model 6 of Table 3.10 we therefore include women's continuously changing level of education, a time-dependent indicator for their enrollment in the educational system, and the cohort-interaction effects of these influences. Again, enrollment in the educational system negatively affects women's propensity to have a first child. There are normative societal expectations that young women who are enrolled in education are 'not ready' to have a child. Finishing education, as one of the important steps towards adult status, thus leads to a steep rise in the rate of entry into parenthood (Blossfeld and Nuthmann 1989).

Again, the level of education has no significant influence on the timing of first birth. The accumulation of human capital investments does not lead to a lower rate of having children, as posited by the 'new home economists'. If there is an effect of educational expansion on entry into first motherhood, then this influence stems from increasing periods of educational enrollment. The conflict between education and first motherhood is largely limited to the period of transition from youth to adulthood and should not continue throughout much of adult life. This is also illustrated in Figure 3.3. This figure shows that beginning at the age of about thirty-four there are almost no differences in the proportion of childless women.[6]

Finally, it is important to note that in Model 6 of Table 3.10 neither the cohort effects nor the cohort-education-interaction effects are significant. The increasing delay of entry into first birth observed in Model 5 for each younger cohort of women can therefore be completely explained by their increasing educational educational enrollment.

Summary

In this analysis we have found a uniform long-term trend in women's educational expansion; not only have women's average levels of educational attainment steadily risen from one birth cohort to another, but their enrollment in the educational system over the life-course has also extended in time.

We have also seen that the long-term trend in ages at entry into marriage and motherhood is not in line with the long-term trend in women's educational attainment in West Germany. Ages at first marriage and first birth fell sharply from the 1919–1923 cohort until the 1944–1948 cohort and have since been rising again until the youngest birth cohort examined.

Moreover, the recent rise in ages at entry into marriage in West Germany seems to be moderate. Up to now, more or less the same pattern for ages of en-

FIGURE 3.3   Estimated Proportion of Childless Women by
              Education in West Germany (survivor function)

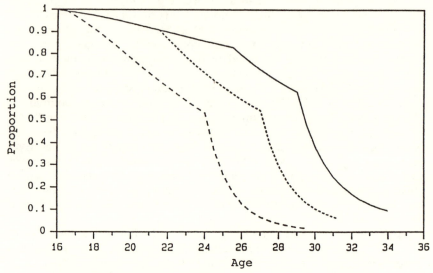

- - -   Lower secondary school qualification without vocational training
        (and marriage at age 24)
...... Upper secondary school qualification with vocational training
        (and marriage at age 27)
—————— University degree (and marriage at 29)

Source: German Socio-economic Panel 1988.

try into marriage is observed as was already established fifty years ago. It is
only relative to the 1944–1948 cohort that the recent marriage patterns appear
so dramatic. It is therefore important in analyzing the effects of women's improvement in educational attainment on the timing of marriage and motherhood to cover a very long historical period.

Consensual unions appear to be more common among the younger respondents and the frequency of cohabitation at the time of the first panel wave in
1984 was modest at about 11 percent. The median of the duration in consensual unions is about three years. For the transition from consensual union to
marriage four factors are especially important: (1) given that consensual
unions are now relatively common, younger couples are under less pressure
to convert a consensual union to a marital one; (2) the birth of a child is closely
connected with the desire to legalize the union; (3) experiences with former
marriages will tend to reduce the probability of remarriage; and (4) enrollment in the educational system delays entry into marriage.

On the basis of this analysis we can say that women's increasing educational attainment accounts for *part* of the changes in the process of family formation in West Germany. In particular, we showed that the delaying effect of
educational expansion on the timing of first marriage is largely confined to

the phase of transition from youth to adulthood; more well-educated women simply marry and have their first child later. After controlling for women's educational attainment, we still see strong cohort effects for women born between 1944–1953. This means that these cohorts have entered marriage far earlier than their predecessors or successors.

Notes

1. The first data collection was carried out in 1984, with a further panel wave annually. Analyses use data from panel waves between 1984 and 1988. In the first wave, 12,245 persons from 5,921 households were questioned. There is an extensive methodological literature on the GSP (see, for example, Hanefeld 1987; Rendtel 1988, 1989).

2. Lower school qualification without vocational training = nine years; lower secondary school qualification with vocational training = eleven years; intermediate school qualification without vocational training = ten years; intermediate school qualification with vocational training = twelve years; upper secondary school qualification (*Abitur*) without vocational training = thirteen years; upper secondary school qualification (*Abitur*) with vocational training = fifteen years; professional college qualification = seventeen years and university degree = nineteen years.

3. The 1964–1968 cohort is not comparable because in 1988—the year of the last available panel wave—many women were still enrolled in education.

4. The 1959–1963 cohort is not comparable because in 1988—the year of the last available panel wave—many were still enrolled in professional colleges and universities.

5. These estimates were obtained from Model 6 of Table 3.4 by holding constant all other variables at the mean and switching the time-dependent variable 'pregnant' at the age where 50 percent of women in different qualification groups had their first child.

6. These estimates were obtained from Model 6 of Table 3.5 by holding constant all other variables at the mean and switching the time-dependent variable 'marriage' at the age where 50 per cent of women in different qualification groups were already married.

References

Becker, G. (1981). *A Treatise on the Family*, Cambridge (MA), Harvard University Press.

Bloom, D.E. (1982). "What's Happening to the Age at First Birth in the United States? A Study of Recent Cohorts," *Demography*, 19: 351–70.

Blossfeld, H.-P. (1985). *Bildungsexpansion und Berufschancen*, Frankfurt and New York, Campus.

Blossfeld, H.-P. (1989). *Kohortendifferenzierung und Karriereprozeß*, Frankfurt and New York, Campus.

Blossfeld, H.-P., A. Hamerle, and K.-U. Mayer (1989). *Event History Analysis*, Hillsdale (NJ), Erlbaum.

Blossfeld, H.-P. and J. Huinink (1989). "Die Verbesserung der Bildungs- und Berufschancen von Frauen und ihr Einfluss auf den Prozess der Familienbildung." *Zeitschrift für Bevölkerungswissenschaft*, 15: 383–404.

Blossfeld, H.-P. and J. Huinink (1991). "Human Capital Investments or Norms of Role Transition? How Women's Schooling and Career Affect the Process of Family Formation," *American Journal of Sociology*, 97(1): 143–68.

Blossfeld, H.-P. and U. Jaenichen (1992). "Educational Expansion and Changes in Women's Entry into Marriage and Motherhood in the Federal Republic of Germany," *Journal of Marriage and the Family*, 54, 5: 302–15.

Blossfeld, H.-P. and R. Nuthmann (1989). "Strukturelle Veränderungen der Jugendphase als Kohortenproze;dss," *Zeitschrift für Pädagogik*, 35: 845–67.

Coale, A.J. (1971). "Age Patterns of Marriage," *Population Studies*, 25: 193–214.

Esping-Andersen, G. (1990): *The Three Worlds of Welfare Capitalism*, Cambridge and Princeton, N.J.: Princeton University Press.

Galler, H.-P. (1989). "Dynamische Mikroanalyse als demographische Forschungsstrategie," in Wagner, Gert, Notburga Ott, and Hans-Joachim Hoffmann-Nowotny (eds), *Familienbildung und Erwerbstätigkeit im demographischen Wandel*, Berlin, Duncker & Humblot.

Gauthier, A. H. (1992): The Western European Government's attitudes and responses to the demographic and family questions, *Paper presented at the European Science Foundation Conference, St. Martin*.

Hanefeld, U. (1987). *Das Sozio-ökonomische Panel—Grundlagen und Konzeption*, Frankfurt and New York, Campus.

Hoem, B. and J. Hoem (1987a). "Patterns of Deferment of First Birth in Modern Sweden," *Stockholm Research Reports in Demography*, No. 42, University of Stockholm.

Hoem, B. and J. Hoem (1987b). "The Swedish Family: Aspects of Contemporary Developments," *Stockholm Research Reports in Demography*, No. 43, University of Stockholm.

Huinink, J. (1987). "Soziale Herkunft, Bildung und das Alter bei der Geburt des ersten Kindes," *Zeitschrift für Soziologie*, 16: 367–84.

Krupp, H.-J. (1985). *Das Sozio-ökonomische Panel. Bericht über die Forschungstätigkeit 1983–1985. Antrag auf Förderung der Forschungsphase 1986–1988*, Frankfurt and Berlin, DIW.

Marini, M.M. (1985). "Determinants of the Timing of Adult Role Entry," *Social Science Research*, 14: 309–50.

Mincer, J. (1974). *Schooling, Experience and Earnings*, New York, Columbia University Press.

Oppenheimer, V.K. (1988). "A Theory of Marriage Timing," *American Journal of Sociology*, 94: 563–91.

Rendtel, U. (1988). Repräsentativität und Hochrechnung der Datenbasis," in H.-J. Krupp and J. Schupp (eds), *Lebenslagen im Wandel—Daten 1987*, Frankfurt and New York, Campus.

Rendtel, U. (1989). "über den Einflu;dss der Panelselektivität auf Längsschnitanalysen," *Vierteljahreshefte zur Wirtschaftsforschung*, 1: 45–61.

Rindfuss, R.R. and C. St. John (1983). "Social Determinants of Age at First Birth," *Journal of Marriage and the Family*, 45: 553–65.

Schwarz, K. (1983). "Die Alleinlebenden," *Zeitschrift für Bevölkerungswissenschaft*, 9: 241–57.

Sørensen, A. (1990). "Unterschiede im Lebenslauf von Frauen und Männern," in K.-U. Mayer (ed.), *Levensverläufe und gesellschaftlicher Wandel—Zwischen Sozialdemographie und Biographie,, Kölner Zeitschrift für Soziologie und Sozialpsychologie*, special edition 31/1990.

Zimmermann, K.F. (1985). *Familienökonomie. Theoretische Untersuchungen zur Frauenerwerbstätigkeit und Geburtenentwicklung*, Berlin and Heidelberg, Springer.

4

France

HENRI LERIDON AND LAURENT TOULEMON

Family Policy and Major Socio-Demographic Changes

For historical reasons (France was the first country in the world where fertility started to decline, during the eighteenth century, and where the population began to age), the pace of population growth has been a concern for many policy-makers in France for about a century. The development of family policy has thus been undoubtedly influenced by pro-natalist views, though it cannot be reduced to this dimension: a concern for the social protection of the members of large families and for a greater degree of economic equality between families has always been present. These aims are supported by influential family associations, whose delegates still exert a strong influence in the *Caisses d'allocations familiales*, channelling money raised from contributions on salaries to beneficiaries.

Family allowances first appeared in France in 1919, and coverage became universal in 1939 with the introduction of the *Code de la famille*. They are payable for children up to the age of sixteen (twenty if the child is still attending school), starting from the *second* child; the amount depends on the birth-order and age of the child but is not means-tested. In addition, there are a variety of allowances which are payable under specific circumstances, such as: the allowance for a young child paid monthly from pregnancy until the child reaches the age of three (becoming means-tested after the birth); the single-parent family allowance; housing aid allowance, paid according to income, family size and rent costs. These specific allowances tend to be more and more often means-tested over time.

A parent who stops working to take care of his or her children at home is entitled to a parental allowance for education. The amount is roughly equivalent to half the minimum wage paid to a full-time worker. Entitlement is restricted to families with at least three children, with one under three years of age, and the parent must have worked at least two out of the previous ten years. Some other allowances are also restricted to families with three or more children, revealing the pro-natalist aspect of family policy. These include, for example, the *complément familial,* a bonus payable to large families, and the *prime de déménagement,* a lump-sum subsidy to cover removal costs.

These allowances are not taxable, and *tax rebates* are also granted to families. The most important feature of the French tax system, especially for medium and high-income households, is the 'family quotient.' This is calculated by taking the total household income, dividing it by a ratio depending upon the composition of the family; tax is then computed by applying a progressive scale and the result is multiplied by the same ratio as before. The progressive nature of taxation (with increasing income) is thus greatly reduced, and the benefit is proportional to the household's income.

Maternity leave lasts sixteen weeks, almost full-paid to the mother (twenty-six weeks for the third child and subsequent children), and hospital costs are fully reimbursed by the social security system. In addition, any parent working in a firm with more than one hundred employees may benefit from unpaid parental leave lasting from one to three years. As mentioned above, the parental allowance for education is a better solution for parents with three of more children.

When both parents continue working after the birth of the child, they need to arrange day childcare. The system of public *crèches* for young children is the solution favored by most families. Although most parents would prefer to use the system of public *crèches* for the care of very young children, due to the shortfall in the provision of this type of childcare, most children are in fact cared for by private *nourrices*, who are unfortunately even more costly. The situation improves markedly when the child reaches the age of two-and-a-half or three years when most of them are accepted into public and free kindergartens (*écoles maternelles*), a very efficient pre- school system.

French family policy is still regarded as one of the most advanced in the world. There are, however, two main criticisms which are often levelled at the present system. First, the rules are becoming increasingly complex, especially in the way the amount of each allowance is related to parental income. Second, the amount of actual support received has dropped slightly; the mean level of allowances has been increasing, on the whole, as fast as retail prices, but more slowly than salaries. We should note, finally, that the entire system of family policy entitlements applies to both married and unmarried couples in the same way; and in the case of taxation, the law actually favors the latter, if both partners request separate taxation.

Long-Term Trends in Socio-Economic Variables

Like many other European countries, France has undergone numerous social and economic changes over the past forty years. The difficult years of the immediate postwar period were followed by about thirty years of economic growth, rapid industrialization and urbanization, increasing net income for employment in all sectors, and important changes in the status of women. The last ten years have been less successful in economic terms, but this has not stopped other developments. In this analysis we will review three key changes: the rise in level of education (especially for women); the increase in women's employment; and the widespread use of contraceptive methods.

The Rise in the Level of Educational Attainment

French boys and girls now start school earlier and earlier, and leave the educational system later and later. Pre-schooling has developed so rapidly that 97 percent of children aged three and 40 percent of children aged two are now enrolled. This might be of some relevance for the analysis of fertility behavior, as it means that parents, and especially women, are not compelled to choose between professional employment and maternity. The lengthening of school enrollment is even more significant at the other end with 42 percent of boys (47 percent of girls) still attending school at the age of eighteen in the 1950 cohort, and 75 percent (83 percent of girls) in the 1970 cohort. In the nineteen to twenty age group, the average jumped from 27 percent to 53 percent for young men over the same period, and from 28 percent to 60 percent for young women. In the twenty-one to twenty-four year age group, where marriage and first birth traditionally took place (at least for women), almost one young person in four is still enrolled in some form of full-time education (Debizet 1990).

Table 4.1 shows the highest diploma obtained by men and women in successive cohorts since 1913–1920. The CEP is the *certificat d'études primaires,* and was once a terminal diploma for a substantial part of the French population when the minimum school-leaving age was fourteen (the minimum is sixteen for cohorts born after 1952). The CAP, *certificat d'aptitude professionnelle,* is the first technical degree (often a terminal one); BEPC is the *brevet d'études du premier cycle* and may be obtained after five years of primary school and four years of secondary school, roughly by the age of fourteen or fifteen; 'Bacc' is the *baccalauréat,* an essential diploma in the French system, after seven years of secondary school ('BP' stands for *brevet professionnel,* a more or less equivalent technical diploma); finally, 'high level' means any diploma beyond the *baccalauréat.* It can be seen, for instance, that the proportion of men with a diploma at least equivalent to BEPC rose from 19 percent to 58 percent, and from 13 percent to 56 percent for women, for the 1919–1921 to 1964–1968 birth cohorts.

In summary then, the levels of educational attainment have risen dramatically during recent decades, especially for girls, so that at university girls are now more numerous than boys.

The Rise in Women's Employment

One consequence (or cause?) of this improving level of education for women has been the rise of female employment over the same period. The most significant figure is for women in the twenty-five to thirty-nine age group, when the competition between maternity and economic occupation is crucial. The rate of employment remained fairly constant in the first half of the century, between 40 and 50 percent; in 1962 it stood at 41.5 percent, and then increased rapidly, reaching 74.0 percent in 1989. Women benefitted greatly from the fast growth of the service sector after the Second World War with two-thirds of the female population—equivalent to 80 percent of all active women—now working in this sector (Marchand and Thélot 1991). The average number of

TABLE 4.1   Educational Attainment by Sex and Birth Cohort

					Year of Birth				
	1913-1920	1921-1925	1926-1930	1931-1935	1936-1940	1941-1945	1946-1950	1951-1955	1956-1960
Men:									
High level (>Bacc.)	5,0	5,9	5,2	6,2	9,7	13,0	13,8	13,0	13,4
Bacc, BP	6,2	9,0	7,9	7,6	10,1	11,9	9,9	10,6	10,1
BEPC	7,6	5,8	11,7	19,8	24,7	28,8	30,6	33,7	34,9
CAP	6,6	5,5	4,5	4,1	4,8	6,0	7,9	7,5	11,4
CEP	39,6	44,7	38,9	29,6	26,9	21,8	21,9	18,0	9,8
No diploma	35,1	29,2	31,8	32,7	23,9	18,5	15,9	17,2	20,3
Total	100	100	100	100	100	100	100	100	100
Women:									
High level (>Bacc.)	1,9	3,0	3,1	3,9	6,2	11,6	13,8	15,6	16,1
Bacc, BP	5,1	4,8	5,6	6,6	8,6	10,7	11,6	12,1	14,2
BEPC	5,8	7,5	10,5	13,7	17,8	23,4	23,3	23,5	25,6
CAP	7,3	6,8	6,7	6,0	7,3	8,2	8,3	11,3	12,6
CEP	38,7	44,6	41,7	37,5	32,7	29,7	25,7	22,0	11,3
No diploma	41,3	33,4	32,3	32,3	27,3	16,3	17,3	15,5	20,2
Total	100	100	100	100	100	100	100	100	100

Note: "Low" level= No diploma, CEP. "Middle" level= CAP, BEPC, Bacc. "High" level= After baccalaureat.

Source: Gollac et al. 1989 (FQP1985 Survey, INSEE).

children has also declined over the same period, but this structural change alone cannot explain the rise in the rate of employment: for each child at least up to the third-order birth, the proportion of employed mothers has been rising constantly since the 1960s. That is, the proportion of women leaving their occupation after the birth of a first or second child has been decreasing (Desplanques 1987).

The Use of Contraception

The freedom of choice for women has also been substantially extended by the spread of new contraceptive techniques and the liberalization of abortion. Contraception became freely available in France in 1967 (law amended in 1974), and abortion became legal in 1975. The typical French woman now starts to take the pill at the age of nineteen, continues for about eleven years (with a couple of interruptions for childbearing), and then switches to an IUD for the same number of years. Sterilization is uncommon and consequently fertility can often be restored. The use of non-medical methods of contraception has declined rapidly, and almost all women exposed to the risk of an unwanted pregnancy practice some form of contraceptive method (Toulemon and Leridon 1991).

Entry into Marriage and Motherhood

The continuation of the baby boom in the late 1950s and early 1960s was largely due to the accelerating *tempo* of marriage and births in the relevant cohorts. The trend was reversed by the end of the 1960s: for women, mean age at first marriage declined from 23.3 in 1956 to 22.4 in 1972, and has exceeded twenty-five years since 1988 (the trend was roughly the same for men, the mean age at first marriage remaining constantly two years over the one for women). During the 1980s, age at first marriage rose by two months every year! But the change has not been limited to the tempo: the intensity of marriage in the recent cohorts has certainly been declining. In the 1919–1923 cohorts, 9 percent of women were still single at the age of forty-eight (Table 4.2); the proportion was near 7 percent in the 1929–1933 cohorts, but will probably exceed 20 percent in the 1959–1963 group (the tentative estimate for more recent generations approaches 30 percent).

The delay of marriage first induced a delay in first-order births. Then, with the dramatic rise in extra-marital births (30 percent of all births in 1990, roughly 40 percent of first births), the picture became more complex, but the trend is still in the same direction: the mean age at first birth rose by two years between 1978 and 1989 (Toulemon 1991). Average family size clearly declined since 1965 (or since the cohort born in 1931), but the reduction almost exclusively applied to third-order and subsequent births. The proportion of women remaining childless at the end of their reproductive period was 19 percent for the 1919–1923 cohorts, 13 percent for the 1929–1933 cohorts, 8 percent in the 1939–1943 cohorts, and it will stand around 10 percent in the 1959–

TABLE 4.2   Changes in the Timing and Intensity of Entry into Marriage, Measured by Proportions of Unmarried Women at Specific Ages (%)

Birth Cohort	Proportion of Unmarried Women at Age							
	20	24	28	32	36	40	44	48
1919-23	76	40	19	14	12	10	10	9
1924-28	75	32	18	13	11	9	9	8
1929-33	72	32	16	11	10	8	8	7
1934-38	74	30	15	11	10	8	8	8
1939-43	71	26	14	11	9	8		8
1944-48	67	27	15	11	10			8
1949-53	69	30	18	14				11
1954-58	69	37	25					
1959-63	78	50						
1964-68	89							

Source: Estimation by Sardon 1990.

TABLE 4.3   Changes in the Timing and Intensity of Entry into Motherhood, Measured by Proportions of Childless Women at Specific Ages (%)

Birth Cohort	Proportion of Childless Women at Age							
	20	24	28	32	36	40	44	48
1919-23	89	58	32	24	21	19	19	19
1924-28	86	49	30	22	19	17	17	17
1929-33	83	48	27	18	14	13	13	13
1934-38	85	47	23	15	12	11	10	10
1939-43	83	42	21	13	10	9		8
1944-48	81	42	21	13	10			8
1949-53	81	44	23	14				9
1954-58	82	50	27					
1959-63	87	57						
1964-68	91							

Source: Rallu, Toulemon 1993.

1963 cohorts (Table 4.3). The proportion of women with only one child has os-cillated between 22 percent and 18 percent for the same generations.

Fewer marriages does not automatically mean less divorces. Whereas the annual number of marriages has dropped by a third (between 1972 and 1987), the annual number of divorces more than doubled. Within cohorts of mar-riages, the *rate of divorce* used to be round 10 percent, whereas it is estimated that it will be over 30 percent for the 1980 cohort (INED 1987). Remarriage has also been declining, the frequency now standing at under 40 percent.

Most of the changes discussed above are obviously largely related to the development of consensual unions, that is of extra-marital cohabitation, and this will be discussed in the next section.

The Rise in Consensual Unions

A survey carried out in 1985–1986 has enabled us to perform a first in-depth analysis of extra-marital cohabitation in France: before this survey, only cross-sectional data from the censuses and the employment surveys were available, and the registration of *de facto* unions was far from perfect in these sources (Leridon and Villeneuve-Gokalp 1988). The questionnaire of the *Enquête sur les Situations Familiales* (hereafter referred to as ESF Survey) included detailed biographies of all unions for the 4091 men and women interviewed (aged twenty-one to forty-five). Three papers have already been published in English on these data (Leridon and Villeneuve-Gokalp 1989; Leridon 1990a and 1990b), and only a brief summary of results produced in these papers will be presented here. In the ESF survey, January 1986 marks the most recent situation, but similar estimates are available for women from the ERN Survey (*Enquête sur la Régulation des Naissances*) until 1988.

Consensual unions have always existed, but their rate began to rise in the late-1960s, just before marriage started to decline. Prior to 1981–1982, there was a full compensation between the two trends, and the proportion of men and women living in a union (married or not) remained fairly constant. Subsequently, this proportion declined, especially for the twenty to twenty-four group. Table 4.4 shows the proportions of women in consensual unions (per hundred women in each age group): they are moving towards a plateau in the twenty to twenty-four age group, and are still increasing in older groups.

Median age for entry into first union was 22.0 for women born in 1941–1945, and almost equal for the 1961–1964 cohort (21.8), but this first union was more often a consensual one. The shift from direct marriage to extra-marital cohabitation for the first union is more spectacular when we classify first unions by calendar year of formation instead of by birth cohort: over a period of only fifteen years (1970–1985), the proportion of first unions begun outside marriage jumped from 20 percent (average for both sexes) to 75 percent. Obviously, a new standard has emerged.

Both ESF and ERN surveys enable analysis of the duration and outcome of unions, before and after—or outside—marriage. The most common reason for the termination of a consensual union is still marriage: in the majority of the cohorts examined, about half of first unions (initiated outside marriage before the thirtieth birthday) led to a marriage within three years, and 10 to 20 percent ended in a separation (without marriage) in the same space of time. In the most recent cohorts, we found a lower propensity to marry, and a slightly higher propensity for the first union to break down; the median duration of a cohabiting union now exceeds two years.

TABLE 4.4 Proportion of Women Living as a Couple, Married or Cohabiting, per 100 Women of Each Age Group, by Period

Year	15-19 Years of Age Living as a Couple			20-24 Years of Age Living as a Couple			25-29 Years of Age Living as a Couple		
	Cohab.	Married	Total	Cohab.	Married	Total	Cohab.	Married	Total
1970	0,9	4,8	5,7	2,6	52,8	55,4	3,6	79,4	83,0
1971	2,0	7,2	9,2	3,7	55,9	59,6	3,5	79,5	83,0
1972	2,0	8,6	10,6	5,1	54,0	59,1	3,7	80,3	84,0
1973	1,3	8,8	10,1	5,5	55,4	60,9	3,1	79,9	83,0
1974	2,2	7,0	9,2	5,5	52,0	57,5	3,7	78,7	82,4
1975	3,7	6,5	10,2	6,0	51,1	57,1	5,7	79,5	85,2
1976	4,1	7,8	11,9	7,5	52,3	59,8	5,3	78,5	83,8
1977	4,1	9,2	13,3	9,1	51,0	60,1	6,8	75,2	82,0
1978	4,0	7,1	11,1	11,2	52,6	63,8	6,7	74,1	80,8
1979	5,7	5,6	11,3	11,2	52,6	63,8	7,7	73,2	80,9
1980	4,5	4,7	9,2	12,8	51,4	64,2	7,4	72,5	79,9
1981	5,6	4,0	9,6	16,0	48,4	64,4	7,1	75,0	82,1
1982	6,3	3,3	9,6	16,3	45,1	61,4	9,1	73,3	82,4
1983	5,5	4,3	9,8	17,4	41,0	58,4	10,4	72,5	82,9
1984	5,5	2,8	8,3	20,1	38,6	58,7	10,7	68,9	79,6
1985	4,9	2,2	7,1	21,6	32,2	53,8	13,6	67,8	81,4
1986				24,7	29,3	54,0	16,1	65,8	81,9
1987				22,4	26,6	49,0	17,1	64,3	81,4
1988				22,6	23,4	46,0	18,3	60,2	78,5

(continued)

TABLE 4.4 (continued)

Year	30-34 Years of Age Living as a Couple			35-39 Years of Age Living as a Couple			40-44 years of Age Living as a Couple		
	Cohab.	Married	Total	Cohab.	Married	Total	Cohab.	Married	Total
1970									
1971									
1972									
1973	2,6	83,7	86,3						
1974	1,9	86,6	88,5						
1975	2,4	83,3	85,7						
1976	2,3	83,2	85,5						
1977	2,8	85,5	88,3						
1978	4,0	85,7	89,7	3,0	83,1	86,1			
1979	4,5	82,1	86,6	3,1	86,2	89,3			
1980	4,6	83,3	87,9	3,5	83,8	87,3			
1981	4,1	80,3	84,4	4,3	83,4	87,7			
1982	6,4	77,7	84,1	3,9	84,4	88,3			
1983	7,1	77,5	84,6	4,9	82,6	87,5	2,8	82,9	85,7
1984	6,3	79,1	85,4	6,2	80,4	86,6	3,0	83,7	86,7
1985	7,9	77,6	85,5	5,4	82,2	87,6	3,5	81,0	84,5
1986	6,6	77,6	84,2	6,2	80,4	86,6	3,3	80,5	83,8
1987	9,6	74,1	83,7	6,4	77,8	84,2	3,4	80,9	84,3
1988	10,1	73,9	84,0	7,1	77,0	84,1	4,9	79,0	83,9

Source: ERN Fertility Survey, INED 1988.

Marriages without previous cohabitation are more stable than consensual unions, probably because this form of union selects couples who attach a high value to the formal (often religious) aspect of marriage. The stability of marriages entered into after a period of cohabitation ranks somewhere between the other two categories. One important methodological issue here is whether we can compare total durations of unions, including years of cohabitation before marriage, or only durations since marriage. It may be argued that marriage marks an important discontinuity in the history of the union, a kind of 'second beginning.' Thus, the first year of marriage, following three years of cohabitation, could not be compared to the fourth year of a (continuing) consensual union. One argument in favor of this position is that we did not find a significant effect of the duration of pre-marital cohabitation on the stability of marriages. Similarly, can we compare the first year of a direct marriage with the first year of a marriage celebrated after a period of cohabitation? These questions certainly deserve more attention, but will not be discussed here.

In our previous analyses of the ESF survey, we concentrated on the differences in the outcome of unions and the birth of the first child by union cohort and, occasionally, by age at the formation of union. Here we have included other variables in the picture: social background, level of education, and current educational status (student or not).

The Impact of Education on Union Initiation and the Role of Women

The emergence of new gender roles is often linked to the increasing educational level of women. More specifically, it has been argued that women with a higher level of education and better career opportunities would prefer to delay or even to avoid living as a couple, getting married and having children (Becker 1981). Indeed, a higher level of educational attainment implies a longer period of educational enrollment, which has in itself a direct and strong negative effect on the likelihood of union formation and of marriage (Blossfeld and Jaenichen 1992).

A pioneer work by Hoem (1985), based on a retrospective survey conducted in Sweden, has shown that no specific direct effect of educational level can be found on marriage and unmarried cohabitation, when education is controlled for. Using hazard models, Hoem described marriage and cohabitation intensities of 4300 'single' (before they ever lived as a couple), parity 0 (before they had a child) Swedish women born in 1936–1960. He found a major effect of 'student/non-student' status (time varying covariate), but no effect of educational level, when student status is taken into account. This result implies that the specific behavior observed for higher educated women may be described as a delay in family formation only due to the longer period of educational enrollment.

Here we have used the Swedish findings as a hypothesis to be tested for France, and built models closely resembling those used by Hoem, testing them using the same statistical software.

Models

Marriage, Cohabitation and Union Initiation Intensities

Data are taken from the 1988 ERN Fertility Survey (see Appendix). The aim of the models is to 'explain' cohabitation, marriage and union formation rates for childless women who never previously lived as a couple. Looking at union intensities and the choice between marriage or cohabitation (in the case of union) highlights other aspects of the data, supplementary to the description of cohabitation and marriage intensities.

Explanatory Variables

The intensities were computed each month, between the ages of seventeen and twenty-five. The 'explanatory' variables are listed below:

- (A) Age in single years, which is the model time variable: 17–24 inclusive;
- (B) Birth cohort: 1941–1945, 1946–1950, 1951–1955, 1956–1960, 1961–1965, 1966–1969;
- (C) Class or Social Background, defined as father's profession when the woman was aged fifteen: unskilled worker, skilled worker, white-collar (low level), white-collar (high level), farmer, self-employed, no answer;
- (E) Educational level: low, middle, higher;
- (S) Student status: student/non-student.

For the class and education variables, we had to make a compromise between the need for comparability with Sweden and the relevance of these categories for France. The variables education and student vary over time. As the French and Swedish educational systems are quite different, it was not possible to guarantee complete comparability. First, adult education is uncommon in France, and we collected only the age at the end of formal education; thus, in the French survey no individual can move from 'non-student' to 'student' status. Second, as we only know the date of the end of education enrollment, the education variable is only unambiguous for the months lived after having completed studies. For years at school, we assumed that middle level (CAP or more) was obtained at the age of seventeen (in June), and a higher level (post-Baccalauréat) at the age of twenty. For social background indicator (class), we favored international comparability against regular French categories of professional activity.

The combinations of all categories of all variables define specific groups where the rates are supposed to be constant. The models are fitted and compared one with the others using the partial log-likelihood ratio criterion (for a precise description of computations made by Loglin, see Oliver and Neff 1976; Hoem 1985, 1989).

Model Notations

All models are derived from a 'basic model,' which takes into account age (A) and birth cohort (B). Following Hoem's notation, we have called this model

AB/-, or simply AB. Introducing an additional effect (for instance of social background, C), gives us the model ABC. The significance of the effect of variable C is tested by checking whether the model ABC improves the fit, compared to AB. Variable C is tested as a whole: there is no specific test for each category.

In the next step, we looked for interactions between two explanatory variables, for instance A and B, which means that the effect of Age is allowed to be specific for each birth cohort; the model is noted AB/AB. The interaction is tested by comparing AB/AB to AB, or ABC/AB to ABC. The variable age is taken as the time variable: as a result, an interaction between age and another explanatory variable induces non-proportional hazard modelling. This treatment is not very common in hazard model software, and can be very helpful.

Main Results

The Impact of Student/Non-Student Status
on Marriage and Cohabitation Rates

Crude Effects of Explanatory Variables. When analyzing marriage, cohabitation and union rates with variables age, birth cohort, class of origin, education and student status, it appears that the 'best' explanatory variables are age, birth cohort, and student/non-student status. When each variable is taken alone (models A, B, C, D, E and S), the estimates are simply the crude intensities, presented in Figure 4.1a and Table 4.5 (part I). Union formation intensities increased from forty-nine per thousand per year at the age of seventeen, to 309 per thousand per year at the age of twenty-two, and decreased for older ages. The proportion of unions entered outside marriage is stable with age (around 40 percent), and the shapes of marriage and cohabitation intensities are very similar.

Changes from one birth cohort to the other are very different for union, marriage and cohabitation intensities. From birth cohort 1941–1945 to 1951–1955, marriage intensities remained stable, while cohabitation rates increased rapidly. Union intensities reached a maximum for the 1956–1960 cohorts, as the dramatic increase in cohabitation compensates for the decline in marriage rates. In the subsequent cohorts (1961–1965), cohabitation intensity reached a maximum (six times greater than for the cohorts born twenty years earlier), while marriage intensities continued to decline down to half the level of the 1956–1960 cohorts. Finally, in the 1966–1969 cohorts, both cohabitation and marriage rates decrease because of a general delay in transition from adolescence to adulthood (Toulemon 1990). From the 1941–1945 to 1966–1969 cohorts, the proportion of first unions entered informally (for childless women) increase steadily from 14 percent to 84 percent (Figure 4.1b).

Non-students' cohabitation and marriage intensities are much higher than those of students. The relative risk of union formation for non- students compared to students is 4.4, mainly due to marriage intensity, which is nine times higher. But cohabitation intensity is also higher for non-students (2.2 times): as in Sweden, it cannot be deduced from the crude intensities that living as a

TABLE 4.5 Union, Cohabitation and Marriage Intensities, and Effects of Some Explanatory Variables (single women without children)

	I Crude Intensities (p. 1000 per year)			II COH/UNI (%)	III Relative Risks			IV Specific Effects		
	UNI	COH	MAR		UNI	COH	MAR	UNI	COH	MAR
Age (A):										
17	51	21	30	(41)	0,23	0,24	0,23	0,30	0,31	0,30
18	119	59	61	(49)	0,54	0,68	0,46	0,63	0,79	0,54
19	158	57	101	(36)	0,72	0,66	0,76	0,77	0,73	0,82
20	220	86	133	(39)	- 1 -	- 1 -	- 1 -	- 1 -	- 1 -	- 1 -
21	271	100	171	(37)	1,23	1,16	1,28	1,17	1,12	1,22
22	318	119	199	(38)	1,45	1,39	1,49	1,34	1,32	1,34
23	306	121	185	(39)	1,39	1,40	1,39	1,25	1,35	1,20
24	215	98	118	(45)	0,98	1,14	0,89	0,84	1,11	0,71
Birth Cohort (B):										
41-45	152	21	132	(14)	0,83	0,35	1,04	0,74	0,34	0,91
46-50	156	28	128	(18)	0,85	0,49	1,01	0,81	0,47	0,97
51-55	184	58	127	(32)	- 1 -	- 1 -	- 1 -	- 1 -	- 1 -	- 1 -
56-60	197	98	101	(50)	1,07	1,68	0,79	1,15	1,68	0,89
61-65	173	127	47	(73)	0,94	2,18	0,37	1,06	2,23	0,45
66-69	88	72	15	(83)	0,48	1,25	0,12	0,89	1,99	0,25
Class (C):										
Farmer	175	46	129	(26)	0,92	0,59	1,15	0,94	0,77	1,02
Self-employed	160	56	104	(35)	0,84	0,73	0,92	0,92	0,90	0,93
Unskilled worker	187	58	131	(31)	0,99	0,74	1,16	0,94	0,82	1,01
Skilled worker	189	78	112	(41)	- 1 -	- 1 -	- 1 -	- 1 -	- 1 -	- 1 -
White coll. lower lev.	173	75	98	(44)	0,91	0,97	0,87	0,99	1,11	0,93
White coll. midd. higher level	136	72	65	(53)	0,72	0,92	0,58	0,94	1,08	0,83
Education (E):										
Low	191	44	147	(23)	- 1 -	- 1 -	- 1 -	- 1 -	- 1 -	- 1 -
Med	150	67	82	(44)	0,79	1,52	0,56	0,91	1,26	0,82
High	203	107	95	(53)	1,06	2,44	0,64	1,04	1,63	0,85
Student (S):										
Yes	54	38	17	(70)	- 1 -	- 1 -	- 1 -	- 1 -	- 1 -	- 1 -
No	229	82	147	(36)	4,22	2,18	8,85	3,39	2,46	5,47

UNI: Union   COH: Cohabitation   MAR: Marriage

Notes:

I = Crude Intensities: Rates estimated by models with only one explanatory variable, for the whole sample per 1000 per year.

II = Proportion (%) of unions entered without marriage.

III = Relative risks deduced from the crude intensities.

-1- = Reference group.

IV = Relative risks deduced from the parameters estimated by model ABCES/- (all variables and no interaction).

FIGURE 4.1a Union, Cohabition and Marriage Intensities
(‰ per year), by Age, Birth Cohort, Class,
Education and Student Status (cruide
intensities, "single" childless women)

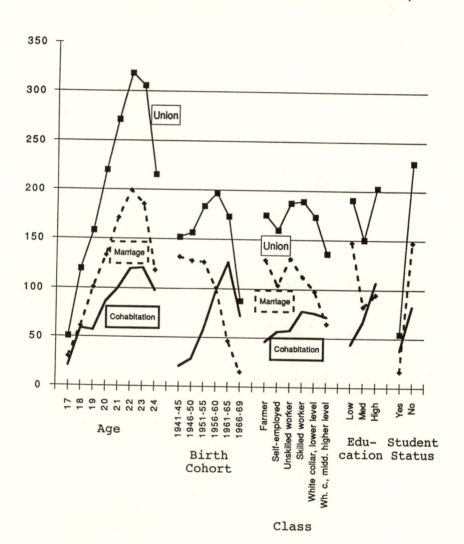

FIGURE 4.1b Proportion (%) of Unions Entered Outside Marriage

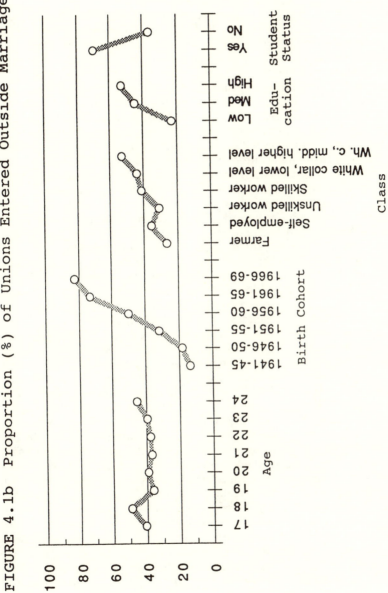

couple without being married constitutes 'campus behavior.' Nevertheless, in our sample taken as a whole, 71 percent of unions begun by students are informal, as against 36 percent of unions begun by non-students.

Compared to age, birth cohort and student/non-student status, the variables class and education appear to have smaller, but non negligible crude effects. Union intensities for unskilled workers' daughters are 1.4 times those for the daughters of white-collars (high level), the latter entering an extramarital union more frequently. Women with a higher educational level marry less (0.6), but cohabit more frequently (2.4) than women with a low level of education, so that union intensities do not vary much by level of education.

Specific Effects. When all variables are used together without interactions (model ABCES), the estimates represent 'specific' main effects. As expected, the range for every explanatory variable becomes smaller (Table 4.5, part IV). The increase of the rates with age is less important than for crude intensities, despite the fact that the introduction of other explanatory variables generally induces an increase of basic hazard derivative by time duration. The reason is that student/non-student status (one of the main explanatory variables) varies with age: as women become older they end their studies, which induces an increase in the hazards. The increase of cohabitation intensity from one birth cohort to the other does not change much in the complete model: the spread of cohabitation cannot simply be attributed to the increase in educational level, which still has a (specific) effect. On the other hand, the decrease in marriage (and union) rates is less dramatic when structural changes (mainly the rise in educational enrollment) are included in the models. Class origin appears to have no specific effect on the hazards, when variations due to age, birth cohort and student status are taken into account.

Looking for the 'Best' Model. More than—or as much as—the range of the contrasts, the likelihood ratio criterion is useful to test specific effects. Relative to model AB (age-birth cohort), the model ABC improves the fit for all the transitions (at the 5 percent level, not shown). However, the addition of term C to model ABS or to model ABES does not contribute to the fit: when taking into account the student/non-student status, no more direct effect of social background can be found. This means that the contrasts in young women's first union formation intensities in different social groups (defined here by father's profession) can be explained by the differences in educational enrollment: for instance, if unskilled workers' daughters marry earlier, it is mainly because they leave school at younger ages than other women. Educational enrollment (for 'single' women with no children) by social background is very similar to the Swedish one: at the age of seventeen, approximately 15–45 percent of unskilled workers daughters are students, as opposed to 70–80 percent for the daughters of higher white-collars. Note that the contrast between social groups is underestimated here, as we restrict the observation to 'single' women with no children. Models ABE and ABS are statistically better than AB, as does ABES relative to ABE and ABS, for union, marriage and cohabitation rates.

Many interactions between explanatory variables appear to be significant, even at the 1-percent-level. First, the student/non-student status has specific effects on marriage and cohabitation intensities at different ages and—significant at the 5-percent-level—in different cohorts. Thus we decided, as did Hoem, to fit separate models for students and non-students. Second, we found an interaction between birth cohort and class, for marriage and cohabitation intensities. This could be explained by the cohabitation diffusion pattern in France (Villeneuve-Gokalp 1990, 1991): in the late 1960s, unmarried cohabitation was as common and more durable for unskilled workers' daughters as for other social groups; during the 1970s and 1980s, cohabitation became increasingly frequent in many social groups, but its diffusion has been less dramatic and less rapid for workers' children. Nevertheless, we did not examine precisely the interactions between B and C before trying specific models for students and non-students (which is similar to allowing any kind of interaction between S and all other explanatory variables). No interaction is found for union intensities: it seems that union formation intensities (married or not) follow simple developments, while the choice between cohabitation and marriage shows more complicated patterns.

We also found significant interactions between age and education level, for marriage, cohabitation and union intensities, and between age and birth cohort for marriage and union intensities. The identification and interpretation of these interactions is greatly simplified by splitting the sample into students and non-students.

The Similarity in Patterns of Students' Union Formation in France and Sweden. The 'best' models for students are very simple: for cohabitation and marriage intensities, no model improves the fit compared to AB. This could be due to the small sample size and to the low level of the rates (few events recorded) when the sample is restricted to students. Nevertheless, students' union initiation seems to depend highly on age and birth cohort, but not much on social background. We did not include education as an explanatory variable for students, as it is a function of students' age in our data. Union formation rates are very low, especially in younger age groups (Table 4.6 and Figure 4.2a): in all cohorts, more than 76 percent of the students did not live in any union before the age of twenty- one, and more than 33 percent were still 'single' at the age of twenty-five (simple decrement life table estimates). Union intensities increased from the 1941–1945 cohort to the 1961–1965 cohort; the subsequent decline (delay) occurred later than for non-students, and the rates in the 1966–1969 cohorts are higher than in the 1941–1950 cohorts.

Students' marriage intensities show a deep and regular decline for cohorts born after 1955: there was even no marriage during educational enrollment recorded in the last cohort (born 1966–1969), while 80 percent of first unions in the 1941–1945 cohort began with a marriage. The proportion of unions begun outside marriage, as estimated by models AB for cohabitation and marriage intensities, does not vary with age (Figures 4.1b and 4.2b): this is contrary to the cross-sectional view on diffusion of unmarried cohabitation. Students' cohabitation can be considered as an interim solution, a compromise between the students' wish to live as a couple and the parents' desire that their children wait until they are financially independent (and to finish their studies) before marrying (Villeneuve-Gokalp 1990). Finally, we can no-

TABLE 4.6   Union, Cohabitation and Marriage Intensities, by Age and Cohort, for Students (Model AB/-) (single women without children)

	I Students' Intensities (p. 1000 per year)			II Students' Intensities: Relative Risks			III STU COH/ UNI	IV NON COH/ UNI	V Students' Intensities (non-students=100)		
	UNI	COH	MAR	UNI	COH	MAR			UNI	COH	MAR
Age (A):											
17	15	7	9	0,16	0,15	0,19	(42)	(29)	15	24	14
18	53	28	23	0,57	0,61	0,47	(55)	(35)	30	46	20
19	53	29	19	0,56	0,64	0,38	(61)	(24)	23	53	11
20	94	46	50	- 1 -	- 1 -	- 1 -	(48)	(28)	33	57	24
21	135	67	70	1,43	1,45	1,40	(49)	(27)	41	76	28
22	213	102	117	2,27	2,20	2,36	(47)	(28)	58	98	28
23	193	69	147	2,05	1,49	2,97	(32)	(34)	55	59	45
24	173	114	39	1,84	2,46	0,79	(74)	(39)	73	126	28
Birth Cohort (B):											
1941-45	51	13	39	0,54	0,29	0,78	(26)	(12)	23	50	20
1946-50	47	21	26	0,50	0,46	0,53	(45)	(16)	19	55	13
1951-55	94	46	50	- 1 -	- 1 -	- 1 -	(48)	(28)	33	57	24
1956-60	106	69	38	1,13	1,49	0,76	(65)	(45)	33	47	21
1961-65	115	103	10	1,22	2,23	0,20	(91)	(67)	39	53	11
1966-69	77	73	0	0,82	1,58	0,00	(100)	(76)	29	36	0

UNI: Union   COH: Cohabitation   MAR: Marriage

Notes:
Rates by age: Model AB/-, estimations for cohort 1951-55.
Rates by cohort : model AB/-, estimations for age 20.

I   = Estimations from model AB/rates per 1000 p. year.
II = - 1 -: reference group.
III = Proportion (%) of unions entered outside marriage, for students.
IV = Proportion (%) of unions entered outside marriage, for non-students.
V   = Rates for students, as a percentage of the rate for non-student (model AB/- for non-students).
       Rates by age: Model AB/-, cohort 1951-55.
       Rates by cohort: Model AB/-, age 20.

FIGURE 4.2a Union, Cohabition and Marriage Intensities
(‰ per year), by Age (cohort 1951-55), Birth Cohort
(age 20), Estimated by Model AB/- for Students and
Non-students

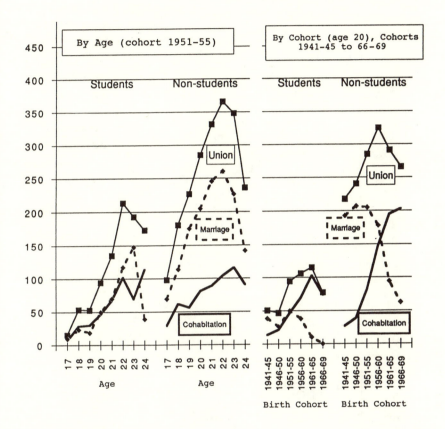

tice a decline in students' cohabitation intensity in the most recent cohort (Figure 4.2a). These results closely resemble those for Sweden, with changes occurring with a ten-cohort lag in France.

The Specific Effects of Educational Attainment on Direct Marriage and Cohabitation in France for Non-Students. The development of union, marriage and cohabitation intensities for non-students do not follow such a simple pattern. Compared to the 'basic' AB model, the fit is improved by taking into account some interaction between A and B (union and marriage), and the effect of class, with an interaction between class and birth cohort, for marriage. Compared to model AB/- at the 5-percent-level, the fit is improved with model ABE/AB+AE for union intensities, model ABCE/BC for marriage, and ABCE/AB+AE+BC for cohabitation. At the 1-percent- level, the 'best' models are respectively AB/AB, ABE and ABE/AB. The main result, however, is a

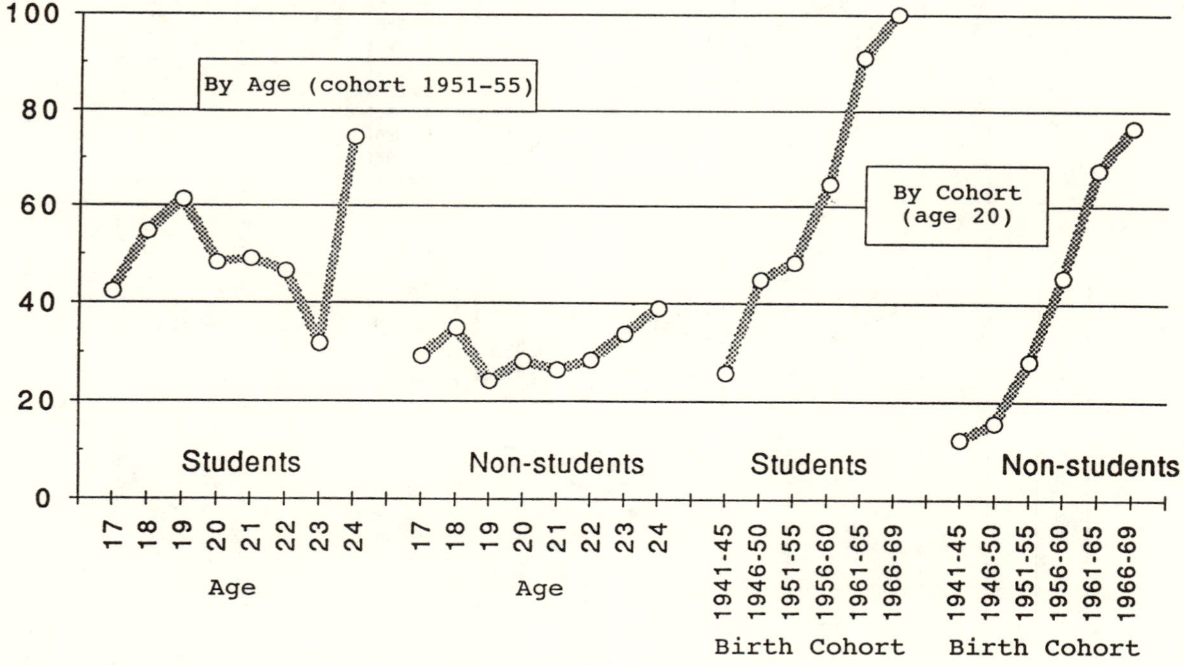

FIGURE 4.2b Proportion (%) of Unions Entered Outside Marriage

major effect of education on non-students' cohabitation and marriage intensities. The relative risks estimated in model ABE are shown in Table 4.7 (part II). Non-students' union intensities do not vary with the level of education: compared to women with a low level of education, the relative risks are 0.95 (0.96) for women with a middle (high) education. But relative risks of cohabitation are 1.35 and 1.62, respectively for women with a middle or high level of education as compared to a low level, and relative risks of marriage are 0.82 and 0.73 respectively. When they have completed their studies, French women with a high level of education seem to continue avoiding marriage. In Sweden, no such effect was found. For the recent cohorts (1966–1969), no decrease in non-students' cohabitation is found—remember that we found an apparent decrease for students—but the survey took place when women of these cohorts were aged eighteen to twenty-one years.

To allow for a comparison with students, it may nevertheless be interesting to describe intensities for non-students taken as a whole, by ignoring the heterogeneity in educational level. Non-students' rates estimated by model AB/- are shown in Figure 4.2.

The interaction between age and birth cohort comes from an earlier entry into first union for non-students from one cohort to the next; cohabitation and union intensities increase more at younger ages than at ages over twenty. This change also applies to the entire cohorts (including students), despite the increase in educational enrollment. For the 1941–1945 to 1956–1960 cohorts, non-students' marriage intensities are more or less stable, but unmarried cohabitation appears as a new opportunity for young men and women to live together as couples. The increase from one cohort to the next is very regular, and quite surprisingly, the same additive effect appears for all ages, as if cohabitation was a behavior with the same meaning at all ages, and was quite independent of marriage. In actual fact, most of the early additional cohabitations (before 1975) ended rapidly with a pregnancy and a marriage, inducing an increase in nuptiality for younger age groups in the 1940–1945 cohorts, and stability in nuptiality from the 1945 to 1955 cohorts, as recorded in vital statistics (Couet and Court 1990). In the most recent cohorts, the dramatic decline in marriage intensities illustrates the disappearance of marriage without previous cohabitation. The AB interaction seems relevant for cohabitation intensities (the variation of the rate from one cohort to the next being more additive than multiplicative), although it is only statistically significant for marriage and union intensities. These interactions do not produce regular patterns, nor do they change the direct effect of education. Finally, the 'best' model for marriage intensities would be ABCE/AB+BC+AE, which is highly complex, despite—or because—it does not include other variables which are relevant for France (Villeneuve-Gokalp 1990). As our goal is to facilitate international comparisons, we will not discuss this model here.

Conclusions

By reproducing as far as possible an analysis made of another country, we wanted to test a specific hypothesis regarding the diffusion of consensual

TABLE 4.7 Union, Cohabitation and Marriage Intensities, by Age and Cohort, for Non-Students (Model ABE/-) (single women with no child)

	I Non-students' Intensities (p. 1000 per year)			II Non-students' Intensities Relative Risks			III NON COH/UNI	IV Non-students' Intensities Model AB/-		
	UNI	COH	MAR	UNI	COH	MAR		UNI	COH	MAR
Age (A):										
17	100	25	75	0,34	0,38	0,32	(25)	98	29	69
18	184	51	127	0,63	0,79	0,54	(29)	180	61	114
19	233	46	199	0,79	0,71	0,84	(19)	226	56	175
20	294	64	236	- 1 -	- 1 -	- 1 -	(21)	285	81	205
21	341	69	285	1,16	1,07	1,21	(19)	331	88	245
22	377	79	309	1,28	1,23	1,31	(20)	366	104	261
23	359	88	268	1,22	1,36	1,14	(25)	348	116	226
24	243	68	168	0,83	1,06	0,71	(29)	236	90	142
Birth Cohort (B):										
1941-45	224	22	215	0,76	0,35	0,91	(09)	218	27	193
1946-50	250	31	236	0,85	0,48	1,00	(12)	240	38	207
1951-55	294	64	236	- 1 -	- 1 -	- 1 -	(21)	285	81	205
1956-60	341	114	209	1,16	1,77	0,89	(35)	325	147	178
1961-65	306	146	112	1,04	2,27	0,48	(56)	291	195	94
1966-69	279	153	75	0,95	2,39	0,32	(67)	266	203	62
Education (E):										
Low	294	64	236	- 1 -	- 1 -	- 1 -	(21)			
Med	279	87	193	0,95	1,35	0,82	(31)			
High	282	104	173	0,96	1,62	0,73	(38)			

UNI: Union   COH: Cohabitation   MAR: Marriage

Notes:

Rates by age: estimations for cohort 1951-55, low level.
Model ABE/-, estimations for cohort 1951-55, low level.
Rates by cohort: Model AB/-, estimations for age 20, low level.
Rates by level of education: Model ABE/-, estimations for cohort 1951-55, age 20.

I   = Estimations from model ABE/- (p. 1000 per year).
II = - 1 -: Reference group.
III = Proportion (%) of unions entered outside marriage, for non-students.
IV = Estimations from model AB/- (p. 1000 per year).
       Rates by age: Model AB/-, cohort 1951-55.
       Rates by cohort: Model AB/-, age 20.

unions: namely that student or non-student status has a major impact on first union initiation, and that educational level does not have a direct specific effect on the choice between cohabitation and marriage of 'single' women. The figures found are very similar to the Swedish ones, with a delay of some ten cohorts in the development. Nevertheless, a major difference appears with a strong effect of educational level on non- students' choice between marriage and cohabitation in France. A similar effect was found for the Netherlands, women with a high level of education marrying less than, and cohabiting as much as, the others (Liefbroer 1991); comparability, however, is limited by Liefbroer's definition of education, where level of education at age sixteen is taken as a time-constant factor. This difference between France and Sweden leads to two different sets of conclusions.

First, the pattern of historical development differs. In France, cohabitation may be more strongly associated with new—less sex-differentiated—roles, whilst married couples adhere to a more traditional pattern. By contrast, in Sweden gender roles have changed for cohabitees and married couples alike.

Second, we should stress that the general pattern is nevertheless very similar for France and Sweden. In both countries, there was a tradition of informal union initiation during the 1960s in the working class, and the increase in the numbers of unmarried couples implied different types of cohabitation (Bernhardt and Hoem 1985, Villeneuve-Gokalp 1990). In that case, the specific effect of our education variable means that this variable pinpoints, more than in Sweden, a specific heterogeneity. For instance, we can note that level of education has a very strong impact on the kind of occupation open to women, so that women with a high level of education may in fact be more specific in so far as they want to have good career opportunities and are thus more reluctant to marry. The absence of a direct strong effect of social background in France may be interpreted in the same way, by making the role of education in social reproduction of women's status more explicit.

However, international comparisons allow us to emphasize certain results which appear to be specific to each country, and others potentially similar to both countries. Such comparisons may generate a 'loss of information' for each country, because variables have to be analyzed in a way which may not be optimal for one of the two countries, but nevertheless they also offer a new perspective on each country.

Appendix: Brief Description of the Surveys

The 1988 INED Fertility Survey

The ERN survey (*Enquête sur la Régulation des Naissances*) was conducted by INED, with the collaboration of INSEE (Institut National de la Statistique et des Etudes Economiques) and INSERM (Institut National de la Santé et de la Recherche Médicale), in January to March 1988 (see Toulemon and Leridon 1991). A total of 3183 women aged eighteen to forty-nine were interviewed, from a random sample of 8700 households; 21 percent of 'eligible' women refused to answer the survey. The interviews included retrospective information on pregnancies, unions (formal or informal) and contraceptive methods used. They were also dealing with fertility projects, past ('wantedness' of each pregnancy, fertility intentions at the beginning of the last union) and present, and with problems of sterility and subfecundity.

The 1985–1986 INED Survey on Family History

The ESF survey (*Enquête sur les Situations Familiales*) was conducted by INED with the collaboration of INSEE in November and December 1985 (see Leridon and Villeneuve-Gokalp, 1988 and 1989). A total of 4091 men and women aged twenty-one to forty-four (on 31 December 1985) were interviewed. The sample was drawn from a larger survey on employment carried out by INSEE in March 1985: households were selected on the basis of the information available on their structure in this first survey, in order to over-represent non-typical families (single-parent families, consensual unions, divorced persons, etc.). The non-response rate was 13 percent, including 5 percent refusals.

References

Becker, G. (1981). *A Treatise on the Family,* Cambridge (Mass.), Harvard University Press.

Bernhardt, E. and B. Hoem (1985). "Cohabitation and Social Background," *European Journal of Population,* 1:4.

Blossfeld H.-P. and U. Jaenichen (1992). "Educational Expansion and Changes in Women's Entry into Marriage and Motherhood in the Federal Republic of Germany," *Journal of Marriage and the Family,* 54, 5:302–15.

Brin, H. (1991): *La politique familiale française,* Rapport du Conseil Economique et Social, séances des 24 et 25 septembre 1991, Journal Officiel de la République Française.

Couet, C. and Y. Court (1990): "La situation démographique en 1989. Mouvement de la population," INSEE Résultats: Démographie- société, 11–12.

Debizet, J. (1990). "La scolarité après 16 ans," *Donnés Sociales 1990,* INSEE, Paris.

Desplanques, G. (1987). "Activité féminine et fécondité," *Donnés Sociales 1987,* INSEE, Paris.

Gollac, M., P. Laulhé and J. Soleilhavoup (1989). *Formation. Enquête Formation Qualification Professionnelle de 1985,* Les Collections de l'INSEE, Série D, 129.

Hoem, J. (1985). "The Impact of Education on Modern Union Initiation," Stockholm Research Reports in Demography, 27, published in the *European Journal of Population,* 2 (1986), 113–33.

Hoem, J. (1989). *User's guide to LOGLIN with Pre- and postprocessors,* Stockholm University, Demographic Unit.

INED, 1987, "Seizième rapport sur la situation démographique de la France," *Population,* 42, 4–5.

Leridon, H. (1990a). "Cohabitation, Marriage, Separation. An Analysis of Life Histories of French Cohorts from 1968 to 1985," *Population Studies,* 44, 1.

Leridon, H. (1990b). "Extra-marital Cohabitation and Fertility," *Population Studies,* 44, 3.

Leridon, H. and C. Villeneuve-Gokalp (1988). "Les nouveaux couples. Annexe 1: Comparaison des résultats de l'enquête emploi et de l'enquête sur les situations familiales," *Population,* 43, 2.

Leridon, H. and C. Villeneuve-Gokalp (1989). "The New Couples: Number, Characteristics and Attitudes," *Population* (English Selection) 1.

Liefbroer, A. (1991). "The Choice between a Married or Unmarried First Union by Young Adults: A Competing Risks Analysis," *European Journal of Population*, 7, 3.

Marchand, O. and C. Thélot (1991). *Deux siècles de travail en France*, INSEE ("Etudes"), Paris.

Oliver, D. and R. Neff (1976). *LOGLIN 1.0 User's Guide, Health Sciences Computing Facility*, Harvard School of Public Health, Boston, Mass. 02115, USA.

Rallu, J.L. and L. Toulemon (1993). "Les mesures de la fécondit transversale. Application la France de 1946 à 1989," *Population*,48, 2.

Sardon, J.P. (1990). "L'évolution de la fécondité en France depuis un demi-siècle," INED, *Dossiers et recherches*, 31.

Toulemon, L. (1990). "Les étapes vers l'âge adulte: vers un nouveau statut des femmes," *International Population Conference*, New Delhi, 1989, IUSSP, Vol. 3.

Toulemon, L. (1991). "Peut-on choisir de ne pas avoir d'enfant?," paper presented at the European Population Conference, EAPS, Paris.

Toulemon, L. and H. Leridon (1991). "Vingt années de contraception en France: 1968–1988," *Population*, 46, 5.

Villeneuve-Gokalp, C. (1990). "Du mariage aux unions sans papiers: histoire récente des transformations conjugales," *Population*, 45, 2.

Villeneuve-Gokalp, C. (1991). "From Marriage to Informal Union: Recent Changes in the Behaviour of French Couples," *Population* (English Selection), 3.

5

The Netherlands

JENNY DE JONG GIERVELD AND AART C. LIEFBROER

In the Netherlands, a rather paradoxical situation exists. The country is characterized by union formation at a relatively late age, a strong prevalence of unmarried cohabitation, a low birth rate, and a very late age at first birth. All these characteristics fit nicely into the image of the Netherlands as one of the forerunners of what Van de Kaa (1987) has termed *the second demographic transition*. The *first* demographic transition took place at the beginning of this century and was characterized by both a decrease in mortality and fertility. This first transition was viewed as being *altruistic* in nature, because the drop in fertility was attributed to a growing concern for the quality of childhood. People opted for fewer children, but made sure that these were raised to the best of their abilities. The second demographic transition is labelled *egoistic*, because the further decline in fertility is thought to result not from a concern for the well-being of children, but from a concern for one's own autonomy and self-fullfilment. What makes the Dutch case so paradoxical is that although it is one of the forerunners in demographic developments, it is at the same time one of the *back-markers* as far as female employment is concerned. Although the percentage of women on the labor market is rising, it is still low compared to other Western countries.

In this chapter, we have placed the emphasis on the trends that make the Netherlands one of the forerunners in the second demographic transition. Its back-marker role concerning female labor market participation will receive less attention, and will be discussed mainly in as far as it influences the demographic trends under consideration. However, in the concluding section we will return to the apparent paradox, and suggest some possible explanations for it.

This contribution is organized as follows. In the first section, we outline the main characteristics of and developments in Dutch family policy. We then highlight changes in educational attainment and labor market participation of women. This is followed by a discussion of trends in union formation patterns. We then go on to deal with fertility trends and conclude our contribution with a brief discussion of the main implications of our survey of family formation in the Netherlands.

The data used are from three different sources. First of all, we used official population statistics provided by the Netherlands' Central Bureau of Statistics (NCBS). Secondly, we employ data from the Netherlands Fertility Survey (NFS), conducted every five years by the NCBS (NCBS, 1990a). This is a representative survey among Dutch women between the ages of eighteen and thirty-seven. We will present results of own analyses that are based on aggregate data from 6026 women, born between 1945 and 1964, who have been interviewed in the NFS. Those born between 1945 and 1949 have been interviewed in the 1982 NFS, the others in the 1988 NFS. In these data, the occurrence of main demographic events, such as leaving the parental home, first union formation, and childbearing, is registered by age, birth cohort, and educational attainment. These data are analyzed using loglinear hazard models. In addition to these analyses, we review some more extensive analyses of these data made by the NCBS itself (Vermunt 1991), and data from a survey conducted by the Vrije Universiteit of Amsterdam on the 'Social Integration of Young Adults' (SI) (Dijkstra 1989). In this study, 1775 young adults aged eighteen, twenty-two and twenty-six were interviewed at the end of 1987.

Family Policy

Dutch governments have been rather reluctant to formulate explicit family policies in general, and population policies in particular (Dumon 1991; Van Nimwegen and Esveldt 1991). Thus, most policies are not strictly designed to stimulate demographic developments, but do have an *indirect* impact on these developments, for instance, by influencing the costs of parenthood or the opportunities for combining parenthood and employment. We have thus focussed on this type of indirect policy, first with a brief discussion of the legal and fiscal differences between marriage and unmarried cohabitation, and have then concentrated on policies concerned with fertility and with the combination of motherhood and employment.

Mainly because the Netherlands lacks a firm tradition of unmarried cohabitation, it took quite some time before a legal framework for this type of union developed. The government's initial reaction to this new union type was one of ignorance. However, as it became clear that cohabitation was not something temporary, the government initiated a policy to equate cohabitation and marriage, both legally and fiscally. As a result of this, unmarried cohabitation and marriage have successively been made equal before the law during the 1980s. If people live together for a year or more, the same tax regulations apply to them as to married couples. In addition, some cohabitors have drawn up a legal contract, in which the property and financial arrangements between the partners are spelt out.

Three important types of policies concerning fertility can be distinguished (Van Nimwegen and Esveldt 1991), one dealing with education on and access to contraceptives, one concerning direct monetary incentives for parents, and one dealing with the combination of parenthood (or more specifically motherhood) and employment.

The first policy issue that may influence the fertility level is the availability of and ease of *access to contraceptives*. For some decades the Dutch government has had a liberal policy concerning the availability of contraceptives, and has subsidized the activities of private organizations that provide information on birth control. These policies have been very successful, making the Netherlands the country with the lowest level of teenage pregnancies in Europe.

The second policy instrument that has already existed for a long time is the payment of *child allowance*. When it was introduced in 1963, this allowance was only provided from the third child onwards, but was soon extended to cover all children. The amount of child allowance depends on the age and parity of the child, but not on parental means. Furthermore, the amount of money parents receive has fluctuated with economic developments in the Netherlands, rising during the economically prosperous 1960s, dropping— especially for the first child—during the recession of the 1970s, and slightly rising again during the 1980s. Van Nimwegen and Esveldt (1991) conclude that, although child allowance promotes a 'parenthood-friendly' climate, its direct long-term demographic impact has been rather limited, partly owing to the arbitrariness of changes in this policy.

The third important set of policy instruments concerns measures that have an impact on the feasibility of combining motherhood and employment; more specifically this covers maternity leave, parental leave, and childcare facilities. *Maternity leave* originated early this century, but was not often used because employers were allowed to fire women when they either got married or pregnant. This practice was not legally forbidden until 1957, the year in which married women gained juridical contractual capacity (De Bruijn 1989). After that time, the use of maternity leave increased. Up to 1990, paid maternity leave was restricted to twelve weeks around childbirth. In 1990, the maximum number of weeks was increased to sixteen. *Parental leave* is a novel phenomenon in Dutch labor regulations. Since 1991, both parents are legally allowed to make use of unpaid parental leave for a period of six months. Their child has to be under the age of four and, in contrast to maternity leave regulations, the parents have to work for at least twenty hours a week. The law does not apply to part-timers with a working week of less than twenty hours. In some industries, parental leave regulations are somewhat more elaborate than what is legally prescribed. For instance, civil servants receive 75 percent of pay during parental leave. Official *childcare facilities* have, until recently, been rather scarce in the Netherlands. If a mother worked, she had to find private forms of assistance for taking care of her children. The Dutch government has recently started promoting childcare facilities, but the gap between demand and supply is still growing. The Emancipatory Commission, an advisory board to the government, has calculated that the need for childcare is about ten times in excess of supply. Not only is there a lack of childcare facilities, but those that exist are often not financially attractive, making it especially hard for women with low-income jobs to combine work and motherhood.

Surveying the past and present policies concerning the combination of employment and parenthood, Van Nimwegen and Esveldt (1991) and Beets

(1991) conclude that the current policies are very *ad hoc*, and not very effective in creating a stimulus for combining parenthood and employment. Furthermore, the Netherlands is lagging behind most other West European countries in this respect.

Educational Attainment and
Labor Force Participation

The role of women, especially the role of married women, has been changing quite dramatically in Dutch society since World War II. These changes can be observed both within the *private sector* of women's family lives and in the public sector. The relationship between spouses has become much more egalitarian, although it has been observed that this is true to a much larger extent with regard to people's *opinions* about partner relationships than with regard to the *actual* balance of power and division of labor. Thus, 83 percent of the Dutch adult population agrees that household chores are the joint responsibility of both spouses, and an even higher percentage (88 percent) agrees that childcare is the joint responsibility of both parents (SCP, Sociaal en Cultureel Planbureau 1988). However, Tavecchio et al. (1984) show that there is a discrepancy between spouses' intentions concerning the sharing of household chores and actual practice. The same point is made by Komter (1985), who reports that men contribute less to household labor than they think. Knulst and Van Beek (1990) report that among men who have a paid job, the amount of time spent on household chores has risen from five to seven hours a week between 1975 and 1985, irrespective of the educational level of the men. Among women with a paid job, the amount of time spent on household chores remained constant between 1975 and 1985 for women with a medium and high level of education, at nineteen and eighteen hours a week respectively. Among women with a low level of education, the amount of time increased from twenty hours in 1975 to twenty-four hours in 1985. Thus, the emancipation of women has, so far, only led to a marginal shift in the distribution of household chores. However, it could be that women have a much stronger say in decision processes within the family household than they had in the past.

Changes in the *public role* of women mainly come to the fore when we concentrate on changes in the educational attainment and the labor force participation of women in the Netherlands during the past decades. Women are now tending to remain longer in education. Of the women born in the late 1940s, 60 percent had already left school by the age of sixteen. Of the women who were born in the early 1960s, not even 20 percent had left school by that age (NCBS 1990b:4). Furthermore, women have caught up with men with regard to the level of their final educational attainment. Table 5.1 provides an overview of the development of the final educational attainment of women from the 1925 to 1974 birth cohorts.

Caution is required when interpreting these figures for cohorts born from 1955 onwards. Not all women in these cohorts have finished their education yet, and therefore the percentages of women having at least a medium level

TABLE 5.1 Educational Attainment of Women from Selected Cohorts (%)

Educational Attainment	Birth Cohort				
	1925-1934	1935-1944	1945-1954	1955-1964	1965-1974
Primary education	42	25	18	12	17
Lower level vocational training	20	25	22	16	15
Secondary education	11	11	10	8	24
Medium level vocational training	18	25	29	36	22
Pre-university education	2	2	3	6	17
High level vocational training	7	11	14	17	5
University degree	1	2	4	5	0

Source: NCBS 1990b.

vocational training is somewhat deflated. However, it is clear that an increase in the percentage of highly-educated women occurs with increasing year of birth. This mainly manifests itself in a higher percentage with an intermediate or higher level college degree, but also applies to women with a secondary, pre-university, and university education. There are increasingly fewer women who have only had a primary education. This pattern is basically similar for men. The poorer 'starting position' of women—of the 1925–1934 birth cohorts, 42.4 percent had only had primary education compared with 27.3 percent of men—has been completely caught up by the 1955–1964 birth cohorts.

Developments in the area of labor force participation are presented in Table 5.2. In this case we present period population data, rather than cohort data. The first column of Table 5.2 does not show the birth cohorts, but the census years. Data is presented for the census years 1899, 1909, 1920, 1930, 1947, 1960, and 1971. Then follows data from the 1981 NCBS Labor Force Census and from the 1988 Survey on the Working Population (NCBS 1989).

Female labor force participation in the Netherlands has been very low for a long time. Even as recently as 1960, only 26 percent of women aged from fifteen to sixty-four years had a job outside the home. After 1960 this percentage increased, first very slowly, but after 1971 somewhat more rapidly. By 1988 this percentage had reached 44 percent. From Table 5.2, it becomes clear that the strongest increase has been among women aged twenty- five to forty-nine. Labor force participation has decreased both in the youngest age group and in the oldest one, among the former as a result of increased educational participation, and among the latter as a result of the establishment of old age pensions.

The increase in female labor force participation as shown in Table 5.2, might look quite impressive, but it should be noted that many more Dutch women than Dutch men hold *part-time* jobs. In 1990, 8 percent of the male employees in the Netherlands held a job of less than twenty hours a week, whereas the same was true for 32 percent of the female employees (NCBS 1992). Another characteristic of female labor force participation is the so-called *childcare interval*, the phenomenon that many women leave the labor force for a number of years to care for their young children, after which they partly resume their jobs (Dykstra 1991). This can be seen in Table 5.2 from the fact that the labor participation of women aged twenty to twenty-four years is about 70 percent, whereas for the twenty-five to thirty-nine age group, this is considerably reduced to 55 percent. This strong interrelation between number of children and labor force participation can be illustrated even more clearly from figures of a study by Allaart, Kunnen, and Van Stiphout (1989). They calculated that the labor force participation rate of married and unmarried women without children is relatively high (65 percent and 78 percent, respectively). However, this rate drops to between 27 percent and 38 percent for women with children, depending somewhat on the age of the children, illustrating the pervasive impact of the 'childcare interval.'

TABLE 5.2 Labor Force Participation of Women by Age in Selected Years (%)

Year	Total			Age Group			
		14-19	20-24	25-39	40-49	50-64	65+
1899	17	37	43	19		17	13
1909	18	41	46	22	18	19	13
1920	18	45	47	21	16	16	9
1930	19	49	50	23	17	15	7
1947	20	49	51	24	21	17	6
1960	16	52	53	18	17	14	3
1971	19	42	56	24	23	17	2
1981	33	31	72	45	37	19	1
1988	37	27	71	55	47	19	0

Source: NCBS 1990b.

Union Formation

We now turn to the analysis of the main changes in nuptiality and fertility patterns that have taken place in the Netherlands after 1945. Firstly, we will take a look at union formation.

After World War II, the age at marriage first showed a decrease, followed by a strong increase. This is exemplified by Table 5.3, which shows the proportion of women who have not married before specified ages for cohorts born from 1932 onwards.

From Table 5.3, it can be observed that the proportion of women that married during their teens increased for cohorts born before the mid-1950s. From then on it decreased. In the youngest birth cohort, only 2 percent has married before the age of twenty. The same pattern can be observed at other ages, with the difference that the decline in the percentage of women that has ever married starts earlier. For instance, the percentage of women ever-married before the age of twenty-five already starts to decline among cohorts born between 1952 and 1956, and the percentage ever-married before the age of thirty starts to decline from cohorts born between 1947 and 1951. From this pattern of change in the proportion never-married it can be concluded that a change in union formation behavior began in the *mid-1970s*. From then on, people started to become more reluctant to marry. From the figures in Table 5.3, it cannot be conluded, however, whether this change only signifies a *delay* in the process of marriage or rather a decline in the overall tendency to marry. The NCBS, however, projects future marriage rates that are considerably lower than those of the past.

Postponement of marriage does not have to imply postponement of union formation altogether. From the 1960s onwards, unmarried cohabitation has become increasingly popular in the Netherlands, and this could have compensated for the decline in marriage. As Table 5.4 makes clear, this is at least partly what happened. The difference between the birth cohorts, born between 1945 and 1959, in the percentage of women that has ever entered a first union is rather small. The percentage of women in the birth cohort 1960–1964 that has ever entered a first union before the age of twenty-three is somewhat lower, however. The percentage of women that has ever entered a first union at that age in this cohort had been reached about one year earlier by the older birth cohorts. Thus, the difference is not that spectacular. It seems, therefore, that a rise in unmarried cohabitation has largely made up for the decline in marriage. However, this raises the question on the extent to which unmarried cohabitation and marriage are comparable phenomena in Dutch society.

Although unmarried cohabitation has never been completely absent, it has been practised by a very small minority during most of this century. During the heyday of the nuclear family, it was something that would have met with strong disapproval. As in a number of other Western countries (Meyer and Schulze 1983), it started to become popular from the second half of the 1960s onwards, at first mainly among young, highly educated people who wanted to show their aversion to the bourgeois ideals of Dutch society. As time went by, cohabitation became increasingly popular. Where only 10 percent of the

TABLE 5.3 Changes in the Timing of Entry into Marriage, as Measured by the Proportion of Women Never-married at Specific Ages

Birth Cohort	Proportion of Never-married Women at Age						
	20	25	30	35	40	45	50
1967-1971	98						
1962-1966	95	62					
1957-1961	90	47	29				
1952-1956	85	30	20	15			
1947-1951	87	25	12	10			
1942-1946	89	26	10	7	8	6	
1937-1941	92	34	10	6	6	5	5
1932-1936	93	41	12	7	6	5	5

Source: Unpublished Population Statistics NCBS.

TABLE 5.4   Changes in the Timing of Entry into a First Union, as Measured by the Proportion of Women Who Never Entered a First Union, at Specific Ages

Birth Cohort	Proportion of Women Who Never Entered a Union at Age			
	18	23	28	33
1965-1969	95			
1960-1964	95	44		
1955-1959	95	35	12	
1950-1954	94	33	10	6
1945-1949	97	39	10	6

Source: Netherlands' Fertility Survey, NCBS.

women of birth cohorts 1945–1949 ever cohabited before the age of twenty-eight, among women of birth cohorts 1950–1954, this figure rose to 23 percent, and among women of birth cohorts 1955–1959, to 38 percent. In a recent survey, Liefbroer (1991a) observed that 51 percent of women born in 1961 had cohabited before the age of twenty-six. Thus the *majority* of women nowadays enter their first union by cohabitation. Among young adults who did not live with a partner, Liefbroer observed that most of them intend to cohabit either temporarily, as a prelude to marriage, or more permanently. He concluded that it is now common practice among young adults to start their union formation by unmarried cohabitation.

Although the majority of young adults intend to cohabit for some time, there are great differences in the significance attached to cohabitation (Liefbroer 1991a). Most young adults still view unmarried cohabitation as a trial period, albeit a very serious one. Because the *institutional barriers* to a break-up are smaller when people cohabit than when they are married, a decision to cohabit may be taken sooner than a decision to marry. As a result, chances of a mismatch, and thus the dissolution rate, are higher among cohabitants than among married couples. Of all respondents who had started a consensual union *before* the age of twenty-six, 36 percent were still cohabiting at the age of twenty-six, 47 percent had married by that age, and 17 percent had experienced a dissolution of their relationship. Although this last percentage is by no means trivial, it signifies that most cohabiting young adults are already seriously involved in their relationship, and that many of them end up getting married. Another important reason for cohabitation, cited by young adults, is that they do not really see many differences between cohabitation and marriage. In that case, it seems logical to opt for cohabitation because this union type is more easily achieved than marriage. A third reason often cited for opting for unmarried cohabitation is that marriage is too restrictive and threatens one's autonomy. In this view, cohabitation is less institutionalized and thus offers better prospects for arranging the partner relationship according to the partners' own preferences. A final set of reasons for opting for cohabitation are practical ones, for example, housing availability or wanting to save money.

From the above, one can conclude that, for many, cohabitation is more than just a prelude to marriage. It has become part of a 'standard' biography, and many young adults postpone marriage until the time they have or seek to have children. In the study by Liefbroer cited earlier, 44 percent of the married respondents who had cohabited before marrying said that they married because they wanted or had children. Thus, for many, an intricate relationship between marriage and parenthood seems to persist. However, whereas in the past people had children because they got married, now they marry because they have children.

In our opinion, cohabitation and marriage are two alternative routes to enter a union. Even if unmarried cohabitation sometimes serves as a prelude to marriage, it is a very serious one. Thus, if one wants to explore the impact of level of education and labor market participation on the process of union formation, it is better to focus on entry into first union than on entry into first marriage only. This is not to deny that differences between cohabiting and married couples do exist. For example, Maas (1987) found that young adults who marry without having cohabited beforehand, have a more traditional view of partner relationships than young adults who have cohabited premaritally. The greater risk of divorce among couples that previously cohabitated that has been observed in a number of countries (DeMaris and Rao 1992; Haskey, 1992; Trussel, Rodríquez, and Vaughan 1992) is often attributed to this difference in attitudes and life-style between those who do and do not cohabit premaritally.

To explore the impact of changing levels of education on women's entry into a first union, we analyzed data from the Netherlands Fertility Survey. The NCBS provided us with information on the occurrence of entry into a first union and on exposure to the 'risk' of entering such a union, both disaggregated by age, cohort (born in 1945–1949, 1950–1954, 1955–1959), union type (cohabitation or marriage), and final level of education (low, medium, high). We analyzed these data using a loglinear competing risks model (Larson 1984). Within such a model, one can test whether the rate of entry into a first union is influenced by the factors under consideration, and one can easily test for proportionality of effects and for interactions between covariates. Simple models did not fit the data very well. The simplest model that gave a satisfactory fit included two second-order interactions, one between union type, cohort, and level of education, and one between union type, age, and level of education, and a first-order interaction between cohort and age (Model COH × UNI × EDU, UNI × AGE × EDU, COH × AGE; likelihood ratio = 101.9; df = 90; p = .18).[1]

First of all, we have concentrated on shifts in the overall rate of entry into a first union. Figure 5.1 shows the proportion of women who have ever entered into a first union, for women with low and high levels of education, respectively, for several birth cohorts.

A first conclusion that can be drawn from Figure 5.1 is that, until their mid-twenties, women with a low level of education have *higher* rates of entering a first union than women with a high level of education. Between the ages of twenty-five and twenty-seven, the differences between women with high and low levels of educational attainment are much smaller. Secondly, interesting *cohort differences* emerge. Women born between 1945 and 1949 have lower rates of entering a first union until they reach the age of twenty-one than women from younger birth cohorts. This difference is mainly due to the stronger propensity among the younger cohorts to cohabit unmarried. The marriage rates at young ages do not differ markedly between cohorts, but the cohabitation rates show a strong increase from one cohort to another. Among women with a low level of education born between 1945 and 1949, this lag is made up for between the ages of twenty-two and twenty-five. Among highly-educated women born between 1945 and 1949, this does not happen until the age of twenty-five. As a result, neither for women with a low level of education nor for women with a high level of education, has the shift from marriage to cohabitation led to a decrease in the overall proportion of women that enter a first union. However, both for women with a low level of education and for

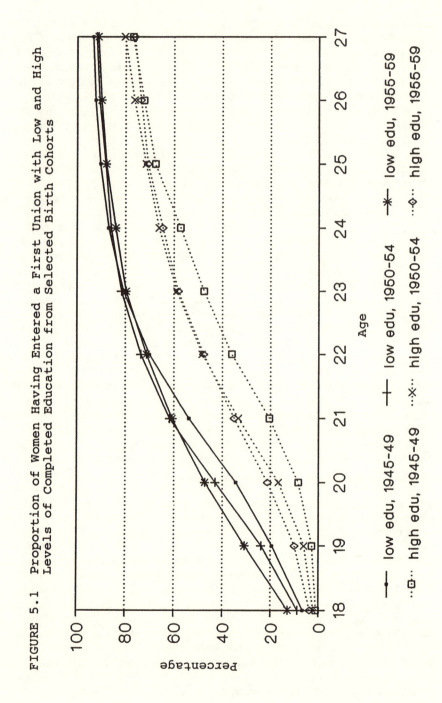

FIGURE 5.1 Proportion of Women Having Entered a First Union with Low and High Levels of Completed Education from Selected Birth Cohorts

women with a high level of education, the rate of entering a union has *increased* at relatively young ages and *decreased* somewhat at older ages.

The estimated model testifies to the strong shift from marriage to unmarried cohabitation. To illustrate this, we calculated the ratio of the rate of entering a first union by cohabitation versus the rate of entering a first union by marriage. The results, again for women with a low and women with a high level of education separately, are presented in Table 5.5.

Among women with a low level of education, the odds ratio of choosing cohabitation as against choosing marriage increases by a factor of almost eleven from birth cohort 1945–1949 to birth cohort 1955–1959. For instance, at the age of twenty-four, women born between 1945 and 1949 with a low level of education were about ten times as likely to marry than to cohabit unmarried. Among women with a low level of education, born between 1955 and 1959, the corresponding risks are about equal. The increase in the relative risks of cohabitation among women with a high level of education are somewhat smaller, though still rather impressive. Their odds ratio increases by a factor of almost four between cohort 1945–1949 and cohort 1955–1959. Among women with a high level of education and born between 1945 and 1949, the risk of cohabitation at the age of twenty-four is about 70 percent of the risk of marriage. Among the same women born between 1955 and 1959, the risk of cohabitation is more than two and a half times as great as the risk of marriage. The relative popularity of cohabitation seems to be particularly high among nineteen-year-olds with a high level of education. This may be due to the fact that a relatively high number of students opt for cohabitation shortly after starting some form of tertiary education. Furthermore, the balance between cohabitation and marriage seems to shift further towards cohabitation with increasing age.

The results presented so far show that the process of union formation greatly depends on the educational level of women. However, because of the crudeness of the operationalization of this indicator, it is not possible to be more specific about the *type* of effect education has. We only have information on the level of completed education. There are two main possibilities with respect to the type of effect prolonged education can have on women's union formation behavior. First of all, it might be that female *attitudes towards family formation* become less positive with increasing education.

This is a central contention within the economic theory of the family as proposed by adherents of the 'New Home Economics' (Becker 1981). According to this view, higher educational attainments lead to a stronger preference for an occupational career. The more important such a career becomes, the less women have to gain from a partner relationship, especially from a married one. A second line of reasoning emphasizes the importance of the delay in union formation that results from the *prolonged participation in education* as women's educational level increases (Blossfeld and Huinink 1991). In this view, the decrease in union formation with increasing level of education results mainly from the prolongation of education, rather than from a change in preferences. Research from Sweden (Hoem 1986) and the Federal Republic of Germany (Blossfeld and Huinink 1991) indeed found participation in educa-

TABLE 5.5 Ratio of the Rate of Entry into a First Union by Cohabitation and the Rate of Entering a First Union by Marriage, for Selected Categories of Women

Level of Education and Birth Cohort	Age									
	18	19	20	21	22	23	24	25	26	27
Low 1945-1949	.03	.03	.03	.03	.07	.06	.10	.21	.24	.96
Low 1955-1959	.43	.32	.36	.35	.73	.67	1.02	2.19	2.52	10.20
High 1945-1949	.84	3.28	.64	.50	.54	.57	.69	.54	.93	4.11
High 1955-1959	3.20	12.58	2.46	1.93	2.08	2.19	2.65	2.05	3.58	15.77

Source: NCBS Population Statistics.

tion to be the most important factor of these two in explaining differences in union formation.

The importance of both factors for the Dutch situation has been assessed by Liefbroer (1991b) using data from the SI survey. He examined how a number of socio-structural variables affect the process of union formation among women born in 1961. He found that educational level has no significant effect on union formation, once one controls for educational participation. However, educational participation does affect the process of union formation. Young adults, men and women alike, in full-time education have an eight times lower risk of entering a first union by marriage, and twice as low a risk of entering a first union by unmarried cohabitation, than young adults who are employed. As employment for most women takes place after they have finished their education, this means that the chance of entering a first union rises sharply after young adults have finished their education and entered the labor market.

Fertility

Not surprisingly, fertility levels have dropped since World War II. First of all, the total birth cohort fertility rate dropped from 2.5 children among birth cohorts born in 1935 to 2.2 among women born in 1940. From then on, it dropped even further to an estimated low of 1.85 among women born in 1955, that is, well below the replacement level. Among younger cohorts, the fertility rate seems to stabilize. In the latest population forecast of the Netherlands Central Bureau of Statistics, 1.8 children per woman is estimated for birth cohort 1985. Secondly, there has been a very significant drop in the number of three- and four-child families for cohorts born between 1935 and 1945. From birth cohort 1945 onwards, they have stabilized at a low level (De Jong 1985). A third indicator of changes in fertility trends is the proportion of childless women. This proportion is shown in Table 5.6, for several birth cohorts at selected ages.

It can be observed from Table 5.6 that the age at which women have their first child dropped slightly from birth cohorts 1932–1936 to birth cohorts 1942–1946. From then on the pattern reversed, showing increased proportions of childless women at the ages of twenty, twenty-five, thirty, and over. Among women born between 1962 and 1966, only 24 percent had at least one child at age twenty-five, whereas this was 58 percent among women born between 1942 and 1946. Thus, a *massive postponement* of getting a first child has occurred, which in turn may lead to a rise in the percentage of women who put off childbearing altogether. To what extent does the decline in the first birth rate result from the rising level of education among women? To answer this question, we again analyzed NFS data, this time on first birth. The effect of three factors, age (AGE), cohort (COH), and achieved level of education (EDU) on the rate of first birth was analyzed within a loglinear framework. The simplest model demonstrating a satisfying fit showed an effect of cohort and an interaction between age and educational level (Model COH, AGE × EDU; Likelihood ratio = 56; d.f. = 52; p = .33).[2] The estimated first birth rates

TABLE 5.6   Changes in the Timing of Entry into Motherhood, as Measured by the Proportion of Childless Women at Specific Ages

Birth Cohort	Proportion of Childless Women at Age						
	20	25	30	35	40	45	50
1967-1971	96						
1962-1966	95	76					
1957-1961	94	69	38				
1952-1956	90	59	31	21			
1947-1951	88	48	23	16	14		
1942-1946	88	42	17	12	11	11	
1937-1941	91	48	18	13	11	11	11
1932-1936	92	54	22	15	13	13	13

Source: Population Statistics NCBS.

of women with a low and a high level of education from these cohorts are shown in Figure 5.2.

Compared to women born between 1945 and 1949, women born between 1950 and 1954 had a 19 percent lower risk of a first birth, and women born between 1955 and 1959 even had a 37 percent lower risk of having a first child before the age of twenty-seven. The effect of educational level shows a much higher overall risk of having a first child among women with a low level of education than among women with a high level of education. However, this difference is most pronounced at relatively young ages. Later on in their twenties, the difference in the rates of getting a first child between women with low and high levels of education becomes much smaller. According to the estimated model, the percentage of women with a low level of attained education, who had a first birth before the age of twenty-eight decreased from 80 percent among women born between 1945 and 1949 to 64 percent among women born between 1955 and 1959. Among women with a high level of education, the figures were 33 percent and 22 percent, respectively.

The fact that the interaction between cohort and educational level is not significant, indicates that the decline in the birth rate for successive cohorts occurs to the same extent among women with different levels of education. As a result, even when the distribution of women among education levels would have been constant across cohorts, the overall rate of first birth would have gone down among these cohorts. However, the overall rate of first birth has decreased even more strongly, because the average level of education of women has increased among these cohorts, causing a shift in the distribution of women towards categories with lower first birth rates.

In the above analysis, we only used a few factors to account for the fluctuations in the first birth rate. Vermunt (1991) performed a more extensive analysis of these data. In a multivariate loglinear rate model, he used eleven covariates to predict the rate of first birth. In this analysis, he included both educational level *and* activity status (with the categories employed, in full-time education, other activity) as covariates. Both factors turned out to have a significant effect on the rate of first birth. However, the effect of activity status was much stronger than that of educational level. As far as *activity status* of the women is concerned, women in the 'other' condition have by far the highest rate of first birth, followed by employed women and women in full-time education. Probably the 'other' condition includes a high proportion of housewives. The effect of the activity status of women varies somewhat, however, according to their age. Between the ages of eighteen and twenty-seven, employed women have first birth rates that are more than twice as high as those of women in full-time education. This difference becomes even larger at higher ages.

The difference between employed women and women who are out of the labor force grows smaller with increasing age. Before the age of twenty-seven, women who are out of the labor force have first birth rates that are more than three times as high as those of working women. Between the ages of twenty-eight and thirty-two, this ratio decreases to two to one. In their late thirties,

120

FIGURE 5.2 Rates of First Birth of Women with High and Low Levels of Completed
Education from Selected Birth Cohorts

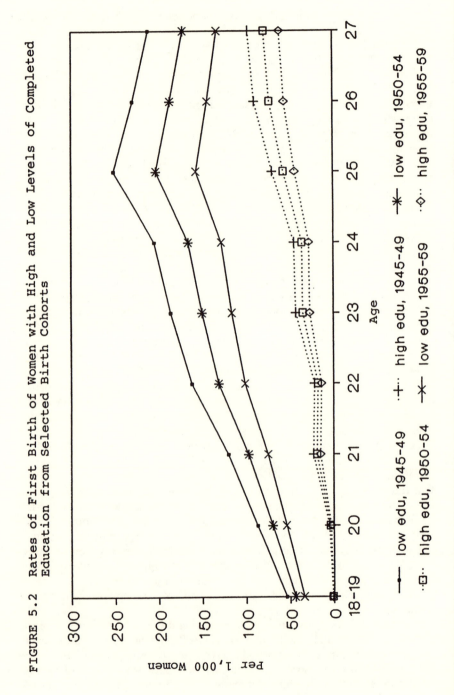

the first birth rates of women who are in and who are out of the labor force are about the same.

The effect that Vermunt observes for women's *level of education* up to the age of twenty-eight corresponds with the effects found in our own analysis of these data. Furthermore, he finds that after the age of twenty-seven, the trend towards a convergence of the first birth rates between women with varying levels of education continues. It seems that many highly educated women postpone their first birth until their late twenties or early thirties. Between the ages of thirty-three and thirty- seven, women with a high level of completed education even show the highest first birth rates of all educational levels.

Conclusions

This chapter has concentrated on the extent to which changes in educational level and female labor force participation have influenced recent changes in demographic patterns in the Netherlands. In examining this issue, we first considered changes which occurred in the past decades in the *labor force participation* and *educational level of women*. From the descriptions of trends, it is clear that the average level of education of women in the Netherlands has risen considerably, and that the labor force participation of young women has also, albeit not as dramatically; compared with other countries, the labor force participation of women is still low, and most of the jobs held by women are part-time.

Union formation in the Netherlands has been characterized by very high marriage rates during the greater part of this century. However, since the early 1970s, marriage rates have dropped and unmarried cohabitation has become increasingly popular among the Dutch population. Among recent birth cohorts, however, the increase in unmarried cohabitation does not completely compensate for the decline in marriage. All *fertility* indicators show a very sharp decline in fertility since the late 1960s. For example, the NFS data show that for each successive (five-year) birth cohort born since 1945, the rates of having a child are lower at each age between eighteen and twenty-seven. Comparing the onset of these changes in fertility and nuptiality, an interesting *difference in timing* can be observed. Whereas the postponement of first marriage and the increase in unmarried cohabitation started in the early 1970s, the postponement of the birth of a first child dates back to the second half of the 1960s. One reason for the 'early' postponement of childbirth is the introduction of contraceptives. However, this difference in timing could also be due to the fact that changing attitudes towards family issues will initially affect types of behavior about which only few strict *norms* exist. Postponing a first child will probably not be met with strong disapproval by significant others, at least as long as those others do not start to doubt one's intentions concerning having children at all. Thus, postponing a first child is something that can be done without risking too many sanctions from others. This certainly is not true with regard to unmarried cohabitation. This is a highly visible type of behavior, that might be met with strong disapproval by significant others. Therefore, it seems logical that it will take somewhat longer for this type of behavior to become popular than for postponing childbirth.

Women's level of education and labor force participation have a strong impact on both nuptiality and fertility. The rate of entering a first union goes down with an increase in educational level. Highly educated women are less likely to enter a union up till their late twenties than women with a low level of education. This pattern is fairly stable across cohorts. Furthermore, an increasing proportion of women enter a first union by unmarried cohabitation. This trend started among the highly educated, but has *diffused* among successive cohorts towards women with low levels of educational attainment. Currently, rates of entering an unmarried cohabitation are even higher among the latter than among the former. Finally, the impact of education on the process of first union formation seems to be mainly due to the delaying impact of educational participation, rather than from differing preferences according to level of education. Compared to being employed, being in full-time education strongly reduces the likelihood that women will enter a first union, either by marriage or by unmarried cohabitation.

The decline in first birth rate can be observed among women of *all* levels of educational attainment. However, at almost all ages, first birth rates are lower among women with a high level of education than among those with a low level of education. Thus, even if the first birth rates were to stabilize within educational levels, the expected growing proportion of women with a high level of completed education would lead to a *further decline* of the overall first birth rates of women in their twenties. The extent to which this decline signals a delay in first childbirth, or the abandonment of childbirth altogether, cannot be deduced from these data, as no information is known yet on the behavior of the youngest birth cohorts at these ages. A third conclusion that can be drawn from these results is that women in the labor force have a much lower risk of having a child than women not in the labor force. Again, this would lead to the conclusion that the increasing labor force participation of women leads to a drop in the overall first birth rate.

The presented figures testify to the profound impact of the increase in educational level and in labor market participation of women on their demographic behavior in the Netherlands. The effects have been twofold. The enormous increase, both in absolute and in relative terms, in the number of women attaining high levels of education and participating in the labor force has mainly affected demographic processes by shifting the *composition* of the cohorts undergoing these demographic transitions. The *strength of the impact* of labor force participation and level of education on demographic processes has, on the other hand, changed to a much smaller extent. A further diffusion of values emphasizing individualization and emancipation, combined with an increase in childcare facilities, could perhaps lead to diminishing differences in demographic behavior between women with high and low levels of education, and even between women in and out of the labor force. Such a diminishing of differences in behavior is already apparent as far as nuptiality is concerned. It would be interesting to see whether the same will happen in the future with regard to fertility processes. This will, to a large degree, depend on the effectiveness of measures designed to combine motherhood and employment.

We conclude with some final observations on the paradox we pointed out at the beginning of this chapter. We signalled that changes in the labor force participation occurred much later and at a slower rate than changes in attitudes on combining paid and unpaid work, and changes in nuptiality and fertility. We would suggest that something like a *structural lag* (cf. Ogburn's 'cultural lag') exists in the Netherlands, which makes it difficult to put modern, emancipatory ideals into practice. From the survey of family policy presented earlier, it can be concluded that the Dutch government has been very reluctant to create conditions favorable to female labor force participation. This reluctance is linked to the dominance of Dutch politics by the Christian Democrats since the World War II. Since 1945 they have participated in every Dutch government. In the 1960s, as a result of the secularization process and the breaking down of traditional religious and socio-political barriers, they lost their grip on the cultural developments in the Netherlands. However, because of their central position in Dutch politics, they could effectively delay policy measures designed to stimulate female labor market participation. At the moment, things appear to be slowly changing. Perhaps current policy measures, combined with changes in the age structure and the growing reservoir of highly educated women, will finally change the backward situation of the Netherlands with regard to female labor market participation.

Notes

The authors would like to thank Eric Beekink for his assistance in preparing this contribution.

1. Due to the complexity of the model, we have not presented parameter estimates, but have instead concentrated on some summary measures derived from the model. Parameter estimates are available on request from the authors.

2. Parameter estimates for this model are available on request from the authors.

References

Allaart, P.C., R. Kunnen, and H.A. van Stiphout (1989). *Trendrapport Arbeidsmarkt 1989* (Labor Market Trend Report 1989), The Hague: OSA. (OSA-Voorstudie V 32).

Becker, G. (1981). *A Treatise on the Family*. Cambridge, Mass.: Harvard University Press.

Beets, G.C.N. (1991). "Population Policy in the Netherlands," in G.C.N. Beets, R. Cliquet, G. Dooghe and J. de Jong Gierveld (eds.), *Population and Family in the Low Countries VII*. Lisse: Swets & Zeitlinger.

Blossfeld, H.-P. and J. Huinink (1991). "Human Capital Investments or Norms of Role Transition? How Women's Schooling and Career Affect the Process of Family Formation." *American Journal of Sociology*, 97, 143–68.

Bruijn, J. de (1989). *Haar Werk. Vrouwenarbeid en Arbeidssociologie in Historisch en Emancipatorisch Perspectief* (Her Job. Female Labor and Labor Sociology in Historical and Emancipatory Perspective). Amsterdam: Uitgeverij SUA.

DeMaris, A. and V.K. Rao (1992). "Premarital Cohabitation and Subsequent Marital Stability in the United States: A Reassessment," *Journal of Marriage and the Family*, 54, 178–90.

Dumon, W. (1991). "Family Policy in the EC Countries: A General Overview," in G.C.N Beets, R. Cliquet, G. Dooghe and J. de Jong Gierveld (eds.), *Population and Family in the Low Countries VII.* Lisse: Swets & Zeitlinger.

Dijkstra, W. (1989). *Het Proces van Sociale Integratie van Jong-volwassenen. De Gegevensverzameling voor de Eerste Hoofdmeting* (The Process of Social Integration of Young Adults. Data Collection for the First Wave). Amsterdam: Vrije Universiteit Uitgeverij.

Dykstra, P.A. (1991). "Arbeidsparticipatie van vrouwen en vruchtbaarheid" (Labor Force Participation of Women and Fertility), in N. van Nimwegen and H. van Solinge (eds.), *Bevolkingsvraagstukken in Nederland anno 1991. Demografische Ontwikkelingen in Maatschappelijk Perspectief.* The Hague: NiDi.

Haskey, J. (1992). "Pre-marital Cohabitation and the Probability of Subsequent Divorce: Analyses Using New Data from the General Household Survey," *Population Trends,* 68, 10–19.

Hoem, J.M. (1986). "The Impact of Education on Modern Family-union Initiation," *European Journal of Population,* 2, 113–33.

Jong, A.H. de (1985). "Vruchtbaarheid naar geboortecohort van de moeder" (Fertility by Birth Cohort of the Mother). *Maandstatistiek van de bevolking,* 85/8, 47–65.

Kaa, D.J. van de (1987). "Europe's Second Demographic Transition," *Population Bulletin,* 42, special issue 1.

Knulst, W.P. and P. van Beek (1990). *Tijd Komt met de Jaren* (Time Comes with Ageing). Rijswijk: Sociaal en Cultureel Planbureau.

Komter, A.E. (1985). *De Macht der Vanzelfsprekendheid. Relaties tussen Vrouwen en Mannen* (The Power of the Obvious. Relations between Women and Men). The Hague: VUGA.

Larson, M.G. (1984). "Covariate Analysis of Competing-risks Data with Log-linear Models," *Biometrics,* 40, 459–4–69.

Liefbroer, A.C. (1991a). "Kiezen tussen Ongehuwd Samenwonen en Trouwen. Een Onderzoek naar Planen en Gedrag van Jong-volwassenen omtrent Relatievorming" (Choosing Between Unmarried Cohabitation and Marriage. A Study of Plans and Behavior of Young Adults Concerning Union Formation). Amsterdam: Centrale Huisdrukkerij Vrije Universiteit (PhD Dissertation, Vrije Universiteit).

Liefbroer, A.C. (1991b). "The Choice Between a Married or Unmarried First Union by Young Adults: A Competing Risks Analysis," *European Journal of Population,* 7, 273–98.

Maas, L.C. (1987). "Opvattingen van jonge mensen in relatie tot hun leefvormen" (Attitudes of Young People Related to Their Living Arrangements). Bevolking en Gezin, 7–31.

Meyer, S., and E. Schulze (1983). "Nichteheliche Lebensgemeinschaften—Alternatieven zur Ehe?" *Kölner Zeitschrift für Soziologie und Sozialpsychologie,* 35, 735–54.

NCBS (1989). *1899–1989. Negentig Jaren Statistiek in Tijdreeksen.* (Historical Series of the Netherlands 1899–1989). The Hague, SDU/uitgeverij.

NCBS (1990a). *Onderzoek Gezinsvorming 1988* (Netherlands Fertility Survey 1988). The Hague: SDU/uitgeverij.

NCBS (1990b). *Arbeidskrachtentelling* (Survey Working Population). Voorburg: NCBS.

NCBS (1992). *Bevolkingsprognose* (Population Forecast). Voorburg: NCBS.

Nimwegen, N. van, and I. Esveldt (1991). "Voorwaardenscheppend beleid" (Policies Aimed at Creatying Better Opportunities), in N. van Nimwegen and H. van Solinge (eds.), *Bevolkingsvraagstukken in Nederland anno 1991. Demografische ontwikkelingen in maatschappelijk perspectief.* The Hague: NiDi.

SCP (1988). *Sociaal en Cultureel Rapport 1988* (Social and Cultural Report 1988). Alphen aan den Rijn: Samsom.

Tavecchio, L.W., M.H. Van IJzendoorn, F.A. Goossens, and M.M. Vergeer (1984). "The Division of Labor in Dutch Families with Preschool Children," *Journal of Marriage and the Family,* 46, 231–42.

Trussel, J., G. Rodríguez, and B. Vaughan (1992). "Union Dissolution in Sweden," in J. Trussel, R. Hankinson and J. Titton (eds.), *Demographic Applications of Event History Analysis.* Oxford: Clarendon Press.

Vermunt, J.K. (1991). "Een multivariaat model voor de geboorte van een eerste kind" (A Multivariate Model for First Birth) *Maandstatistiek van de bevolking,* 91/5, 22–33.

6

Great Britain

KATHLEEN E. KIERNAN AND ÉVA LELIÈVRE

Traditionally, as young people move through their teens and twenties the majority make two key demographic transitions: they marry and they become parents. In Britain, the generation of men and women born during the 1940s had one of the earliest age patterns of marriage ever recorded (Kiernan and Eldridge 1987) and they also commenced childbearing at younger ages than their predecessors born during the 1920s and 1930s (Thompson 1980). In demographic terms the 1940s cohorts were a 'watershed' generation. The normative pattern of demographic behavior for this generation was to marry, and to marry young, to start their families around two years after marriage and to have two children. Cohabitation and remaining celibate or childless was relatively rare (Kiernan 1989). Broadly speaking, their behavior was the culmination of a long-term trend towards earlier and near universal marriage and parenthood. The family formation behavior of cohorts born since the 1940s, particularly those born since the mid–1950s, has been markedly different.

In this analysis we examine the quite dramatic changes in family formation behavior that have occurred in recent decades. The complex mosaic of social, economic, technological, cultural and ideational factors underlying these changes have not yet been satisfactorily unravelled. We have no such ambitions for this analysis, rather we will mainly consider two elements: the changing educational and employment contexts of these demographic changes.

Data

The primary source of data for this study is the British General Household Survey (GHS) an annual sample survey of private households which has been carried out by the Office of Population Censuses and Surveys (OPCS) since 1971. It is a cross-sectional general purpose survey with all the drawbacks that this entails for the detailed analyses of specific behaviors. Britain, unlike the USA and many other European countries, has no recent survey dedicated to the study of fertility and/or family and households. The last such survey was the 1976 Family Formation Survey carried out by OPCS as part of the

World Fertility Survey series (Dunnell 1979). Consequently, we do not have at our disposal a series of histories on unions, fertility, education and employment which would allow us to assess more directly issues such as the effect that increased participation of women in higher levels of education and extended employment may have on their partnership and fertility behavior. However, the General Household Survey is an up-to-date source for looking at some of the issues, albeit indirectly. Here we make use of a range of data particularly from the 1988 survey. There are data on whether the respondent is currently cohabiting and the duration of the union. Additionally, there is information on whether respondents cohabited with their spouse prior to their current or most recent marriage and for how long. For those in a second or later marriage we do not have information on whether they cohabited prior to their first marriage. This has been rectified in the 1989 and later surveys. Moreover, we have no information on cohabiting unions that have broken-up. There is information on dates of marriages and births of children. Turning to the non-demographic variables we have information on age at leaving full-time education and level of highest qualification achieved and current employment activity. Where applicable we will supplement our analyses and interpretations from other data sources.

Changing Patterns of Family Formation

First Marriage Trends

In the postwar period the general trend in first marriage behavior was towards an increasing tendency to marry and for first marriages to occur at increasingly younger ages. This trend continued until the beginning of the 1970s, since when young people have been marrying less and those who are marrying are doing so at later ages. In 1971, the median age at first marriage amongst women was 21.4 years, by 1980 it had increased slightly to 21.8 years but by 1988 it stood at 23.6 years. The analogous figures for men were 23.4 in 1971, 24.0 in 1980 and 25.6 years in 1988 (OPCS, Marriage and Divorce Statistics, Series FM2).

Table 6.1 shows the proportions of women not married by a specified age according to cohorts (age-group in 1988). Consideration of the experiences of cohorts provides insights and highlights some of the subtleties in changing marriage patterns. Let us look at our 'watershed' generation first. Compared with their predecessors born in the 1930s (particularly those born in the early 1930s), women born during the 1940s (1939–1943 and 1944–1948 in the table) were more prone to marry in their teens, their marriages were more concentrated between the ages of twenty and twenty-four years, and 80 percent were already married by the age of twenty-five.

We also have detailed micro-data for one of the 1940s cohorts which come from a longitudinal study of a sample of children born in one week in 1946 who have been followed from birth to the present day (The National Survey of Health and Development). Earlier analyses of the 1946 cohort data showed that women of widely differing socio-economic backgrounds all married very

TABLE 6.1   Proportions of Unmarried by Specified Age

Age in 1988	Birth Cohort	Proportion Unmarried at Age						
		20	24	28	32	36	40	44
20-24	1964-68	80						
25-29	1959-63	68	38					
30-34	1954-58	61	29	18	9			
35-39	1949-53	57	21	13				
40-44	1944-48	58	20	10	6	5	4	
45-49	1939-43	60	21	9	7	6	5	4
50-54	1934-38	62	23	12	8	6	5	5
55-59	1929-33	67	24	12	8	7	7	7

Source: 1988 General Household Survey.

rapidly (Kiernan and Eldridge 1987). For example, unqualified factory work-ers began to marry at an earlier age than office workers with low-level qualifi-cations and these in turn married sooner than highly qualified women in pro-fessional occupations but once a particular group started to marry, what can best be described as a 'lemming effect' was triggered and they plunged into marriage very rapidly. This suggests that during the 1960s there were strong social norms governing the timing of marriage. Marriage appeared inevita-ble. All women regardless of background could be expected to have married by their early twenties. A similar pattern of behavior was observed for men of this generation. It is relative to this pattern of marriage that recent changes seem so dramatic.

Returning to Table 6.1, we can observe some of these recent changes. Rela-tive to the 1940s generation, it can be seen that women born during the 1950s married to a similar extent in their teens but they had a much more protracted pattern in their twenties. For example, we know from vital registration data that the median age at first marriage, for example, for the 1958 cohort of women was 22.5 years, one year older that that observed for the 1946 cohort, and the proportions married by age thirty was 81 percent as compared with 92 percent in the 1946 cohort. One notes that the earliest reaction to the women who postponed marrying until their twenties. It is not until the 1960s cohorts, that the avoidance of teenage marriage is seen. The timing of this change in teenage marriage may be linked to the economic recession of the early 1980s, with its attendant rates of high youth unemployment. Again from vital registration data we know that the median age of marriage amongst, for example, the 1964 cohort, was 25.5 years, some three years older than that of their predecessors born in 1958, and the proportions married by age thirty (in 1994) may be as low as 70 percent (Kiernan 1991). There is little doubt that the tide of youthful marriage has receded in Britain; young people born since the 1960s have marriage patterns that are more like those of their grandparents than either their immediate predecessors or their parents generation. Despite these major changes Britain still has a lower average age at marriage than many other European countries, so there may well be room for further change.

The Rise of Cohabitation

Reductions in youthful marriage and more protracted marriage patterns amongst recent generations are likely to be related to the rise of cohabitation. Few developments relating to marriage and family life have been quite as dramatic as the rapid rise in unmarried cohabitation. Given this let us con-sider the phenomenon in more detail. Cohabitation encompasses a wide range of living arrangements. Before the 1970s, it was largely statistically in-visible and probably socially invisible outside the local community or social milieu. Cohabitation was probably practised by three main groups: those whose marriages had broken-up but were unable to obtain a divorce under the more stringent divorce legislation then in force; the *avant garde,* and the very poor.

FIGURE   6.1   Proportions of Women Having Cohabited by Age

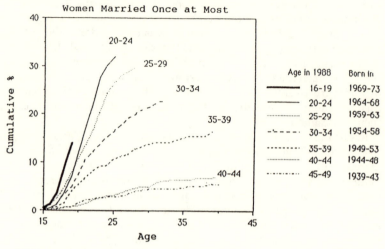

Source: 1988 General Household Survey.

However, the form of cohabitation that came to the fore in the 1970s and escalated during the 1980s is a recent development. We refer to this as 'nubile cohabitation,' whereby young people predominantly in their twenties and early thirties, live together either as a prelude to, or as an alternative to marriage. Data for 1988 from the General Household Survey show that two out of three of those cohabiting had never been married and three out of four were under thirty-five years of age. The emergence and rapid rise of cohabitation can be clearly seen in Figure 6.1.

The GHS first started collecting information on cohabitation from women in 1979 and from men in 1986. During the 1980s the proportions of single (never-married) women, between the ages of eighteen and forty-nine, cohabiting increased from 8 percent in 1981 to 20 percent in 1988. Nowadays, it is virtually a majority practice to cohabit before marrying. For example, amongst never-married women marrying in 1987, 48 percent had cohabited prior to marriage as compared with 19 percent of women marrying in the late 1970s and 7 percent of women marrying at the beginning of the 1970s (Haskey and Kiernan 1989). The cohabitation behavior of different generations will be discussed in more detail in the trajectories section.

The British public still recommend marriage for young people and there is a good deal of approval for cohabitation as a prelude to marriage. Respondents to the 1989 British Social Attitudes Survey were asked, *"What advice would you give—first to a young woman, then to a young man—as to whether they should live alone, live with a steady partner without marrying, live together then marry, or marry without living together first?"* As Table 6.2 shows, the most pop-

TABLE 6.2   Advice Respondent Would Give to Young People
              Regarding Choice of Union/Non-union

| | Advice Would Give to: | |
| | Young Woman (%) | Young Man (%) |
Advice		
Live with a steady partner for a while and then marry	43	42
Marry without living together	37	36
Live alone without a steady partner	4	5
Live with a steady partner without marrying	4	5
Can't choose	11	11

Source: 1989 British Social Attitudes Survey.

ular response, by a small margin, was to cohabit and then marry (Scott 1990). One notes that there is little difference in the advice that would be given to a young man or young woman.

In Britain cohabiting unions tend on average, to be short-lived, less than two years in the case of the never-married. Such unions either convert into marriages or break-up with few, as yet, continuing for extended periods.

Transition to Motherhood

One major feature of childbearing in recent years is the postponement of motherhood, and another is the striking growth in extra-marital childbearing. We will discuss each in turn.

Age at First Birth. Women are now starting their families later in life: for example, in 1964 the mean age at first child was 24 years, by 1980 it had risen by six months to 24.5 years, and by 1988 it stood at 25.1 years. Amongst married women, the average age at first birth has risen even more sharply, from 24.3 years in 1964 to 25.2 in 1980 and 26.6 in 1988 (OPCS, Birth Statistics, Series FM1).

The movement to a later start to motherhood is clearly seen in Table 6.3. Compared with the generations of women born in the 1930s and 1940s, women born since the mid–1950s have been becoming mothers at a later age and at a slower pace than their predecessors. Later-born cohorts have been continuing this trend. Whether these women with a later start to childbearing catch-up at older ages remains an open question. There are signs of some growth in childlessness amongst those born in the early 1950s (aged thirty-five to thirty-nine in 1988).

Extra-marital Childbearing. Since the beginning of the 1980s the number of children born outside marriage has more than doubled; the illegitimacy ratio

TABLE 6.3   Proportions Childless by Specified Age

Age in 1988	Birth Cohort	Proportion Childless at Age						
		20	24	28	32	36	40	44
20-24	1964-68	81						
25-29	1959-63	80	55					
30-34	1954-58	80	54	34				
35-39	1949-53	73	50	28	18			
40-44	1944-48	77	45	23	14	12	11	
45-49	1939-43	81	47	21	15	13	12	11
50-54	1934-38	82	48	26	18	15	14	14
55-59	1929-33	87	51	28	18	15	15	15

Source: 1988 General Household Survey.

has increased from 12 percent in 1980 to 27 percent in 1989; and illegitimate fertility rates doubled at most ages under thirty-five. The majority of extramarital births are to women under twenty-five years of age: two out of three in 1989, and the bulk of these births are first births to single women. Extramarital births at older ages tend to be to divorced women.

Changes in extra-marital childbearing across cohorts amongst never-married women and the recent nature of the development can be seen in Figure 6.2. Having a child whilst single was relatively rare amongst the 1940s and 1950s cohorts: less than 5 percent had done so. Amongst those born since the 1960s it has become more common and the trend looks set to continue.

Not all these births are to women living on their own. More and more children born outside marriage are being registered by both parents. The proportion of joint registrations has risen from 49 percent in 1975 to 71 percent in 1989. Of the joint registrations made in 1989, seven out of ten were made by parents living at the same address (OPCS, Birth Statistics, Series FM1). In Britain, cohabitation generally precedes rather than substitutes marriage, but it would appear that a growing proportion of couples are no longer marrying prior to the birth of their children.

Trajectories of Family Formation

To get a clearer picture of the extent of the changes in the timing and sequencing of family formation behavior a series of trajectories for women included in the 1988 GHS have been derived from the timing of first marriage, first child and cohabitation. There are some drawbacks to the data. Cohabitation may not be strictly a first cohabitation, but evidence from other sources suggest that at younger ages the vast majority are likely to be so. Only never-married and women married once only are included in the analysis. The small group of women in a second or later marriage (9 percent of the total) have been excluded as we do not have the relevant cohabitation information. Finally, some of the cells in Table 6.4 are based on a small number of cases (twenty or less and are marked with an asterisk) which is to be expected given

FIGURE 6.2 Proportions of Women with a Birth Whilst Single

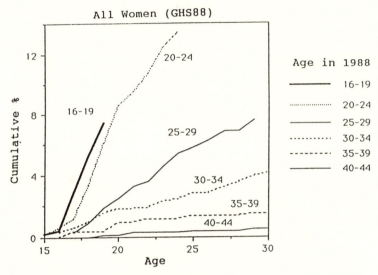

Source: 1988 General Household Survey.

the rarity of some of the events, consequently the proportions should be viewed as order of magnitude rather than as precise estimates. The most frequently observed trajectories are depicted in Table 6.4. In order to compare the trajectories of the different cohorts, experiences were truncated at the age of twenty-five.

Let us start with cohabitation, as this is increasingly the first element in family formation behavior. From Table 6.4 we see that 'nubile cohabitation' was rare amongst the 1930s and 1940s generations, less than 3 percent had cohabited whilst single, the proportions increased to 8 percent for the early 1950s generation, and then the proportions began to increase rapidly. Of the later born 1950s and early 1960s generations, 14 and 22 percent respectively had cohabited by the age of twenty-five. This is in marked contrast to marriage behavior where the proportions married by the age of twenty-five have fallen from around 80 percent for the 1930s to early 1950s generation to 60 percent amongst women born in the early 1960s. There are even sharper contrasts when we consider the groups who married and had a child post-marriage. By age twenty-five, just over 50 percent of women born in the 1930s and 1940s had pursued the conventional life-cycle of marriage followed by motherhood, compared with only 30 percent of the early 1960s cohorts. Overall, 46 percent of the early 1960s cohorts had had a child by age twenty-five, compared with 51 percent of the early 1950s and nearly 60 percent of the 1930s and 1940s cohorts. One also notes the rise in extra-marital childbearing amongst the most recent cohorts. Amongst women born during the early

TABLE 6.4 Family Formation Trajectories Attained by Age 25 by Age Group/Cohort
(women; excludes remarried)

Age Group:	20-24	25-29	30-34	35-39	40-44	45-49	50-54	55-59	Total
Cohort:	64-68	59-63	54-58	49-53	44-48	39-43	34-38	29-33	
Family Formation									
Single	45.7	19.6	19.4	15.4	16.1	16.5	17.5	21.3	17.9
Cohabitation (only)	10.7	6.8	3.4	1.6	0.4*	0.3*	0.2*	0.2*	2.1
Married (only)	10.7	15.5	19.6	24.6	23.2	22.0	23.0	23.9	21.4
Child (only)	7.0	4.4	3.4	2.9	1.4	0.9*	1.2*	0.4*	2.2
Married->Child	8.0	27.3	37.2	42.5	52.8	55.5	53.9	52.8	44.9
Cohabitation->Marriage	4.7	5.7	5.5	3.9	0.7*	0.5*	0.2*	0.0	2.6
Cohabitation->Marriage ->Child	4.0	7.5	4.2	2.9	1.1*	1.4*	0.7*	0.0	2.8
Marriage->Child->Break	1.3	3.7	0.9*	2.2	1.2	0.9*	0.3*	0.2*	1.5
Single->Child->Marriage	0.5	1.0*	1.9	1.1*	2.1	1.4*	2.0	0.05*	1.5
Cohabitation->Child	2.7	1.8	0.8*	0.1*	0.1*	0.0	0.2*	0.0	0.5
Other combinations	4.7	6.7	3.7	2.8	0.9	0.6	0.8	1.15	2.60
Number of cases	876	872	795	696	803	649	588	568	5847

* Estimates based on less than 20 cases.

Source: 1988 General Household Survey.

1960s, 7 percent had a child whilst unmarried as compared with 4 percent of women born during the early 1950s. However, it is worth noting that amongst the women born during the late 1960s, who as yet have not reached the age of twenty-five, 10 percent had already had a child outside marriage.

The most recent generations of young women are more likely to be single, more likely to be cohabiting, more likely to have a child whilst single (either on their own or in a cohabiting union), more likely to cohabit before marriage and less likely to be married or to be mothers by their mid-twenties than are preceding generations, and these trends seem set to continue. In sum, the family formation behavior of recently born women is more varied and complex than that of their predecessors.

Education and Employment Patterns

In this section we consider the educational experiences and employment patterns of British women.

Education: Participation

Young people in Britain have the option of leaving school at the age of sixteen. The minimum school leaving age was raised from fourteen to fifteen years in 1947, and from fifteen to sixteen in 1973. Compared with many other developed countries, Britain has one of the lowest full-time participation rates in education and training for sixteen-to-eighteen-year-olds. In 1988, 35 percent of British youth between the ages of sixteen and eighteen were in full-time education and 31 percent were in part-time education. In contrast, around the same period, 47 percent of (West) German and Italian sixteen-to-eighteen-year-olds were in full-time education and between 70 and 80 percent of young people from Belgium, France, Sweden, the Netherlands and the USA were in full-time education between the ages of sixteen and eighteen (*Social Trends*, No. 20, Table 3.17).

In Britain, prior to the Second World War the proportions of an age group entering full-time higher education (typically at age eighteen for courses lasting from three to four years) was less than 3 percent, the proportions then increased steadily during the 1950s to stand at 8 percent in the mid–1960s. Thereafter, there was a major expansion in the higher education sector and the approximately analogous proportion for the early 1970s was 14 percent; it has remained about this level throughout the 1970s and 1980s (*Social Trends*, No. 20; Halsey 1988). In 1939, women constituted less than one-quarter of all full-time university students, and by the mid–1980s they constituted 44 percent of all higher education students (Halsey 1988; "Social Portrait of Europe," *Eurostat*, 1991).

Educational Qualifications

Over the postwar period, men and women have been staying on in education to older ages, and acquiring more and higher-level qualifications. Table 6.5 shows the trends in the acquisition of qualifications amongst men and women

TABLE 6.5   Level of Qualification Achieved Across Cohorts by Sex

| Age in 1988: | 55-59 | | 50-54 | | 45-49 | | 40-44 | | 35-39 | | 30-34 | | 25-29 | | 20-24 | |
| Cohort: | 1929-33 | | 1934-38 | | 1939-43 | | 1944-48 | | 1949-53 | | 1954-58 | | 1959-63 | | 1964-68 | |
Type of Qualification	M	F	M	F	M	F	M	F	M	F	M	F	M	F	M	F
None	53.2	66.1	44.8	61.4	39.7	52.9	36.9	44.8	26.8	34.9	25.2	31.3	17.7	20.9	15.6	13.1
O Levels or equivalent	20.1	18.0	25.0	21.6	22.6	27.2	22.0	32.8	26.8	34.2	25.2	38.7	38.8	50.3	44.5	55.0
A Levels or equivalent	4.6	1.9	6.9	2.7	9.2	4.3	11.0	4.4	13.6	7.7	18.1	7.5	17.2	10.3	21.3	18.2
Advanced non-degree qualification	2.5	8.5	1.5	6.6	1.5	7.8	2.7	8.4	1.7	9.1	1.3	9.4	0.4	5.5	0.1	3.3
Degree or Higher	15.4	3.1	16.2	4.0	22.3	4.2	23.8	6.4	27.8	9.8	28.0	11.0	23.6	11.4	16.6	9.5
Number	603	635	611	679	685	743	865	919	766	805	763	884	775	905	788	877

Source: 1988 General Household Survey.

born since the 1930s. These data are derived from the 1988 General Household Survey. The meaning of these categories, and the proportions in each category, have changed over time, as have the life chances of people with different levels of qualification. The proportions of men and women with no
qualifications have declined dramatically amongst the most recent cohorts,
such that compared with times past the unqualified group is becoming an increasingly residualized group. Although differences between the sexes have
tended to lessen with the passage of time, men are still more likely than their
female contemporaries to acquire high-level qualifications.

To illustrate and consider the changes let us focus in on two sets of female
cohorts (Table 6.5): those born during the latter half of the 1940s (1944–1948)
and those born during the early 1960s (1959–1963). The most striking difference between these two cohorts is in the proportions with no qualifications at
all; down from 45 percent amongst women of the 1940s generation to 21 percent in the early 1960s generation. Complementing this reduction, there has
been a substantial increase in the proportions with low level qualifications
('O'-Ordinary level or equivalent), a moderate increase in those with 'A'-Ad-
vanced levels or equivalent, but the proportions with high level qualifications
has not grown so rapidly. There is likely to be further growth in the proportions of graduate women as the proportions with A-levels (typically taken at
age eighteen) are still growing and these qualifications are an almost essential
pre-requisite for entry into university.

Female Employment Patterns

Over the 1970s and 1980s the economic activity rates for men under sixty fluctuated slightly around the 90 percent level. The labor force participation rates
of women showed more variation: the overall level of activity for all women
under sixty rose from 60 percent in 1973, to 66 percent in 1985, and 70 percent
in 1988. The proportion of British women who enter the labor market is very
high (96 percent) and age at entry tends to be young, given early exits from
full-time education, with the great majority of women commencing work at
or before the age of eighteen (Kempeneers and Lelièvre 1991). With the advent of parenthood, employment-careers are disrupted. The majority leave
the labor market at this juncture, at least for a time, but the majority return to
work, in the main part-time, typically when their children reach school age
(age five years). Currently, the position seems to be that each successive group
of new mothers returns to the labor market more quickly than the one before.
The number of children, but particularly the age of the youngest child, tend to
be constraints. In 1988, 32 percent of mothers with a child under the age of
two were working (21 percent part-time and 11 percent full-time), amongst
women with a child aged from three to four years, 34 percent were working
part-time and 13 percent full-time. Amongst those with a child aged from five
to nine years the proportions were 47 percent part-time and 18 percent full-
time. Of women with a dependent child aged ten or older, 73 percent were in
employment; 30 percent in full-time and 43 percent in part-time employment.
Highly educated women (with A-levels or higher qualifications) are more

likely to work when their children are young (under the age of five) than lesser qualified women and the more qualified women are more likely to work full-time.

Mothers with dependent children opt for part-time work either through choice or through the lack of adequate child-care provision. Britain has amongst the poorest child care facilities in Europe (Cohen 1990). Government policy is that the care of children is the responsibility of parents, and if they want to make other arrangements for their care they should take the necessary action and must expect to meet the costs. This applies especially to the provision of day care and nursery education for pre-school age children. As such there is no state provision for child care when parents are away from home. For pre-school children the main form of child care used in Britain is relatives. Data from the 1990 British Social Attitudes Survey (Witherspoon and Prior 1991) showed that amongst women employees with a child under the age of five, 64 percent were cared for by a relative, 17 percent used the services of a child-minder and another 17 percent of children went to day nurseries. Britain lags behind most EC countries with a lack of child-care facilities, parental leave, little financial concessions for parents and the diminishing value of child benefit. Amongst members of the EC only Britain and Ireland have neither a formal parental leave system nor one planned.

Another major theme with respect to female employment is the concentration of women in a relatively few occupational groups (Joshi 1989). Data from the 1988 General Household Survey Report shows that amongst female employees, 78 percent were in just four occupational categories: personal services (for example, cleaners and hairdressers); clerical; selling (mainly shop assistants) and professional workers in education, health and welfare (school teachers, nurses and social workers). Only 22 percent of men are to be found in these four occupational groups.

The General Household Survey only collects information on current employment activity. Surveys which combine both marriage and fertility and employment histories are rare in Britain, so we are unable to provide an examination of how type of employment may affect the timing of marriage and becoming a parent and how this may have changed over time. However, there is some evidence from analyses of National Survey of Health and Development that both level of highest qualification and occupational status before marriage were important determinants in the timing of marriage, and educational and occupational achievements amongst women were directly related to the probability of their remaining single (Kiernan and Eldridge 1987, Kiernan 1988). Educational attainment was generally the more influential of the two effects.

Educational Change and Family Formation Behavior

In most studies of family formation, educational attainment has been found to be a powerful influence on the timing of the transition to marriage and parenthood (Kiernan and Diamond 1983, Kiernan and Eldridge 1987 on Britain; Blossfeld and Jaenichen 1992 on Germany; Hoem 1986 on Sweden; and

Rindfuss, Bumpass and St. John 1980 on the USA). Here we examine the relationship between educational attainment and age at marriage, age at first birth, extent of cohabitation and life-course patterns across cohorts, using data from the 1988 General Household Survey. Since 1986, questions on cohabitation and marriage have been put to male respondents to the General Household Survey, no information on their fertility is collected, thus for marriage and cohabitation we can compare and contrast the experiences of men and women. After this descriptive tour we proceed to test the cohort and education effects on ages at marriage and first birth and propensity to cohabit.

Relationship Between Education and Family Formation

Marriage and Cohabitation. Figures 6.3a and 6.3b show the proportions of women and men who had not married by a given age, the Figures 6.4a and 6.4b show the proportions who had not cohabited by a given age, according to level of highest qualification achieved. It is apparent that educational attainment has a stronger and more lasting impact on women's than on men's propensities to marry and cohabit.

Unqualified women enter marriage at a faster pace and in greater proportions than those with qualifications. Graduate women marry less rapidly and are more likely to remain single. In contrast, the variation in men's marriage patterns according to educational level are much less marked and it is the unqualified who are most likely to be single at older ages.

Analyses based on current cohabitation suggest that there is little systematic difference in the proportion of men and women cohabiting according to level of educational qualifications (Haskey and Kiernan 1989). analyses based on a life-history perspective provide alternative insights.

Women with degrees are ultimately the most likely (30 percent) to have entered an unmarried union and seemingly continue to enter such unions to a relatively advanced age (over twenty-five years). Women with other types of qualifications cohabit to a lesser extent overall and cohabitation is relatively more popular at younger ages (under twenty-five). Women with A-level qualifications behave like their graduate sisters to the age of twenty-five when their propensity to cohabit slackens; overall 27 percent had cohabited by age twenty-five. Only 10 percent of women with no qualifications had experienced cohabitation. Women with O-levels appear to hold a median position with 20 percent having ever cohabited whilst those with Advanced qualifications, in the main nursing and teaching qualifications, are seemingly more traditional in their union formation behavior (18 percent had ever cohabited).

As for marriage, there was little variation in propensity to cohabit amongst men with qualifications of different levels. Unqualified men, as well as being the most likely to remain single, were also the least likely to have cohabited. This may be the result of two forces. Unqualified men are more likely to enter marriages at young ages and therefore to have lower exposure time to form cohabiting unions, and they are also less likely to form a couple, perhaps because their human capital in the marriage market is less than their more qualified peers.

140

FIGURES 6.3a and 6.3b   Proportion of Never-Married by Level of
                        Highest Qualification (survival analysis)

(a)

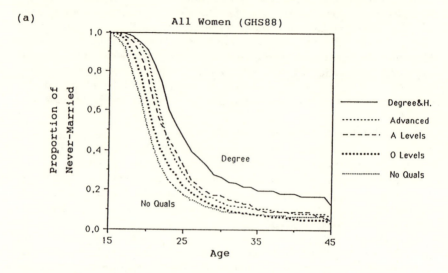

Source: 1988 General Household Survey.

(b)

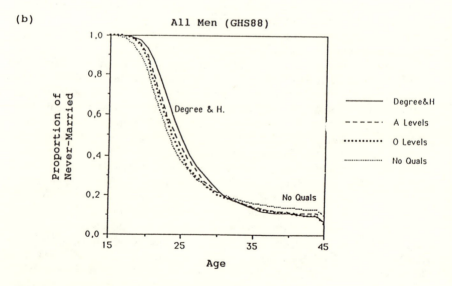

Source: General Household Survey.

FIGURES 6.4a and 6.4b Proportions Who Have Never Cohabited
by Level of Qualification

(a)   Singles and Women Married Once (GHS88)

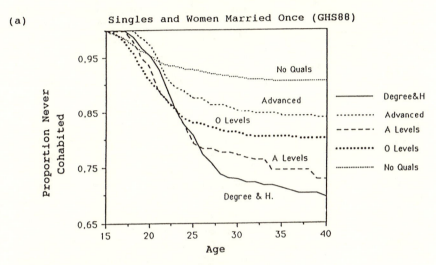

Source: 1988 General Household Survey.

(b)   Singles and Men Married Once (GHS88)

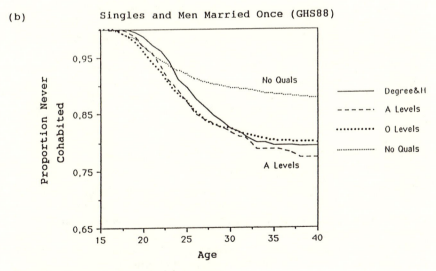

Source: General Household Survey.

First Birth. Turning our attention to childbearing we see in Figure 6.5 that their are systematic differences in the timing of childbearing and in the proportion of women who become mothers, according to level of qualification. With one exception, the higher the level of qualification the greater the likelihood of the woman becoming a mother at an older age and generally speaking the more likely she is to remain childless. The exception is the group of women with Advanced level qualifications (in the main, nursing and teaching qualifications) who have a pace of childbearing commensurate with their level of qualifications at ages under twenty-five and then have an accelerated pace thereafter. The distinctive behavior of this group of women may be in part due to being in occupations that allow them to more readily combine having children and working or it may be that the attributes which underlie the choice of profession also foster marriage and relatively early motherhood.

Family Formation Trajectories. Earlier we examined the family formation trajectories attained by the age of twenty-five amongst women from different birth cohorts. Table 6.6 shows the more common trajectories amongst women with different levels and types of qualifications. This provides only crude insights into the relationship between family formation patterns and educational level, as it is essentially an average picture across cohorts, in which changing educational patterns and family formation patterns are confounded. Nevertheless, we will highlight a few points. The great majority of women have no or O-level (low level) qualifications, (41 and 33 percent respectively). The most common trajectory (achieved by age twenty-five) by unqualified women was to have married and had a child, cohabiting prior to marriage was relatively less common amongst this unqualified group but more popular amongst women with qualifications. Compared with unqualified women those with low-level qualifications were relatively less likely to make the traditional trajectory marriage—child by age twenty-five; more having integrated cohabitation into their marriage and childbearing histories. Amongst women with A-levels and above, following a cohabitation—marriage—child trajectory was more common than a marriage—child one. There are signs which suggest that the cohabitation—marriage—child trajectory may become the normative one for the very recent generations of young women.

The Impact of Cohort and Education on
Age at First Marriage and First Birth

To measure the changing effect of education on the mean age at first marriage, an analysis of variance was conducted for the different cohorts. The strength of the effect was measured by the F-ratio. A further comparative test between the means corresponding to different educational levels was conducted using Scheffe's procedure. This allowed us to distinguish the significant differences between means for each level of education within each cohort. The education variable is grouped, in order to reduce the estimation biases which would arise from very different cell sizes. Hence we distinguish three educational groups: those with A-levels or higher qualifications; those

FIGURE 6.5 Proportions of Childless Women by Level of Qualification

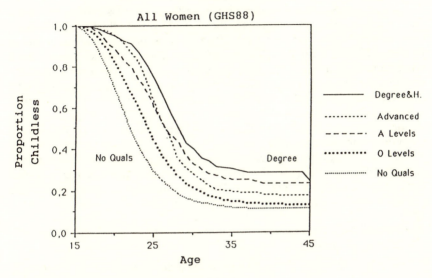

Source: 1988 General Household Survey.

TABLE 6.6 Family Formation Trajectories Attained by Age 25 by Level of Qualification

	Degree 2 H	Advanced	A Levels	O Levels	No Quals.	Number
Women:						
Single	16.2	11.2	8.3	29.0	31.0	(890)
Married	10.3	11.9	7.3	36.2	32.0	(1058)
Cohab	24.0	11.5	12.5	34.6	11.5	(104)
Cohab→Married	22.9	13.7	10.7	38.9	11.5	(131)
Child	2.7	2.7	2.7	36.0	52.3	(111)
Married→ Child	2.5	5.9	4.0	32.2	52.6	(2221)
Cohab→Married→ Child	7.1	9.3	9.3	49.3	25.0	(140)
Total 25 y +	8.0	8.6	6.1	33.4	41.0	(4680)
Men:						
Single	26.2	1.9	11.3	24.8	30.9	(1841)
Married	20.6	1.5	11.6	26.3	36.9	(2347)
Cohab	31.5	1.4	15.4	22.4	25.2	(143)
Cohab→Married	22.7	0.4	16.2	35.4	23.6	(229)
Total 25 y +	23.3	1.6	12.0	26.0	33.4	(4560)

Source: 1988 General Household Survey.

with O-levels, equivalent and lesser qualifications; and those with no qualifications (Tables 6.7 and 6.8).

The effect of education on the mean age at marriage amongst women was
significant across all the cohorts. The overall effect across cohorts increased
and seemingly reached a climax for those aged thirty to thirty-four—cohorts
born between 1954 and 1958—the effect then declined but remains higher
than that observed for the older generations. The differences observed for
older women distinguish the most qualified group from those without qualifications, for younger women the means for all three groups are significantly
different from one another. The observed effect of education on men's mean
age at marriage is of a lesser magnitude. It is non-significant for older cohorts.
As for women, the maximum effect is to be seen amongst those aged thirty to
thirty-four and then declines.

The effect of educational level on mean age at first birth (Table 6.8) is similar to that observed for marriage. But the difference between each educational
level is significant across all cohorts. The less qualified were and remain significantly more likely to bear children at younger ages.

The Impact of Cohort and Education on the Propensity to Cohabit

'Nubile cohabitation' was rare amongst the older generations in our sample
consequently we have limited our analyses to the most recent cohorts of men
and women. A logit model was fitted to identify the effect of education after
controlling for the effect of cohort. Table 6.9 shows the odds (or exponentiated
parameter estimates) of cohabiting before age twenty-five. Models 1 and 2 estimate the effect of education and cohort separately and Model 3 their combined effects. For both men and women the cohort or generation effect is
stronger than the education effect. Younger generations of men have a greater
propensity to cohabit than older generations and this propensity is largely in-
variant with respect to educational achievement. Amongst women the cohort
(or time period) effect is also the stronger effect but there is still a heightened
propensity amongst the more educated women to cohabit.

Discussion

There have been quite dramatic changes in family formation behavior
amongst recent generations of young people; they are cohabiting more, marrying later and becoming parents at older ages.

A number of factors might account for the trend towards later family formation. The long term trend for young people to prolong their education continues; the minimum school leaving age has been raised, increasingly young
people are acquiring formal qualifications and the sex differential in continuation rates has largely disappeared. Nevertheless young people who stay in
full-time education beyond the minimum school leaving age are still a minority in Britain. Women's working lives are tending to lengthen as attitudes to
taking paid work outside the home have changed and the period during

TABLE 6.7 Analysis of Variance: Difference in Mean Age at Marriage for Different Educational Levels

Cohort	Age in 1988	Women		Men	
		F-ratio	Significant Differences	F-ratio	Significant Differences
1959-63	25-29	30.60	Between all groups	9.67	A levels + from the 2 other groups
1954-58	30-34	38.29	"	17.38	Between all groups
1949-53	35-39	28.23	A Level + from the 2 other groups	3.96	A levels + from No Qualifications
1944-48	40-44	22.80	"	6.54	No Qualifications + from the 2 other groups
1939-43	45-49	20.84	"	1.87	No difference
1934-38	50-54	15.43	A Level + from No Qualifications	2.27	No difference
1929-33	55-59	15.69	"	3.01	A Levels + from No Qualifications

<u>Source</u>: 1988 General Household Survey.

TABLE 6.8   Analysis of Variance: Difference in Mean
Age at First Birth for Women with Different
Educational Levels (by cohort)

Cohort	Age in 1988	F-ratio	Significant Differences
1959-63	25-29	39.53	Between all groups
1954-58	30-34	45.32	"
1949-53	35-39	64.51	"
1944-48	40-44	48.78	"
1939-43	45-49	23.21	"
1934-38	50-54	19.23	"
1929-33	55-59	17.61	"

Source: 1988 General Household Survey.

which they are responsible for young children is reduced. Such changes involve some reassessment of the roles, opportunities and responsibilities of men and women. Nowadays, young women are less likely than earlier generations to view marriage and parenthood and employment outside the home as mutually exclusive. Their educational and labor market experiences as young adults may increasingly have as important implications for their future careers and levels of remuneration as for men. Prevailing ideology encourages young women to seek the economic independence equivalent to that normally achieved by young men. One may recollect that the greatest reaction to the previous pattern of early marriage and motherhood was first visible amongst older women. Many of the elements we have outlined as being conducive to delayed family formation are more likely to have had a greater impact on these women than on women prone to marry in their teens or to have children in their early twenties. In the particular context of Britain one might also highlight some other factors. These include the economic recessions that have peppered the last two decades and the uncertainty this engenders, higher unemployment rates amongst young people than amongst older people, and the increased tendency to purchase one's own home which requires some capital accumulation.

In recent decades the axiomatic nature of marriage and parenthood has been brought into question; they are seemingly no longer inevitabilities but considered choices. We might infer from our analyses that a later start to marriage and particularly parenthood appears to be more significant for the lives of women than those of men. Delays give women increased opportunity to obtain educational qualifications, occupational training and job experience. Women perhaps had more difficulty in investing in 'human capital' when they married and had children early. In our analyses, level of qualification was important in distinguishing between women who married and became moth-

147

TABLE 6.9   Exponentiated Parameter Estimates of Cohabiting by Age 25
(logit analysis)

	Women			Men		
	(1)	(2)	(3)	(1)	(2)	(3)
Age group in 1988:						
25-29	1.705**		1.714**	1.890**		1.909**
30-34	0.963		0.962	0.997		0.993
35-39	0.606**		0.606**	0.531**		0.528**
Educational Attainment:						
A levels		1.206**	1.206**		0.970	0.980
O levels		0.995	0.925		1.024	0.935
No Qualifications		0.833	0.896		1.007	1.091

Note: ** Significant at the 0.05 level.

Source: 1988 General Household Survey.

ers at different ages. It remains to be seen whether at the individual level educational attainment continues to discriminate amongst more recent cohorts;
and at the aggregate level whether changing educational and occupational
opportunities make further impacts on family formation behavior. As more
women obtain qualifications, and a wider range of qualifications, and enter, to
a greater extent than hitherto, a wider range of occupations, qualification level
and occupational status may become more powerful discriminators. On the
other hand, if similarly qualified women choose to marry and become mothers over a wider range of ages than in the past, its impact may be diluted. In
this case, the association between educational attainment and family formation behavior may become more like that currently observed for men.

Marriage is probably no longer the dominant romantic dream of young
women. The so-called 'golden age' of marriage which predominated during
the 1960s and early part of the 1970s which in turn boosted early parenthood,
is over. Youthful and near universal marriage and parenthood are unlikely to
return in the near future. With the rise in cohabitation and 'visiting unions,'
conjugal links have become more varied in recent times. Our knowledge and
understanding of the genesis of nubile cohabitation is scant. Undoubtedly,
there are many factors to take into account in explaining its rise, but it may
symbolize, particularly for women, the avoidance of the notion of dependency that is typically implicit in the marriage contract. For example, women
may be anxious that the legal contract may alter the balance of power in their
partnership arrangements and make the relationship less equitable. This may
be among the reasons why cohabitation is relatively more prevalent amongst
the very highly educated, a group who are the most likely to be economically
self-sufficient. Cohabitation is still evolving. Currently, most cohabiting
unions are short-lived; they convert into marriages or break-up. But there is
as yet no sign of a steady state. The incidence of cohabitation seems set to continue on an upward course, but the extent to which such unions become more
long-term arrangements or unions within which children are increasingly
born and reared is more difficult to foresee. Young people who move directly
into marriage may increasingly be an atypical group.

The current directions of social, economic and cultural change in Britain
point to further movement towards later and more varied patterns of family
formation and at a minimum the maintenance of the current situation.

Notes

This work was carried out under a grant from the ESRC (UK) Number R000–23–
2161. We are also grateful to the OPCS and ESRC Data Archive for making available the
GHS data.

References

Blossfeld, H.-P. and U. Jaenichen (1992). "Educational Expansion and Changes in
    Women's Entry into Marriage and Motherhood in the Federal Republic of Ger-
    many," *Journal of Marriage and the Family*, 54, 5:302–15.

Central Statistical Office (1990). *Social Trends*, No. 20, London, H.M.S.O.

Cohen, B. (1990). "Caring for Children: The 1990 Report," Report for the European Commission's Childcare Network on Childcare Services and Policy in the United Kingdom, London, Family Policy Studies Centre.

Dunnell, K. (1979). "Family Formation: 1976," OPCS, London, H.M.S.O.

Eurostat (1991). "Social Portrait of Europe," Luxembourg.

Halsey, A.H. (1988). "Higher Education," in A.H. Halsey (ed.), *British Social Trends since 1990: A Guide to the Changing Social Structure of Britain*, London, Macmillan Press.

Haskey, J. and K.E. Kiernan (1989). "Cohabitation in Great Britain—Characteristics and Estimated Numbers of Cohabiting Partners," *Population Trends*, 58.

Hoem, J. (1986). "The Impact of Education on Modern Union Initiation," *European Journal of Population*, 2, 2.

Joshi, H. (1989). "The Changing Form of Women's Economic Dependency," in H. Joshi (ed.), *The Changing Population of Britain*, Oxford, Basil Blackwell.

Kempeneers, M. and E. Lelièvre (1991). "Employment and the Family," Commission of the European Communities, *Eurobarometer*, 34.

Kiernan, K.E. and I. Diamond (1983). "The Age at which Childbearing Starts: A Longitudinal Study," *Population Studies*, 37, 3.

Kiernan, K.E. and S.M. Eldridge (1987). "Inter and Intra-cohort Variation in the Timing of First Marriage," *British Journal of Sociology*, 38. 1.

Kiernan, K.E. (1988). "Who Remains Celibate?," *Journal of Biosocial Science*, 20, 3.

Kiernan, K.E. (1989). "The Family: Fission or Fusion," in H. Joshi (ed.), *The Changing Population of Britain*, Oxford, Basil Blackwell.

Kiernan, K.E. (1991). "Changing Marriage Patterns," *Journal of Social Work Practice*, 5, 2.

OPCS (annual). *Birth Statistics*, Series FM1, London, H.M.S.O.

OPCS (annual). *Marriage and Divorce Statistics*, Series FM2, London, H.M.S.O.

OPCS (annual). *General Household Survey Reports*, London, H.M.S.O.

Rindfuss, R.R., L. Bumpass and C. St.John (1980). "Education and Fertility: Implications for the Roles Women Occupy," *American Sociological Review*, 45, 3.

Scott, J. (1990). "Women and the Family," in R. Jowell, S. Witherspoon and L. Brook (eds), *British Social Attitudes Survey*, 7th Report, Aldershot, Gower.

Thompson, J. (1980). "The Age at which Childbearing Starts: A Generation Perspective," *Population Trends*, 21.

Witherspoon, S. and G. Prior (1991). "Working Mothers: Free to Choose?," in R. Jowell, L. Brook and B. Taylor (eds), *British Social Attitudes*, 8th Report, Aldershot, Gower.

7

United States of America

VALERIE KINCADE OPPENHEIMER, HANS-PETER BLOSSFELD,
AND ACHIM WACKEROW

During the past 25–30 years dramatic changes in American marriage and fertility behavior have occurred in the United States. Marriages have become increasingly delayed for both men and women and the proportion who will remain unmarried may be growing as well, if many of the apparent postponers never marry (Rodgers and Thornton 1985; Espenshade 1985). Marital instability has also risen enormously so that now some demographers estimate that as many as two-thirds of recent first marriages may end in separation or divorce (Martin and Bumpass 1989). Although it has levelled off in the 1980s and even shown some signs of rising recently, fertility dropped substantially after the early 1960s, partly because of increasing delays in both marriage and the start of childbearing after marriage, and partly because of declines in the total number of children women bear (National Center for Health Statistics 1993; Westoff 1986). All in all, the changes in family behavior have been so diverse as well as so extensive that social scientists have started to view each demographic shift as but one example of an underlying transformation in the American family system. Hence, the theoretical thrust of recent work has been to develop a single overarching explanation of these changes. This, in turn, makes the empirical analysis of any particular demographic phenomenon, say marriage formation, achieve a much broader theoretical significance than has heretofore been the case.

Probably the most widely accepted explanation of the demographic trends of the past 30 years is that the growing earning power of women in American society has increased the opportunity cost of childbearing and childrearing. Furthermore, it has also decreased the benefits of the traditional division of labor in marriage, thereby reducing the desirability of marriage for both men and women (Becker 1981). For convenience sake, we will dub this approach the "independence argument" because of its emphasis on the economic independence of marriage that women's rising labor-market involvement presumably affords them. Our goal in this paper is to undertake both a theoretical and empirical examination of this perspective, focusing particularly on marriage formation. We will use several types of data as well as the results of previous analyses but will primarily rely on two types of data for our analyses. One is the cross-sectional time series data from the Currently Population Surveys (CPS) conducted by the U.S. Census Bureau. We have utilized both published data from the CPS as well as utilizing public use samples of these data covering 1964 to 1990.[1] Our second major source of data is the from the National Survey of Family and Households (NSFH), collected in 1987-88 (Bumpass and Sweet 1989). NSFH obtained extensive retrospective information on family behavior from a relatively large representative sample of American men and women, thereby facilitating inter-cohort comparisons of important life course transitions. The data thus make it possible to investigate marriage and fertility behavior over a lengthy historical period and analyze its relationship to basic socioeconomic characteristics.

The Independence Argument

Becker's theories of marriage and family behavior all hypothesize that women's increasing labor-force participation has had a critical and presumably irreversible impact on the family (1981). In the case of fertility, he argues that the major component of the cost of children is the "indirect" costs–the costs of the mother's time. Hence as women's wages rise, the cost of children increases, thereby contributing to the observed long-term decline in fertility experienced by industrial societies. Furthermore, declining fertility also reduces the desirability of marriage since children represent the major source of marriage-specific capital; hence as fertility declines the gains to marriage are reduced.

In his theory of marriage, Becker argues that the major gain to marriage arises out of the mutual dependence between the spouses that results from each specializing in certain functions–the woman in domestic production and the man in market work. Marriage then involves trading the fruits of these different skills. In response to rising wages, however, women's labor force participation also rises. As a consequence, women become less specialized and more economically independent, leading to a decline in the desirability of marrying or of staying married. As a variant of this theme, Becker also argues that government transfer payments to women provide another means of achieving economic independence and, hence, the growth of the welfare state, along with women's rising employment, discourages stable marriages and fosters nonmarital childbearing.[2] Moreover, the growing prevalence of divorce increases the importance of a woman developing marketable skills while the desirability of investing heavily in marriage-specific capital (i.e., children) is further reduced. An additional consequence of the decreasing gain to marriage is the rise in nonmarital cohabitation and female-headed families and the large growth of the ratio of the illegitimate to the legitimate birth rate.

Not all researchers necessarily subscribe to Becker's emphasis on the role of specialization per se in providing the gain to marriage and the ensuing reductions in such a gain, once women's employment increases. Nevertheless, an economic independence argument of one sort or another, whether it be expressed in the terminology of exchange theory or some other perspective, such as feminism, has had wide appeal since it can easily be incorporated into extremely diverse theoretical and ideological positions (Ross and Sawhill 1975; Cherlin 1980, 1981, 51ff; Preston and Richards 1975; Waite and Spitze 1981; Fuchs 1983; Espenshade 1985; Goldscheider and Waite 1986; Farley 1988; Schoen and Wooldredge 1989; McLanahan 1991). Even where scholars do not specifically espouse a particular position themselves, the independence hypothesis plays a prominent role in their discussions of the major determinants of changes in marriage behavior (Espenshade 1985; Cherlin 1981; 1988). In sum, more and more, married women's rising employment is being seen as the single most critical factor transforming the family system of American society.

On the face of it, there is considerable empirical support for the independence hypothesis in the United States, judging from recent trends in women's employment, on the one hand, and their marriage and fertility behavior, on the other. Although the labor-force participation rates of married women were rising throughout the twentieth century, by 1940 the highest work rates were still quite low—below 20 percent for those aged 25–34 (Figure 7.1). After that date, however, work rates rose extremely rapidly. Between 1940 and 1960 alone, wives' labor-force participation either doubled or tripled, depending on the age group. Between 1960 and 1980 there was another quantum leap in the rates, especially for younger wives and participation rates have continued to increase during the 1980s. By 1990, almost 70 percent of wives between the ages of 20 and 54 were in the labor force compared to less than 20 percent in 1940 and only about five percent in 1900. It is true that these figures somewhat exaggerate the extensiveness of married women's employment because, even today, many do not work year-round full time; nevertheless, the data attest to a really enormous increase in women's labor-market involvement, particularly after 1960.

Dating from the 1960s, changes in demographic behavior also became quite dramatic. Between 1960 and 1990, the proportion of women who had never married by age 22 increased from 26 to 63 percent; the corresponding change in the proportions single at age 27 rose from 10 to 30 percent (U.S. Bureau of the Census 1991). The divorce rate also rose rapidly—going from 9.2 divorces per 1000 married women in 1960 to a high of 22.8 in 1979, after which it declined somewhat to 20.7 in 1988 (National Center for Health Statistics 1991.[3] Meanwhile, nonmarital cohabitation has emerged as a major social phenomenon for the first time. Using retrospective data from the 1987–1988 NSFH, Bumpass and Sweet (1989) estimate that the proportion of Americans who had ever cohabited rose from 14 percent for those who were aged 50–59 at the time of the interview to 42 percent for those who were 25–29; comparing the same age cohorts, the proportions who cohabited before their first marriage rose from 5 to 36 percent. Finally, fertility has dropped precipitously; the total fertility rate decreased from 3.6 births per woman in 1960 to a low of 1.7 in 1976, remaining at roughly that level until exhibiting a slight rise around 1989–90 (National Center for Health Statistics 1974; 1993). In sum, it is primarily in the postwar period that the rise in women's employment really took off

FIGURE 7.1   Labour Force Participation Rates of
U.S. Married Women, 1900-1990 and of
Single Women and All Men, 1990 by Age

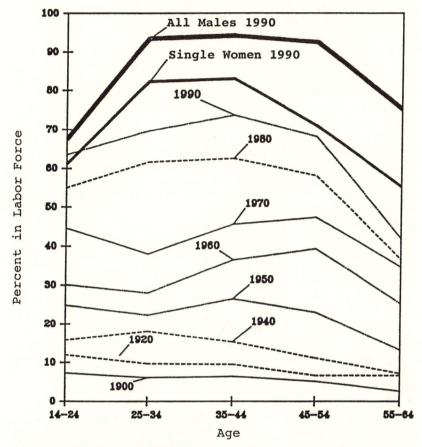

Sources: Smith and Ward, 1985; U.S. Censuses; Current
Population Surveys.

in the United States and, after some lag, this is a period when marriage and
family behavior also underwent dramatic changes as well. On the basis of
time series comparisons, then, the evidence seems very persuasive that wom-
en's increasing economic independence has been a major factor in the striking
shifts in marital and family behavior observed since the early 1960s. In this
chapter we will argue, however, that the evidence supporting the theory is really rather weak once it is subjected to a more rigorous conceptual and empirical analysis than simple comparisons of time series afford.

Another Look at the Independence Hypothesis

What Is the Appropriate Benchmark?

Just as we have done in our initial review of recent demographic trends and their relationship to women's rising employment, most discussions of the independence hypothesis take as their starting point the early postwar period (Becker 1981; Davis 1985; Espenshade 1985; Goldscheider and Waite 1986; Farley 1988).[4] In effect, the marriage and family behavior of the 1950s and early 1960s has been used as the bench mark against which subsequent changes are compared. Even more, this bench mark has come to exemplify the "traditional" American family. The problem is that this standard is based on the demographic behavior of the baby-boom period which started right after the war in the United States and lasted for 15 years or more. However, viewed within a broader historical context, the baby boom era hardly epitomizes the typical patterns of a so-called traditional American family characterized by extensive sex-role specialization. On the contrary, in some cases, it represented a sharp contrast to the demographic behavior of a more traditional era; in other cases, it actually reversed long-run trends that had their inception well before any significant rise in women's employment.

With regard to fertility, the total fertility rate for white women was continuously declining since 1800 until the sharp and prolonged rise in fertility starting in the 1940s and continuing up to the late 1950s. Between 1800 and 1900, for example, the total fertility rate dropped from 7.0 to 3.6 children per woman; by 1940 it had further declined to 2.2, although this low a level partly reflects the exceptionally sharp drop in fertility during the Great Depression of the 1930s (Coale and Zelnick 1963). The baby boom era brought the rate back to a high of 3.6 in 1957 but, since the total fertility rate is a period measure, this partly reflects shifts in timing rather than in completed family size. With regard to marital instability, although the proportion of all marriages ending in divorce has risen substantially since the 1950s and 1960s, the trend toward increased marital instability is of long-standing in American society, as Preston and McDonald (1979) have shown; marriages contracted during the baby-boom era were more stable than marriages contracted somewhat *earlier* as well as *later*. In short, declining fertility and rising marital instability seem to be part of the economic development and modernization process in the United States, long preceding major changes in married women's employment. Given these historical trends, relying solely on the independence argument to explain the recent shifts, in effect, posits an entirely different set of causal mechanisms for the pre- and post-baby boom trends in demographic behavior. This may very well be the case, but it would be preferable to first rule out the importance of causal process that might underlie both sets of trends and included the patterns of the baby-boom era as well.

Changes in marriage formation present a somewhat different picture. Although historical data on marriage timing are limited, the evidence indicates that it fluctuated considerably over time. Sanderson (1979) has estimated that the singulate mean age at marriage for white women in 1800 was only 19.3

years. By the end of the 19th century, however, age at marriage had risen considerably (Thornton and Rodgers 1983). For the white female birth cohorts of 1880, for example, just 50 percent had married by age 23.4 and 25 percent were still single by age 29.6. The age by which half the cohorts had married declined gradually after that time and, in particular, the age at which late marriers married decreased sharply. Thus the age by which 75 percent had married dropped from 29.6 years for cohorts reaching age 20 in 1900 down to age 27.7 for those reaching that age in 1930. This trend continued even for cohorts reaching young adulthood during the Great Depression with the 75th percentile declining to age 25.6 for those who were age 20 in 1940. This decrease in the age at marriage and in the variability of marriage timing continued for the baby-boom era reaching the lowest level for the cohorts of 1936–37—for them 50 percent had married by age 20.2 and 75 percent by age 22.7. From that point on, age at marriage and the variability in it have been rising to levels approximating and in some cases exceeding those of late 19th century cohorts (see Tables 7.1 and 7.2).[5]

In sum, women's age at marriage was quite young in the early years of the republic but then rose during the 19th century. It subsequently declined pretty steadily throughout a good part of the 20th century, reaching an extremely young age for those entering adulthood during the baby boom era and is now rising again. Hence, the process of economic development and modernization per se by no means ushers in a monotonic trend toward delayed marriage. All this suggests that it is probably not very meaningful to talk about any particular age at marriage as characteristic of a "traditional" family type marked by extensive sex-role specialization, at least the American version of this family system. Instead, what was really traditional was the sensitivity of marriage formation to varying circumstances. Hence, the very fluctuating nature of the trend data raises serious doubts about whether the late age at marriage currently observed is better explained by women's presumed rising economic independence today any more than this was a factor in the later marriages of turn-of-the-century cohorts. Time series data are particularly inadequate here and determining the importance of the independence effect on marriage formation really requires a micro-level multivariate analysis.

Nonmarriage or Delayed Marriage?

The argument that women's increasing economic independence sharply reduces the desirability of marriage may or may not be true but it is essentially an hypothesis about *whether* people marry, not *when*.[6] So far, researchers have paid little attention to the important analytical distinction between delayed and non-marriage and how this should affect empirical investigations of the hypothesis. But people may need or desire to postpone marriage without wanting to forego it. Hence, if most of the substantial changes in marriage formation patterns are really marriage delays rather than primarily indicating eventual nonmarriage, then the independence hypothesis is not addressing the critical empirical issue. Moreover, by glossing over the important distinc-

TABLE 7.1   Changes in the Timing of Entry into Marriage, as
            Measured by Proportions of Unmarried Non-Hispanic
            White Women at Specific Ages (percentages)

Birth Cohort	Proportion of Unmarried Women at Age								
	16	20	24	28	32	36	40	44	48
1964-68	100	-	-	-	-	-	-	-	-
1959-63	99	71	40	-	-	-	-	-	-
1954-58	99	71	35	19	-	-	-	-	-
1949-53	99	72	30	14	7	-	-	-	-
1944-48	98	66	21	9	7	5	-	-	-
1939-43	98	57	18	8	5	4	4	3	-
1934-38	97	55	17	10	5	4	4	4	4
1929-33	98	53	20	8	6	5	4	4	4
1924-28	98	69	23	14	8	5	5	4	4
1919-23	99	72	32	16	11	7	6	5	5
1901-18	98	76	41	26	15	11	9	8	8

Source: NSFH 1988.

TABLE 7.2   Changes in the Timing of Entry into Motherhood, as
            Measured by Proportions of Childless Non-Hispanic
            White Women at Specific Ages (percentages)

Birth Cohort	Proportion of Childless Women at Age								
	16	20	24	28	32	36	40	44	48
1964-68	100	-	-	-	-	-	-	-	-
1959-63	99	84	57	-	-	-	-	-	-
1954-58	100	86	60	41	-	-	-	-	-
1949-53	100	84	57	38	25	-	-	-	-
1944-48	98	82	47	26	17	14	-	-	-
1939-43	100	80	36	19	12	9	8	8	-
1934-38	99	76	36	21	13	11	10	10	10
1929-33	99	77	37	16	9	8	8	7	7
1924-28	100	86	49	26	19	14	14	14	14
1919-23	100	87	53	32	23	15	12	12	12
1901-18	99	88	63	44	31	24	20	20	20

Source: NSFH 1988.

tion between delayed and nonmarriage, the hypothesis garners far more apparent empirical support for its position than is analytically warranted.

There is little doubt from the evidence already cited that age at marriage has been rapidly rising in the United States. Furthermore, delayed marriage promotes a certain amount of nonmarriage, particularly for women as the supply of eligible males tends to decline sharply with age (Goldman, Westoff, and Hammerslough 1984). So we should expect some rise in the proportions never marrying simply because of the poorer marriage market position of delayers. Whether it will exceed the proportions never marrying in a more traditional era cannot yet be determined because the cohorts involved are still fairly young.[7] However, among whites at least and for those who have already reached their thirties, there are some indications that the delaying factor is far more important than any shift in the proportions never marrying. For example, for those cohorts reaching ages 20–24 in 1975, the proportion still single five years later at ages 25–29 was 17 percent compared to 11 percent for those reaching 20–24 in 1970; however, by ages 35–39, only two percentage points separated the two cohorts. For those reaching their early twenties in 1980, the proportion never married at that age was up to 40 percent compared to 30 percent for those reaching this age range in 1975. However, by ages 30–34 (the latest age we could compare), the difference was, once again, only two points—11 and 13 percent respectively for those reaching ages 20–24 in 1975 and 1980.[8] Hence, it is by no means clear that a high proportion of these marriage delays are really indicative of a major decline in the desirability of marriage per se.

Cohabitation

A critical issue affecting whether there will be a substantial rise in nonmarriage in the United States is the relationship of trends in nonmarital cohabitation to those of marriage formation. Does the rise in cohabitation signify an increasing rejection of marriage and the substitution of a more informal and less committed relationship or has cohabitation become another stage of the courtship process leading up to marriage but perhaps operating to delay it? The paucity of data on cohabitation precludes a definitive answer to this question. Nevertheless, the fact that an increasing proportion of first marriages started as cohabitations (up to 39 percent for the marriage cohorts of 1980–1984) indicates that cohabitation is playing an important role in the marriage formation process (Bumpass and Sweet 1989). Moreover, in a multivariate event-history analysis Lichter et al. (1992) found that cohabiting had a strong net positive effect on the log-odds of marrying in the following year, suggesting that it was operating as a proxy for being engaged. Cohabiting unions also do not last very long; Bumpass and Sweet (1989) found that only 33 percent of first cohabiting unions survived for two years and only nine percent for five years—41 percent of cohabiters married their partner within 2 years while 56 percent did so within five years. In sum, it seems unlikely that, so far, the rise of nonmarital cohabitation signifies a major rejection of or indifference to marriage in American society. However, it undoubtedly delays it. Cohabitors who plan to marry may be under little pressure to formalize the union and only do so at the time of some critical life transition—e.g., the desire to have a child or the imminent geographical relocation of one of the partners due to job mobility. There is just not the same push to marry in the immediate future that once existed in an era when the every-day intimacy of living together was confined to the married state. The date of the marriage ceremony may increasingly represent the time when it is most convenient to publicly cement the bond between two persons rather than signifying the date that a socially meaningful commitment took place.

Effect of Women's Labor Market Position on Marriage Formation

According to the independence hypothesis, women in a better labor-market position (and hence who are presumably more economically independent) should be less likely to marry than women in a poorer labor market position. However, the evidence is mounting that a superior labor market position has little effect on marriage formation but what effect it does have is usually positive rather than negative. Since this volume stresses the role of education as a proxy for the woman's long-term labor market status, we will place the greatest emphasis on education in our discussion but will also mention findings using other measures of labor-market status.

Micro-Level Analyses of Panel Data

It is well known that the more educated tend to marry later than the less educated. But this phenomenon can be due to two reasons, only one of which has much bearing on the independence hypothesis. The first is when educational attainment is directly indicative of labor-market position and this is obviously highly relevant to the hypothesis. However, a second reason why the more educated may marry later is that they have necessarily stayed in school longer and it is school enrollment which discourages marriage. Moreover, a later school-leaving age is only likely to lead to an inverse association between educational attainment and marriage formation in populations where everyone goes to school until young adulthood, regardless of educational attainment, and/or people marry relatively soon after leaving school. If that is the case, however, an extensive increase in educational attainment is likely to produce a rise in the age at marriage resulting from increasing school-leaving ages.

Due to the growing availability of longitudinal data in recent years, a fair amount of research is being done on the determinants of marriage formation. Most of the surveys employed follow birth cohorts of young people over several years of their life course and the analyses have generally employed event history modeling of one sort or another. Two sets of panel studies have been particularly useful in the study of marriage and first birth timing. These are the NLS (National Longitudinal Survey of Labor Market Experience) and the NLSY (National Longitudinal Survey of Labor Market Experience, Youth Cohorts). The NLS consisted of cohorts of young men and women, aged 14–24 at the first interview (1966 for men and 1968 for women) and who were reinterviewed yearly for over 15 years. The NLSY is a new set of cohorts of men and men, first interviewed in 1979 when they were aged 14–21. They have been reinterviewed annually ever since then (Center for Human Resource Research 1990).

All these studies have found that school enrollment greatly discourages marriage formation, but in no case has educational attainment had a negative impact, net of enrollment or other factors (Cherlin 1980; Goldscheider and Waite 1986; Lichter et al. 1992; Oppenheimer and Lew, forthcoming). In fact, most of the studies have reported that educational attainment has a positive effect on marriage formation. Moreover, this same lack of support for the independence hypothesis is found when other proxies for a woman's labor-market position are used. For example, Lichter estimated that women's earnings had a positive effect on the probability of marrying in any yearly interval. One of us (Oppenheimer) tried to directly address the delayed vs. nonmarriage issue by conducting a logistic regression analysis for the NLSY cohorts when they were younger (aged 17–22) and then when they were older (23–32), reasoning that if an independence factor were promoting nonmarriage rather than just delayed marriage, it would have to have a negative effect on marriage formation for women in their late twenties, whatever its impact for younger women. She found, however, that although earnings had no significant effect for the marriage probabilities of the cohorts when they were young, it had a substantial *positive* effect for women in their late twenties. Moreover, other indicators of labor-market position also had no significant influence on marriage timing—those in high-level white-collar jobs were no less likely to marry in a year than those in lower-level white-collar occupations who were themselves not significantly different from semi-skilled blue-collar workers. Moreover, women who seemed to have a strong work attachment (as indicated by year-round full-time employment) were no less likely to marry than those who worked part-time and/or part-year. However, there was evidence that women in the worst labor-market position were *less* likely to marry—for example, high school dropouts, those in unskilled jobs and those not working at all in a year.

Education and Cohabitation

Since cohabitation is often considered a substitute for marriage or, at the very least, a major contributor to delayed marriage, is there any evidence of a special relationship between education and the propensity to cohabit? The lack of a significant negative relationship between educational attainment and marriage timing suggests that cohabitation, as a substitute for marriage, is not disproportionately popular among the better educated. However, it is possible to investigate this issue more directly.

A common misconception about the rise of cohabitation in American society is that the pattern was pioneered by young single people who were college educated. Hence, a popular picture is of the young rebellious well-educated cohorts of the 1960s starting a whole new behavioral pattern that then spread to the rest of the population in the 1970s and 1980s. This perception also fits in well with the idea that a better labor-market position for women has led to a decrease in the desirability of marriage and the substitution of co-habitation as a more palatable alternative. The major problem with this argument is that the evidence shows just the opposite. Retrospective data from the NSFH indicate, first of all, that those entering their first marriage (and hence who were younger) were much less likely to have first cohabited with their spouse than those entering a second marriage. For example, taking the marriage cohorts of 1965–1974, only 9 percent of those marrying for the *first* time had cohabited with their spouse while 29 percent of the cohorts entering their *second* marriage had. Even for the marriage cohorts of 1980–1987, cohabiting first was much more common among people going into their second marriage—54 percent compared to 39 percent for the first marriers (Bumpass and Sweet 1989). In short, cohabiting was pioneered by somewhat older couples, not the young.

With regard to the relationship of educational attainment to cohabitation, the NSFH data show that the pattern was "pioneered" by the *least* rather than the *most* educated and this pattern has continued for all the cohorts studied. For example, of the birth cohorts who reached their twenties in the early 1960s, over 10 percent of high school dropouts had cohabited before age 25 while only one or two percent of college graduates had. For those entering young adulthood in the early 1970s, the proportion who had cohabited before their 25th birthday had risen substantially for all educational groups but was still only about 20 percent for college graduates while it was over 30 percent for the dropouts. And for those entering their twenties in the 1980s, the proportion of college graduates who had cohabited had actually declined while it continued to rise for all less educated groups, reaching almost 50 percent for dropouts and over 30 percent for high school graduates (Bumpass, Sweet, and Cherlin 1991). One drawback of these findings is that, if cohabitation is largely limited to those already out of school, then college graduates will not have had as much time before age 25 as less educated groups to have ever cohabitated. However, in a multivariate regression analysis Bumpass and Sweet (1989) also found a strong inverse association between educational attainment and having cohabited before marriage among those under age 45 at the interview.

In sum, there is no evidence that in American society, the trend towards nonmarital cohabitation was started by the arrival of a new generation of intellectual cultural elites and thence spread out to older and less educated groups. On the contrary, cohabitation caught on much early among somewhat older people who had already achieved independence of their parents in a first marriage and among those of lower socioeconomic status and, to this day, it remains a much more common phenomenon among these same groups. The reason for the perception that it was pioneered by the young and the college educated probably stemmed from the fact that the pioneering *studies* of cohabitation were done on college students—a very convenient sample for academic social scientists. But the group which was first selected for study is not necessarily the group who first instituted a new behavioral pattern. Moreover, cohabitation might indeed be more common among the very highly educated—a segment which is not well represented in a general sample because of its relatively small size but which is, once again, a very salient one for academics. In addition, those college and graduate students who were most likely to cohabit were also highly visible to the media in the sixties because of their well-publicized protests about the Viet Nam War and the "flower children" behavioral pattern of this era.

Multi-Cohort Analysis of the Effect of Education on Marriage

All the longitudinal data analyses that we have discussed so far have utilized relatively short-term panel studies that only cover the transition to adulthood of a very limited group of birth cohorts. A further question is whether the nature of the education/enrollment effect is a stable one over a long period of time. If so, then this indicates that not only does the independence effect appear to be a relatively unimportant factor in today's marriage behavior but that this was always the case with the possible exception of very highly educated women. In addition, if the impact of education is mainly due to later school-leaving ages, and always has been, changes in the school-leaving age may be an important factor in recent trends in marriage timing. We could then go on to explore how much of the changes in marriage formation might be accounted for by the increasingly delayed school leaving age of American women.

Our long-term cohort analysis uses data on non-Hispanic white women from the 1988 National Survey of Families and Households (NSFH). This study was designed to provide detailed information on different aspects of family life. Topics covered include family background, adult family transitions, education and work (see Sweet et al. 1988).

Since the aim of this book is to compare the results across countries, we designed the hazard rate analyses for the US as similar as possible to the model used in other chapters (Table 7.3). As described in detail in the chapter on German women, we have used an exponential model with time-constant and time-dependent covariates. After age 14, we follow the women until their first marriage (equation 1 in Table 7.3) and their first birth (equation 2 in Table 7.3), or at most until they are censored. Censoring occurs after age 46 or at the time of the interview, whichever occurs first.[9]

The following covariates were included in the two models: (1) two time-dependent variables which control for the well-known age-dependence of the process of entry into marriage and motherhood (Log(current age - 14) and the Log (46 - current age)) (for further information see the chapter on German women); (2) a set of dummy-variables controlling for the influence of social origin in terms of fathers' occupation (omitted category: operators, fabricators, and laborers); (3) a detailed set of birth cohort dummies to capture the change across cohorts (omitted category: women who were born in 1918 or earlier); a time-varying control variable of whether a woman is pregnant (in the marriage equation) or married (in the motherhood equation); (4) a time-

TABLE 7.3 Estimates for Models of the Rate of Entry into Marriage and
Motherhood (only non-hispanic white women)

Variables	Entry into Marriage	Motherhood
Intercept	-21.84*	-19.77*
Log (current age - 14)	0.55*	-0.02
Log (46 - current age)	2.58*	2.26*
Managerial and professional specialty occ. [a]	-0.07	-0.02
Technical, sales, a.admin. support occ.	-0.04	0.00
Service occ.	0.01	0.00
Farming, forestry, and fishing occ.	0.10	-0.07
Precision production, craft, and repair occ.	0.06	-0.03
Cohort 1964-68 [b]	-1.53*	-0.53
Cohort 1959-63	-0.49*	0.35
Cohort 1954-58	-0.32	0.32
Cohort 1949-53	-0.41	0.23
Cohort 1944-48	0.04	0.37
Cohort 1939-43	0.10	0.28
Cohort 1934-38	0.42*	0.53*
Cohort 1929-33	0.42*	0.27
Cohort 1924-28	0.32	-0.12
Cohort 1919-23	0.14	-0.20
Pregnant (time-dependent covariate)	1.13*	
Married (time-dependent covariate)		3.41*
In school (time-dependent covariate) [c]	-2.03*	-1.13*
Schooling interrupted (time-dependent covariate) [c]	-1.79*	-2.56*
Completed schooling (time-dependent covariate)	0.03*	0.02
Cohort 1964-68 * In school	0.74*	0.27
Cohort 1959-63 * In school	0.70*	-0.21
Cohort 1954-58 * In school	0.53*	-0.41
Cohort 1949-53 * In school	0.22	-0.45
Cohort 1944-48 * In school	0.76*	-0.19
Cohort 1939-43 * In school	0.56*	-0.27
Cohort 1934-38 * In school	0.17	-0.39
Cohort 1929-33 * In school	0.26	-0.26
Cohort 1924-28 * In school	0.26	-2.80*
Cohort 1919-23 * In school	-0.56*	-1.78*
Cohort 1964-68 * Completed schooling	0.09*	0.04
Cohort 1959-63 * Completed schooling	0.06*	-0.02
Cohort 1954-58 * Completed schooling	0.05*	-0.02
Cohort 1949-53 * Completed schooling	0.09*	-0.01
Cohort 1944-48 * Completed schooling	0.04*	-0.02
Cohort 1939-43 * Completed schooling	0.05*	0.00
Cohort 1934-38 * Completed schooling	0.03	-0.02
Cohort 1929-33 * Completed schooling	0.03	0.01
Cohort 1924-28 * Completed schooling	0.01	0.02
Cohort 1919-23 * Completed schooling	0.02	0.03
Number of events	4,228	3,715
Number of episodes	85,130	112,404
Chi-Square	1,225.4	1,274.5

Notes:
[a] Omitted category: Operators, fabricators, and laborers.
[b] Omitted category: Cohort born in 1918 or earlier.
[c] Omitted category: Out of school.
* Significant at the 0.05 level.

Source: NSFH 1988.

varying dummy-variable of whether a woman is still enrolled in school (omitted category: out of school); (5) a time-varying dummy variable of whether a woman is enrolled in school again after she had left school for more than half a year (omitted category: not in school); (6) a time-varying variable for a woman's changing level of education over the life course; (7) a detailed set of variables for the interactions between cohort membership and "In training" as well as "Level of education."

In our study, the interest focuses on the effect of a woman's level of education for the marriage (motherhood) rates across a large set of successive birth cohorts and the impact of school enrollment. To make the analyses comparable across countries and to bring out the partial effects of these two different aspects of women's educational attainment, we have at first included all the control variables described above. The effects of these variables will only get summarizing attention here (equation 1 in Table 7.3).

In the marriage equation, we obtain at first a right-skewed 'bell-shaped' age pattern for the rate of entry into marriage because the coefficient of Log (46 - current age) is greater than the coefficient of Log (current age - 14). Social origin has no significant impact on the rate of entry into marriage, which is in sharp contrast to the result for West Germany, where differences in social origin not only have been transformed over the life course into differences in schooling, but have also kept an autonomous "class-specific" influence on the timing of marriage. As in all other countries, we also observe a non-monotonic age pattern of entry into marriage across cohorts. The lowest age at marriage is found for the cohorts born between 1929 and 1938. After these cohorts, there is an progressive delay of entry into marriage for each younger generation. The delaying effect is even significant for the two youngest cohorts. This indicates that women's changing marriage timing cannot only be explained by changes in women's educational attainment, since completed schooling did rise monotonically across all cohorts. As expected, the time-dependent covariate "pregnancy" has a positive impact on the marriage rate which indicates that for women experiencing a premarital pregnancy the marriage rate increases sharply.[10]

Given the effects of the above controls, we can now turn to the impact of the two aspects of completed schooling. First, school enrollment has the expected negative impact on entry into marriage. This is in accordance with the results of most of the other studies in this book and with US studies on the timing of adult role entry (see, for example, Marini 1985). Thus, women's higher educational attainment across cohorts promotes later marriage because of longer participation in the school system itself. However, as shown by the interaction effects between cohort membership and school participation, the strength of this effect decreases significantly for the younger birth cohorts. Thus, this factor becomes less important over time. A delaying effect on the timing of marriage is also obtained when a woman re-enters school after she has left the school system for more than a half year.[11] However, what is most important for testing the independence hypothesis is the effect of educational attainment on marriage timing rather than the impact of school enrolment. Here we find that increasingly higher levels of completed schooling do not decrease but rather increase the rate of women's entry into marriage. In addition, there is evidence that this positive effect is getting somewhat stronger for the younger birth cohorts.

Since Becker's (1981) theory implies that women's investments in marketable qualifications might lead to a delay or even to an avoidance of entry into motherhood, we have also studied the two effects of completed schooling on the rate of women's entry into motherhood (column 2 in Table 7.3). Again, the only long-term important dimension of educational attainment seems to be school enrollment itself. As long as a woman is in school, her rate of entry into first motherhood is very low. Finishing schooling, which is one of the most important steps for entering into adulthood status, leads to a steep rise in the rate of entering into motherhood. The level of a woman's education, her general human capital, however, has no significant effect at all. As the rate always reflects both delayed motherhood and childlessness, there seems to be no empirical evidence for Becker's hypothesis that the "indirect" costs, the costs of mother's time, do influence fertility in the US.

First marriage and first motherhood are closely connected life events. They form what statisticians call a system of interdependent qualitative variables in which change in a woman's marital status depends on her fertility status and in which change in marital status also depends on the woman's marital status. This coupling between first marriage and first motherhood was modeled in our dynamic anylsis by the two rate equations including the respective other process as a time-dependent covariate (Tuma/Hannan 1984; Blossfeld/Hamerle/Mayer 1989). Our results in Table 7.3 show that the effect of being married on entry into motherhood is three times as large as the effect of being pregnant on entry into marriage. This means that marriage events seem to be much more important for entry into motherhood than the motherhood events for marriage decisions. Some effects of the covariates on the marriage process are, therefore, indirectly transposed to the motherhood process by the time-dependent variable "Married."

School-Leaving Age and Delayed Marriage

Let us summarize our findings so far. The evidence from a large variety of studies utilizing longitudinal data fails to provide support for the independence hypothesis in the United States. Focusing particularly on educational attainment, the research to date indicates that although higher educational attainment may promote later marriage, this is because the more educated have a later school-leaving age and it is school enrollment which inhibits marriage formation. Once enrollment is controlled for, there is no evidence that educational attainment has a negative impact on marriage formation; if anything, its impact is positive. This finding not only emerges from panel data covering the years of the transition to adulthood for the narrow range of cohorts included in the NLS and NLSY studies but also from our analysis of the multi-cohort retrospective data from the NSFH. Hence it is a long-standing pattern and one which raises the strong possibility that a major factor in the rising age at marriage of American women is their increasingly later age at school completion. It is to this issue that we now turn.

Because of the large sample sizes, cross-sectional time series data provide an excellent resource for further exploring the role of educational attainment vs. school enrollment on first marriage formation and of assessing what proportion of the changes in marriage timing could be accounted for by the increasingly delayed age at leaving school. To start with, we use information on trends in the percentage of non-Hispanic white women who were ever married, by educational attainment and time out of school, covering the March Current Population Surveys (CPS) for 1964–1990.[12] We roughly control for time out of school by examining marital status for women who we estimate to be out of school 1–3 years as well as those out 4–6 years (Figure 7.2).[13]

Looking first at women just out of school, these time-series data, like the longitudinal analyses, do not exhibit major differences among educational groups in the proportions ever-married. However, as in the longitudinal studies, what differences there are do not support the independence hypothesis. Throughout the period, those with a college education were somewhat *more* rather than *less* likely to be married shortly after leaving school; the least likely were high school dropouts (those with less than 12 years of schooling completed). Moreover, quite substantial proportions of all these women were married within three years of leaving school—over 70 percent for college graduates, for example, in the mid-sixties. Thus in the United States there has been a long-standing pattern of women marrying fairly soon after school completion and this is true whatever the level of schooling achieved. Turning to those out 4–6 years, the curves for the different educational groups are even more tightly intertwined. Hence, once we control for school enrollment in this rough way, educational attainment up through college completion has no negative effect on marriage timing for white women and there is no evidence of a change in this pattern over the entire 1964–1990 period.[14]

A second important finding, however, is that for *all* educational groups, the proportions ever married dropped considerably, starting sometime in the early 1970s. Moreover, the change was greater for those out 1–3 years, indicating that delayed marriage more than nonmarriage is playing a major role in these changes. The fact that the proportions ever married dropped sharply for those already out of school also indicates that increases in the school-leaving age cannot be the only important factor in the growing delays in marriage timing. However, since we are holding constant time out of school in these figures, we cannot use them to assess just how big the role is of rising school-leaving ages on trends in marriage timing. To roughly estimate this, we employ the well-known demographic technique of standardization—in this case standardizing the percentage of women who were married in subsequent years by the school enrollment distribution of 1965 (Table 7.4). What this does is to keep the proportion enrolled in school at the 1965 level but allows the proportion of the enrolled and non-enrolled who were married to change over time in the observed manner. If the only factor operating to increase the age at marriage were changes in school enrollment (i.e., the movement of women from higher to lower marriage-propensity enrollment groups), there

FIGURE 7.2   Percentage Ever Married, by Education, Non-Hispanic White Women
Out of School 1–3 and 4–6 Years, 1964–1990

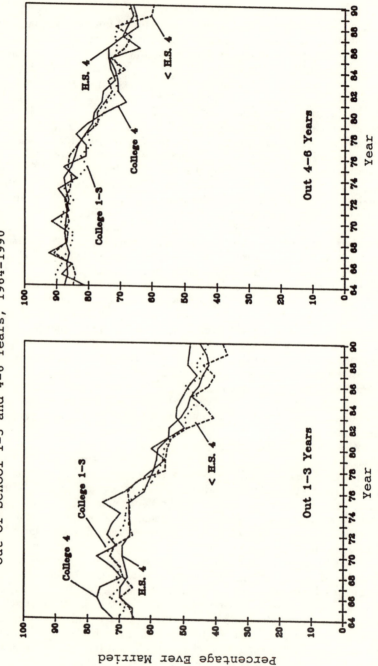

Source: U.S. Bureau of the Census, Current Population Surveys, 1964–1990.

would be no change in the standardized proportions over time. On the other hand, if the standardized proportions changes almost as much as the observed proportions, then most of the increase in delayed marriage is due to changes in the probability of marrying by either the enrolled or not-enrolled groups or both.

In addition to the observed and standardized percentages married, Table 7.4 also shows the percent enrolled and the percent of those not enrolled who were married. As expected, we find substantial increases in the percentages enrolled for each of three age groups (18–19, 20–21, and 22–24) in the 1964 to 1990 period. For example, for those aged 20–21, the percentages enrolled rose from 19.8 to 39.2 between 1965 and 1990. Moreover, rising school enrollment did contribute a considerable proportion of the rather modest decreases in the proportions married between 1965 and 1975—accounting for about 48 percent of the shift for 18–19 year olds and 33 percent for those aged 20–21.[15] However, it only accounted for a very small proportion of the large decreases between 1975–1990—5 percent or less for all the age groups considered. The reason is that the proportions of the non-enrolled who were married declined so much that this swamped the effect of the substantial rise in school-leaving age. Thus the percent of not enrolled 22–24 year olds who were married plummeted from 74 percent in 1965 to 39 percent in 1990. Hence, while more extended schooling has undoubtedly played some role in women's marriage trends in the United States, especially early on in the shift to a more delayed marriage, most of the recent and greatest changes seem to be due to factors *post*-dating school completion.[16]

Conclusion

This chapter has investigated the role of women's educational attainment in marriage and first-birth timing, focusing particularly on marriage timing. Educational attainment has long been used by social scientists as an indicator of labor-market position and, in the case of women, as a measure of their potential economic independence of marriage. The independence hypothesis has argued that women's rising employment has reduced the gain to marriage which in itself is primarily based on sex-role differentiation and the trading of women's home production skills for the man's market skills. While this independence argument has been extremely popular among social scientists, the evidence which is gradually accumulating does not really empirically support it. Most relatively short-term longitudinal analyses completed within the last ten years, and particularly the most recent studies (Lichter 1992; Oppenheimer, forthcoming), indicate that it is school enrollment and the age at completing school, rather than educational attainment per se, which delays marriage. This finding is also borne out by our analysis of the long-term retrospective data of the NSFH as well as the time series data from the CPS. Moreover, other investigators have found that indicators of women's labor-market position, other than education, also show that a better labor-market position either has no negative effect on marriage formation or a positive one. In short, this study, as others, provides no support for the independence hypothesis.

TABLE 7.4 School Enrollment, Marital Status, and Observed and Standardized Percentages Married, Husband Present, by Ages, 1965-1990

Age	1965	1970	1975	1980	1985	1990
18-19						
Observed	23.9	21.1	19.7	14.9	11.5	7.7
Standardized	23.9	22.3	21.7	16.7	14.1	10.2
% enrolled	37.7	41.6	44.2	45.8	51.0	56.3
% of not enrolled married	35.3	33.9	33.0	25.0	21.3	15.6
20-21						
Observed	50.9	45.3	39.6	29.0	24.9	19.5
Standardized	50.9	46.9	42.7	31.9	28.8	23.7
% enrolled	19.8	23.6	27.4	29.5	34.1	39.2
% of not enrolled married	58.9	55.6	50.5	37.7	34.0	27.9
22-24						
Observed	70.9	66.9	59.8	48.6	42.7	35.1
Standardized	70.9	67.9	61.6	51.3	45.4	38.0
% enrolled	6.4	9.4	12.6	14.9	15.1	19.9
% of not enrolled married	73.7	70.1	63.5	53.3	47.4	39.3

Sources: U.S. Bureau of the Census. Current Population Reports. Series P-20, School Enrollment, Nos. 162, 222, 303, 400, 426, and 460.

If rising educational attainment, operating as a measure of economic independence, was not a significant factor in the rise of delayed marriage, could it still be playing a major role in recent marriage trends because it has led to increasingly later ages at school completion? As far as we could determine, the answer to this question is also no. Our analysis of cross-sectional time series data indicated that a rising age at school leaving has only accounted for a very small proportion of the recent changes in marriage timing. The enormous declines in the proportions of *not* enrolled young people who had married has been the major factor in recent trends. Hence, we must look to other possible explanations of the post-1960s trends in marriage and family behavior.

With so much of the focus on woman's labor market characteristics and behavior as the major factors determining recent demographic trends, little attention is being paid to the economic position of young men and how this has been changing over time. As it turns out, young men's labor-market position deteriorated considerably throughout the 1970s and, except for college graduates, in the 1980s as well (Welch 1990; Juhn 1992; Juhn et. al. 1993). A major feature of these changes is not only the worsening position of high school dropouts but also that of high-school graduates, a far larger group and one which has been growing due to rising educational attainment. And in the 1970s the economic position of college graduates also suffered extensively. Hence, the worsening position of young men has by no means been limited to marginal groups and should be an important contender for helping explain the kinds of demographic changes we have been observing throughout the society (Oppenheimer 1994). Not only will it affect the financial ability of young couples to set up an independent household but it greatly increases the uncertainties surrounding men's transition to work—when they will obtain a stable job, their long-run socioeconomic status, and so forth. Rising uncertainties about the nature of people's long-run socioeconomic characteristics, in turn, increase the difficulty of mating assortatively and for this reason, as well as the income problems associated with a weak labor-market position, should be having an impact on marriage formation (Oppenheimer 1988).

Notes

1. More specifically, we have used the public use sample computer files prepared by Mare and Winship (1989) called the *Current Population Surveys: Uniform March Files, 1964–1988. Computer File.* The uniform file only goes up through March 1988 but we have updated the file through 1990. These files permit us to prepare tables with much more exacting specifications than is possible from using published data alone.

2. The kind of transfer payments Becker particularly had in mind were welfare payments—most specifically, the program for Aid to Families with Dependent Children (AFDC) which mainly assists female-headed low income families. More generally, the United States has very little in terms of a family policy. There are no legally mandated paid maternity or paternity leaves nor any family allowances. However, the federal Family and Medical Leave Act was recently passed. It allows for unpaid family leaves up to 12 weeks a year for reasons such as child birth, adoption or a serious health condition suffered by an employee, a spouse, parent or child under age 18. There is no government sponsored system of child-care facilities, although childcare expenditures for

working parents are deductible items on income taxes. Of course, the lack of a family policy is itself a policy. It greatly raises the cost of children and together with the availability of abortion should depress fertility and probably marriage formation as well since abortion of nonmarital pregnancies have become a common option. For example, it is estimated that about 71 percent of unmarried pregnant women of zero parity aborted their pregnancies in 1980 compared to 6.6 percent of married women (Trent and Powell-Griner 1991).

3. Martin and Bumpass (1989) argue, however, that this decline may be more apparent than real since it does not take into account poor reporting of marital disruptions.

4. For a more extended discussion of these issues see Oppenheimer (1994).

5. A similar development my be observed for entry into first motherhood (see Table 7.2).

6. This view is not limited to economists, of course. Goldscheider and Waite argue, for example, that "the recent decline in marriage rates should not be seen as resulting primarily from increased barriers to marriage but from decreases in women's relative preference for marriage because of their increased options outside of marriage" (1986: 107).

7. Thornton and Rodgers (1985, pp. 38–39) estimate that about 88 percent of the cohort of white females born in 1880 had ever married by age 44; this proportion increased to a high of 97 percent for the cohort of 1934. They projected a decline to 90 percent for the cohorts of 1954. However, marriage postponed has continued its rapid rise after the studies completion so the proportions never marrying may go even higher. Whether they will exceed that of the 19th century cohorts is unclear.

8. This discussion is based on an analysis of data from the *Current Population Surveys: Uniform March Files, 1964–1988. Computer File* prepared by Mare and Winship (1989), supplemented by data from the public use samples of the March 1989 and 1990 Current Population Surveys.

9. This means that we have excluded a few first marriage and first motherhood events after the age of 46. However, we suspect that this concerns a specific group of women which behaves differently from the rest.

10. This control variable does not take into account pregnancies which end in abortion and, therefore, reflects only "successful" pregnancies. Thus, the positive effect is biased upward.

11. This effect might be biased because the rate of re-entry into school may be strongly dependent on being unmarried.

12. This figure is based on an analysis of data from the March Uniform Files with updates with the 1989 and 1990 Current Population Surveys (Mare and Winship 1989).

13. Time out of school is estimated as Age - number of school years completed - 7.

14. Women with post-graduate schooling are omitted from this figure because it was impossible to estimate time out of school without making unwarranted assumptions. These women are probably the most likely to delay marriage; however, they are also a very small segment of the female population, albeit an increasing one.

15. The percentage of the total change in the proportions married "accounted" for by the changes in school enrollment is the observed change in the percentage married minus the change in the standardized proportion married divided by the total observed change in the percentage married. Between 1965 and 1975, the percent of 18–19 year olds married dropped from 23.9 to 19.7, a change of 4.2 points; the change for the standardized rates was 2.2 points. The difference between the two (2 points) is the amount of change "explained" by the shift in the percentages enrolled which amounted to 48 percent of the total change for this age group.

16. Increasingly delayed marriage may itself have encouraged more extensive schooling; hence the standardization procedure of Table 7.4 cannot really determine causal direction. It is simply a "what if" exercise showing how much the changing composition of the population could contribute to the observed marriage trends.

References

Becker, G.S. (1981). *Treatise on the Family*, Harvard University Press, Cambridge, Mass.

Blossfeld, H-P., A. Hamerle, and K. U. Mayer (1989). *Event History Analysis*, Erlbaum, Hillsdale, N.J.

Bumpass, L. and J. Sweet (1989). "National Estimates of Cohabitation," *Demography*. 26, 615–625.

Bumpass, L., J. Sweet and A. Cherlin (1991). "The Role of Cohabitation in Declining Rates of Marriage," *Journal of Marriage and the Family* 53, 913–927.

Center for Human Resource Research (1990). *NLS Handbook 1990*, Center for Human Resource Research, Ohio State University.

Cherlin, A. (1980). "Postponing Marriage: the Influence of Young Women's Work Expectations," *Journal of Marriage and the Family*, 42, 355–365.

———. (1981). *Marriage, Divorce, Remarriage*, Harvard University Press, Cambridge, Mass.

———. (1988). "The Weakening Link Between Marriage and the Care of Children," *Family Planning Perspectives*, 20, 302–306.

Coale, A. and M. Zelnik (1963). *New Estimates of Fertility and Population in the United States*, Princeton University Press, Princeton, New Jersey.

Davis, K. (1985). "The Future of Marriage," Chapter 1 in *Contemporary Marriage*, ed. by Kingsley Davis, New York: Russell Sage Foundation.

Espenshade, T. (1985). "Marriage Trends in America: Estimates, Implications, and Underlying Causes," *Population and Development Review*, 11, 193–245.

Farley, R. (1988). "After the Starting Line–Blacks and Women in an Uphill Race," *Demography*, 25, 477–495.

Fuchs, V. (1983). *How We Live: An Economic Perspective on Americans from Birth to Death*, Harvard University Press, Cambridge, Mass.

Goldman, N., C. Westoff and C. Hammerslough (1984). "Demography of the Marriage Market in the United States," *Population Index*, 50, 5–26.

Goldscheider, F. and L. Waite (1986). "Sex Differences in the Entry into Marriage," *American Journal of Sociology*, 92, 91–109.

Juhn, C. (1992). "Decline of Male Labor Market Participation: The Role of Declining Market Opportunities," *The Quarterly Journal of Economics*, 107, 79–121.

Juhn, C., K. Murphy and B. Pierce (1993). "Wage Inequality and the Rise in the Returns to Skill," *Journal of Political Economy*, 10, 410–442.

Lichter, D., D. McLaughlin, G. Kephart and D. Landry (1992). "Race and the Retreat from Marriage: A Shortage of Marriageable Men?" *American Sociological Review*, 57, 781–699.

Mare, R. and C. Winship (1989). *Current Population Surveys: Uniform March Files, 1964-1988. Computer File*, University of Wisconsin, Center for Demography and Ecology, Madison, WI.

Marini, M. (1985). "Determinants of the Timing of Adult Role Entry," *Social Science Research*, 14, 309–50.

Martin, T. and L. Bumpass (1989). "Recent Trends in Marital Disruption," *Demography*, 26, 37–51.

McLanahan, S. (1991). "The Two Faces of Divorce: Women's and Children's Interests," pp. 193-207 in Joan Huber (ed.), *Macro-Micro Linkages in Sociology,* Sage Publications, Newbury Park, CA.

National Center for Health Statistics (1991). "Advance Report of Final Divorce Statistics, 1988," *Monthly Vital Statistics Report,* 39, 12.

———. (1974). "Advance Report of Final Natality Statistics, 1970," *Monthly Vital Statistics Report,* 22, 12.

———. (1993). "Advance Report of Final Natality Statistics, 1990," *Monthly Vital Statistics Report* 41, 4.

Oppenheimer, V.K. (1988). "A Theory of Marriage Timing: Assortative Mating Under Varying Degrees of Uncertainty," *American Journal of Sociology,* 94, 563–591.

Oppenheimer, V.K. (forthcoming 1994). "Women's Rising Employment and the Fate of the Family in Modern Industrial Societies," *Population and Development Review,* 20 (June).

Oppenheimer, V.K. and V. Lew (forthcoming). "American Marriage Formation in the Eighties: How Important Was Women's Economic Independence?" In *Gender and Family Change in Industrialized Countries,* edited by Karen Oppenheim Mason and An-Magritt Jensen, Oxford University Press.

Preston, S. and J. McDonald (1979). "The Incidence of Divorce within Cohorts of American Marriages Contracted Since the Civil War," *Demography,* 16, 1–25.

Preston, S. and A. Richards (1975). "The Influence of Women's Work Opportunities on Marriage Rates," *Demography,* 22, 265–279.

Rodgers, W. and A. Thornton (1985). "Changing Patterns of First Marriage in the United States," *Demography,* 22, 265–279.

Ross, H. and I. Sawhill (1975). *Time of Transition: The Growth of Families Headed by Women,* Washington, D.C.: The Urban Institute.

Sanderson, W. (1979). "Quantitative Aspects of Marriage, Fertility and Family Limitation in Nineteenth Century America: Another Implication of the Coale Specifications," *Demography,* 16, 339–358.

Schoen, R. and J. Wooldredge (1989). "Marriage Choices in North Carolina and Virginia, 1969-71 and 1979-81," *Journal of Marriage and the Family,* 51, 465–81.

Smith, J. and M. Ward (1985). "Time-Series Growth in the Female Labor Force," *Journal of Labor Economics,* 3, S59–S90.

Sweet, J., L. Bumpass and V. Call (1988). "The Design and Content of the National Survey of Families and Households," *NSFH Working Paper No. 1,* Center for Demography and Ecology, Madison, Wisconsin.

Thornton, A. and W. Rodgers (1983). "Changing Patterns of Marriage and Divorce in the United States," *Final Report, prepared for National Institute for Child Health and Human Development, Contract No. NO1-HD-02850.*

Trent, K. and E. Powell-Griner (1991). "Differences in Race, Marital Status and Education Among Women Obtaining Abortions," *Social Forces,* 69, 1121–1141.

Tuma, N. and M. Hannan (1984). *Social Dynamics,* Orlando et al., Academic Press.

U.S. Bureau of the Census, Current Population Reports, Various Dates. *School Enrollment–Social and Economic Characteristics of Students: October,* 162 (1967); 222 (1971); 303 (1976); 400 (1985); 426 (1988); 460 (1992).

U.S. Bureau of the Census (1991). "Marital Status and Living Arrangements: March 1990," *Current Population Reports,* Series P-20, No. 450. U.S. Government Printing Office, Washington, D.C.

U.S. Bureau of Labor Statistics (1988). *Labor Force Statistics Derived from the Current Population Survey, 1948-1987,* Bulletin 2307, Government Printing Office, Washington D.C.

Waite, L. and G. Spitze (1981). "Young Women's Transition to Marriage," *Demography*, 18, 681–694.

Welch, F. (1990). "The Employment of Black Men.," *Journal of Political Economy*, 8, 526–574.

Westoff, C. (1986). "Fertility in the United States," *Science*, 234, 554–559.

8

Italy

ANTONELLA PINNELLI AND ALESSANDRA DE ROSE

Recent Trends

Changes in the Italian family system have been slight compared to those which are taking place in many other developed countries, although the general direction of the change is much the same. The most important change has been in the number and frequency of marriages. In the early 1960s these had increased to 420,000 (1963) with an annual rate of 8.2 marriages per thousand inhabitants, and an average age at first marriage of 28.3 for men and 24.6 for women. Nuptiality subsequently dropped, falling to an annual rate of 7.1 in 1969, but picked up slightly at the beginning of the 1970s, bringing the rate back up to 7.7 per thousand. It started to fall continuously thereafter, reaching a rate of 5.2 per thousand in 1986, that is, to less than 300,000 marriages annually. It appears that this decline has been arrested recently, and the rate has risen somewhat, to 5.4 in 1989.

During this decline, which lasted over twenty years, marriages started to take place at a progressively younger age. In 1979 the average age at marriage reached a minimum of 26.8 for men and 23.7 for women, that is, about a year and a half less for men, and nearly a year less for women in respect of the 1963 figures. Subsequently, however, it began to pick up, and the most recent data reveals an increase of a little over a year for both sexes. The difference in age between spouses is now a little under three years.

In addition to the overall drop in nuptiality since the early 1960s, there has been an increase in non-religious marriages although the majority of marriages are *still* celebrated in church. In the early 1960s the figure for purely civil marriages was as low as 2 percent, but subsequently, and especially after the introduction of the 1970 law legalizing divorce, there was a steady increase in the frequency of registry office marriages, which constituted 16.9 percent of all marriages by 1989. It appears that there is a link between the two phenomena of divorce and registry-office marriage as the divorce rate is considerably higher for purely civil marriages than for church marriages.

On the whole, however, marriage is very stable. Separation and divorce are still relatively rare events; after an increase—due to a change in the law which reduced the time of separation prior to filing an application for divorce, from five to three years—the first accounts for little over 10 percent (total separation rate is equal to the sum of separation rates by marriage duration) and the second for 6.5 out of 100 marriages (total divorce rate).

Marriage usually leads to the setting up of a new household, and indeed, multi-generational families are now in constant decline. But what is the family situation of young people who are not married? In many other developed countries young people often leave home for reasons other than marriage, but in Italy this is a rare event; of young people aged twenty to twenty-four, over 90 percent of men and 65 percent of women still live with their parents (De Sandre 1988). The marked difference between Italy and many other countries also reveals a marked difference in mentality and perhaps also a difference in economic status and in the impact of the educational system in Italy.

On the other hand, young people not living with their parents, while usually living alone or living with a partner in many other countries, are almost always married in Italy (90 percent of young men, and 97 percent of young women) (De Sandre 1988). This confirms the persistence of a behavioral norm whereby the breaking-away of children from the family is marked by marriage, and rarely takes place for other reasons.

The rarity of other forms of union is confirmed by the data of a survey undertaken by the National Statistical Institute in 1983 (ISTAT 1985), which reveal that only 1.3 percent of Italian couples (of all ages) lived together without being married. In nearly half the cases, moreover, these were couples where the partners were over forty-five years of age. This marks Italy off from those other developed countries, where cohabitation has become a relatively frequent form of union, especially for younger people.

The situation in Italy is not, however, homogeneous from a geographical point of view. In the larger centers of North-West Italy, which are wealthier and at the vanguard of modernization in patterns of social behavior, 4.6 percent of unions were consensual. This is much higher than the national average.

ISTAT repeated the survey in 1988 (ISTAT 1989), and the results showed that although there had not been any appreciable increase in the number of unmarried couples living together, there was a higher proportion of younger people (only just over a third were over forty-five years old in comparison to nearly half in 1983). This nevertheless confirms that alternative patterns of family formation have yet to become established among the Italian population overall, and remain marginal.

As regards fertility, this is mainly legitimate and the percentage of children born outside marriage is very low. Nevertheless, this phenomenon is on the increase: initially the percentage of illegitimate births decreased throughout the 1950s, reaching a minimum of a little under 2 percent in 1966, and then rose again to nearly 6 percent at the end of the 1980s. Illegitimate fertility rates increased from 5.3 per thousand unmarried women aged from fifteen to forty-five in 1973, to 6.5 in 1985. Despite this increase, the position of Italy is still very different from that of the other countries in Western Europe, where the rate of illegitimate births has leapt from 20 to 50 percent of total births (Austria, Denmark, France, Norway, the UK and Sweden; see Council of Europe 1990b). The characteristics of illegitimate births have changed over time, however, now children born outside of marriage are generally recognized by both parents while in the past this percentage was very low.

In contrast to the modest changes in the pattern of family formation, within the family there has been a marked change in the number of children born: after the 'baby boom' of the first half of the 1960s, which took the total fertility rate to 2.8, fertility fell steadily to 1.3 children per woman in the mid-1980s. The drop in nuptiality in Italy does not have the same implications as in those European countries where the drop has been accompanied by an increase in alternative forms of union and resulting extra-marital births. That is, the drop in nuptiality in Italy constitutes a real drop in union formation, and has an important role in the decrease of fertility.

However, in Italy even legitimate fertility has declined, albeit at a slower rate than total fertility, particularly since the end of the 1970s (Muñoz Pérez 1987). Only more recently, in 1987 and 1988, has this decline halted (as was also the case for nuptiality), and it may be that, as has occurred in other Western European countries since the mid-1970s, we are at the beginning of a phase of stability or uptake. This long-term decline has, however, completely changed Italy's image, turning it from a country with a traditionally high fertility to a country with one of the lowest fertility rates in the world. The drop in fertility, which has long affected the third child onwards, is now affecting the second and first born, and the percentage of childless couples has therefore gone up (Santini 1988; Muñoz Pérez 1987).

Changes in Patterns of Family Formation
Across Cohorts

The cross-sectional approach used so far gives a great deal of information about the demographic contemporary context but does not allow us to see whether the observed values are due to real long-term changes in marital and reproductive behavior or to the timing effect of the conjunctural situation. Thus, in order to develop our analysis further, we will look at the female cohorts' experience of marriage and first motherhood.

Measures of the cohorts' completed nuptiality do not show evidence of a disinclination to marry: the total nuptiality rate for the cohorts born during the 1940s and the first half of the 1950s has never dropped, but on the contrary it increased to over 95 percent. Only the most recent data indicate that some changes are occurring in the nuptiality patterns of the younger cohorts: the specific nuptiality rates show a decreasing trend at the youngest ages among successive cohorts, while at older ages, there are some signs of an increase (Santini 1986). If we prolong the observed trends and sum the rates again we obtain a total nuptiality rate of 86.5 percent for the 1956 cohort, far beyond that for the previous cohorts (Table 8.1).

In order to have an overall look at the evolution by cohorts in the *quantum* and *tempo* of nuptiality, taking into account the fact that many young women have not yet completed their experience (that is, they are censored), we calculated the proportion 'surviving' the events 'first marriage' or 'first birth' after

TABLE 8.1   First Marriages per 100 Women
            Across Cohorts

Cohort	First Marriage
1919	84.8
1924	87.2
1929	88.7
1934	91.9
1939	93.3
1944	93.4
1949	91.7
1953	95.2
1956	86.5

Source: Santini, 1986.

TABLE 8.2 Proportion of Single Women at Specific Ages

Birth Cohort	Age						
	24	28	32	36	40	44	48
1919-23	57	26	15	12	11	11	10
1924-28	58	33	24	17	14	12	10
1929-33	52	27	14	9	8	7	6
1934-38	51	21	13	9	7	7	6
1939-43	46	19	11	9	7	6	-
1944-48	47	21	13	9	-	-	-
1949-53	41	18	11	-	-	-	-
1954-58	39	20	-	-	-	-	-
1959-63	57	-	-	-	-	-	-

Source: Blossfeld and De Rose, 1992.

the sixteenth birthday (Blossfeld and De Rose 1992) by specific age for all cohorts of women born between 1919 and 1968.

First Marriage

Apart from women born in the period 1924–1928, who were in an unfavorable position *vis-à-vis* the 'marriage market' because of the many young men who lost their lives during the Second World War, over 70 percent of young women were married at twenty-eight years of age, regardless of the cohort considered (Table 8.2).

Marriage was more frequent and took place earlier for women born in the 1930s: the proportion of unmarried women at any age fell continuously from the 1929–1933 cohorts to the 1949–1953 cohorts.

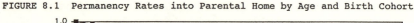

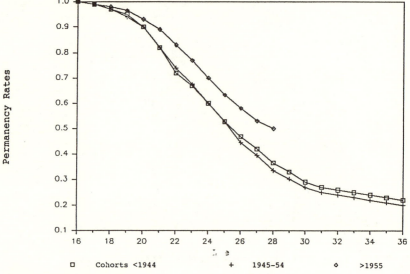

FIGURE 8.1   Permanency Rates into Parental Home by Age and Birth Cohort

Source: De Sandre 1991.

It is only with the cohorts of women born at the end of the 1950s and early 1960s that we observe an inversion in the nuptiality trend. The proportion of unmarried women under twenty-eight increased from 18 to 20 percent (1954–1958 cohorts), and at twenty-four years of age reached 57 percent (1959–1963 cohorts); however, in the latter case events only refer to women born in 1959 who were exactly twenty-four in 1983, the life histories of the other women being censored.

Because of the relatively low incidence of extramarital cohabitation in Italy, the postponement of marriage for the younger cohorts has thus meant a delay in leaving the parental home. At age twenty-eight, 50 percent of young people born after 1955 still lived with their parents, while the same proportion was about 30 percent for the previous cohorts (Figure 8.1).

First Birth

Since in Italy fertility is mainly legitimate, the increase in nuptiality and the earlier age pattern for cohorts of women born between 1919 and 1943 explains the drop in the proportion of childless women at all ages (Table 8.3).

For the younger cohorts, the overall drop in the number and the delay in the timing of first births is more evident and somewhat anticipated compared to nuptiality trends. At the age of thirty-six, while they already recuperated the delay in marriage (the proportion of unmarried women is the same as for the previous cohorts), 16 percent of women born in the period 1944–1948 remained childless, as opposed to 12 percent for the older cohorts.

TABLE 8.3   Proportion of Childless Women at Specific Ages

Birth Cohort	Age						
	24	28	32	36	40	44	48
1919-23	70	37	23	19	17	16	16
1924-28	71	47	30	21	18	15	15
1929-33	65	34	21	15	12	11	11
1934-38	68	32	19	13	11	10	10
1939-43	63	29	15	12	10	9	
1944-48	61	33	21	16			
1949-53	56	27	17				
1954-58	66	56					
1959-63	71						

Source: Blossfeld and De Rose, 1992.

While the percentage of unmarried women aged twenty-four continued to drop for the 1954–1958 birth cohorts, the proportion of childless women in the same cohorts rose from 56 percent (1949–1953 cohorts) to 66 percent.

This can be explained with reference to the fact that, in addition to the postponement of first birth caused by the postponement of marriage, more recently married couples tend to extend the interval between marriage and first birth (De Rose 1988) so that the delay and decline of first-order fertility become 'real' phenomena.

To conclude, measures taken using cohort data give a less dramatic picture of the trends in family formation than those taken using period data, although the behavior of the youngest women shows some clear signs of change, at least as far as timing is concerned. While waiting for these cohorts to conclude their experience, we can suppose that the drop in the cross-sectional measures, which allow us to assume a deeper-rooted change, is mainly due to the fact that Italian women tend to form a family later than their older counterparts.

In the following section we shall analyze a number of factors which help explain the observed changes in the family-formation habits of the youngest cohort examined. We will also examine factors which could 'fasten' the downward trends, as the period measures seem to suggest.

The Impact of Women's Education on the Timing of First Marriage and First Birth

Much empirical research has demonstrated that the improvement in the educational level of women since the end of the Second World War plays an important role as a structural conditioner in social organization and in women's labor-market opportunities and other non-family oriented activities (Blossfeld and Jaenichen 1992).

In Italy, the proportion of women with no school education at all decreased fivefold, dropping from 84 percent for the 1919–1923 cohorts to 13 percent for

TABLE 8.4   Distribution of Women by Educational Level

Birth Cohort	Level of Education			
	Elementary	Middle	High School	University
1919-1923	84.0	8.4	5.9	1.8
1924-1928	80.0	10.7	6.6	2.8
1929-1933	77.3	12.1	7.6	2.8
1934-1938	72.2	19.7	8.8	3.1
1939-1943	63.5	19.0	13.0	4.5
1944-1948	53.6	23.1	15.7	7.5
1949-1953	39.0	27.2	23.5	10.2
1954-1958	23.4	33.6	34.7	8.3
1959-1963	13.0	35.7	48.8	-

Source: Survey on Family Structure and Behavior, ISTAT, 1983.

the 1959–1963 cohorts (Table 8.4). In the same period, the percentage of women with a high school diploma increased fivefold (from 10 percent to 48.8 percent) and the same is true for university education, which, however, is still only obtained by a minority.

The increase in education contributed to the upward trend in female labor force participation. Currently, the presence of women in the labor market—which is much lower than that of men—is highly differentiated by level of education. In 1983, labor force participation rates for women with a university degree or high school diploma were higher than for those with lower levels of completed education (Figure 8.2). What is more interesting, the age distribution of labor participation rates for women with a better education was markedly different from that for the average of Italian women. The maximum—which is about 60 percent in the twenty to twenty-four age range for all women—amounts to 80 percent for those with a better education, and is reached at thirty to thirty-four years of age (cohorts born in the early 1950s); at the same age, less educated women have already begun to leave the labor market.

One promising international line of research supposes that the impact of the increase in the level of women's education on demographic behavior lies with two different processes (Blossfeld and Jaenichen 1992). First of all, better educated women spend more time in the educational system, and this implies a delay of entry into marriage and motherhood. Second, the higher the level of education, the higher the level of women's human capital, and the greater their job and career opportunities. This increases the opportunity costs of women's time and reduces the convenience of marriage and childbearing (Becker 1981). While the effect of educational enrollment is confined to the period of transition from youth to adulthood, and therefore only leads to a postponement of family events, the effect of the level of education will continue throughout much of adult life and reflects a persistent role conflict be-

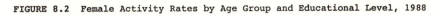

FIGURE 8.2 Female Activity Rates by Age Group and Educational Level, 1988

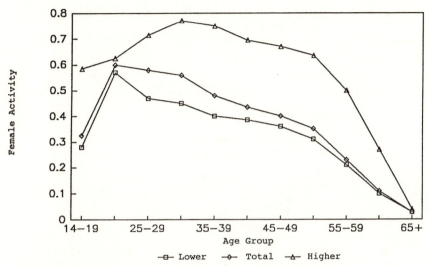

Source: Zanatta 1988.

tween women's growing economic independence and their traditional family roles.

First Marriage

From an analysis carried on the life histories of a sample of Italian women (Blossfeld and De Rose 1992) it emerged that both a high level of completed education and the time devoted to training tend to discourage women from marrying and thus induce a delay of this event.

The estimated coefficients that measure the effects on the probability of marrying over the age of sixteen of the two variables 'level of education' (measured as number of years of study) and being 'in educational enrollment,' are significant and negative; that is, the probability of marriage decreases for all ages (Table 8.5).

However, these two factors alone cannot account for the variability in the family-formation habits of Italian women, or explain the recent trends in cohort behavior. Indeed, besides the expected bell-shaped age effect, we model by means of the first two covariates reported in Table 8.5 for many empirical and theoretical reasons (Blossfeld and Jaenichen 1992), and the known regional differences (women in the North and Centre of Italy tend to marry later than in the South, especially in the major towns), there is also an interesting cohort effect.

The dummy covariates which measure the difference in the behavior of the specific five-year cohorts relative to older women born in the period 1919–

TABLE 8.5   Estimates for Model of Women's Entry
into Marriage

Variable	Estimated Coefficient
Intercept	-17.24 *
Log(current age-16)	0.87 *
Log(46-current age)	1.60 *
Place of residence:	
N-W <100.000 in.	-0.17 *
N-W >100.000 in.	-0.27 *
N-E <100.000 in.	-0.17 *
N-E >100.000 in.	-0.26 *
CNT <100.000 in.	0.01
CNT >100.000 in.	-0.27 *
SOUTH <100.000 in.	-
SOUTH >100.000 in.	-0.24 *
ISL <100.000 in.	-0.16 *
ISL >100.000 in.	-0.10
Birth cohort:	
1919-23	-
1924-28	-0.09
1929-33	0.16 *
1934-38	0.24 *
1939-43	0.41 *
1944-48	0.43 *
1949-53	0.57 *
1954-58	0.71 *
1959-63	0.37 *
1964-68	-1.09 *
In education	-0.63 *
Level of education	-0.04 *
Pregnant	1.78 *
Number of events	2630
Chi-Square	634.90 *
Degrees of freedom	23

* = Significant at the p-value: 5%.

Source: Blossfeld, De Rose 1992.

1923, are nearly all significant. This is because the younger cohorts have a system of norms and values which makes their behavior different from that of older cohorts, quite apart from the structural changes in modern society, witnessed by the growth of female education. The values and signs of the coefficients are consistent with the observations made in a previous section: starting with women born after 1924, the coefficients are positive and increasing (more frequent and earlier marriage), until the 1959–1963 cohort. For these, the coefficient is much lower than for previous cohorts.

The previous life-cycle events also have a strong impact on the timing of marriage. Although the phenomenon is less common now, marriage due to premarital pregnancy, has been a constant in the Italian pattern of family formation. Thus, the high value estimated for the covariate 'being pregnant' (0 until pregnancy and 1 thereafter) is not surprising. In Italy, the 'awareness' of being pregnant together with the social conditioning related to that event are strong incentives to marry.

First Birth

The longer educational enrollment of women has no direct effect on the timing and intensity of first-order fertility—and the level of education, although still significant—influences first-order fertility to a lesser extent.

As expected, first birth is tightly linked to marriage: as soon as a woman marries, the risk of becoming pregnant and of a first birth becomes almost five times higher than at any previous time in her life (Table 8.6). In Italy, being married is the expected moral, and cultural precondition to childbirth. Moreover, controlling for a number of factors, recent trends in first-order fertility observed above for the youngest cohorts, are no longer evident, as the estimates for the 1955 and later cohorts are not significant.

On the whole, the analysis of women's life histories illustrates that the changes in family formation are strongly related to the shift in the timing of nuptiality for Italian couples, and this, in turn, is consistent with the strong patterns existing in the cross-sectional demographic context. This is partly explained by the increased time women devote to education and professional training. However, the significantly different behavior of the youngest cohorts that remains once education is controlled for, suggests that further explanations should be sought. These are probably to be found in the changed attitudes of the younger cohorts towards family, on the one hand, and in the conjunctural constraints which discourage young people from marrying young on the other.

Some Interpretations

We will now attempt to assess the objective contexts which could encourage couples in Italy at this particular time to delay or avoid marriage or other types of union and parenthood.

TABLE 8.6   Estimates for Model of Women's Entry
             into Motherhood

Variable	Estimated Coefficent
Intercept	-18.57 *
Log(current age-16)	0.25 *
Log(46-current age)	1.74 *
Place of residence:	
N-W <100.000 in.	-0.16 *
N-W >100.000 in.	-0.37 *
N-E <100.000 in.	-0.03
N-E >100.000 in.	-0.12
CNT <100.000 in.	0.02 *
CNT >100.000 in.	-0.18
SOUTH <100.000 in.	-
SOUTH >100.000 in.	0.08
ISL <100.000 in.	-0.10
ISL >100.000 in.	0.09
Birth cohort:	
1919-23	-
1924-28	0.00
1929-33	0.18 *
1934-38	0.19 *
1939-43	0.26 *
1944-48	0.04
1949-53	0.24 *
1954-58	0.12
1959-63	0.00
1964-68	-0.15
In education	0.06
Level of education	-0.03 *
Married	4.67 *
Number of events	2423
Chi-Square	1982.16 *
Degrees of freedom	23

* = Significant at the p-value: 5%.

Source: Blossfeld, De Rose 1992.

Opinions and Attitudes

According to the results of a national survey conducted by IRP (Istituto di ricerche sulla popolazione) in 1983, marriage remained the preferred form of union, both in expressed public opinion and in fact (Palomba 1987). Marriage was still regarded as a very serious bond, with over 50 percent of the population believing that it should only be dissolved in serious cases (58.7 percent), and less than a third (30.8 percent) believing that it should be dissolved simply because the spouses desire this. Moreover, the proportion of the population who considered the current divorce legislation too restrictive and in need of a liberalizing reform was relatively low (32.0 percent).

All these opinions were strongly influenced by age, level of education, and above all, by the degree of 'commitment' to the Roman Catholic Church.

Most of the population (67.5 percent) believed the ideal number of children for a family to be two, and almost a quarter (21.0 percent) thought it to be three, with this number being lower for the young, the more educated and the less religious, but never falling short of replacement level.

One therefore cannot help feeling that there may be objective factors which inhibit—in Italy as elsewhere in Europe—a tendency towards greater diversification and flexibility in alternative forms of union and a level of fertility approaching replacement level.

Economic Conditions

Education, work and women's position in society are frequently cited as key factors in explaining the changes witnessed in demographic behavior over the last twenty years. The role of education has been analyzed above, and an analysis of the situation in Italy suggests that labor market conditions partly absorb the other two factors cited (work and women's position in society), and that, even on their own, they provide a convincing explanation of why the situation is so different in Italy compared to that found overall in Western Europe.

The most recent change in the process of family formation is later and lower nuptiality, in the absence of other forms of union, while the delay or even avoidance of first birth has once existed for longer. The origin of the problem must lie with the status of young adults.

If we look at the overall rate of employment for men, we see no great difference between Italy and other European Member States (EUR10), but if we examine rates among the young, we find that the rates of employment are consistently and appreciably lower for this age group in Italy, up to the age of twenty-four in comparison to those of their non-Italian counterparts. As far as women are concerned, activity rates have steadily increased over time—there no longer being the fluctuation which existed between the ages of twenty and thirty—and the pattern by age is beginning to resemble that of males. However, the employment rates for Italian women, particularly younger women, are very low in comparison to the other EUR10 countries (Eurostat 1989).

Hence, unemployment rates are particularly high amongst the under–twenty-fives for both sexes, but especially for women, and between the ages of twenty-five and twenty-nine for women only. Moreover, the percentage of people under twenty-five seeking work is much higher in Italy than in other EUR10 countries. In short, while in other countries people of all ages are looking for employment, in Italy this is specific to young adults. The consequences cannot be wholly appreciated unless we also remember that in Italy those seeking employment are therefore usually people who have never yet been employed, that less than one in five of the unemployed receive benefits (as opposed to 80 percent in Belgium, 70 percent in Denmark, and 60 percent in Holland and Germany), and that other mechanisms of social assistance only function for those who have lost a job and not for those who have never had one (the state redundancy fund is an example). Thus, if we classify the unemployed according to their household position, we find that in Italy they are mainly 'children,' while in other EUR10 countries they are mainly 'heads of household' if male, and 'spouses' if female. This confirms the belief that unemployment is mainly juvenile, and that it is a burden borne almost entirely by the family (Martini 1988). This situation prevents young people from assuming the responsibilities of adult life (working, living alone or with a partner, or marrying), and simultaneously reinforces the function of the family.

Thus, it emerges that the condition of women in Italy is not yet equal to that of women in many other countries, given that, despite undeniable progress, the elimination of discrimination in education has not been accompanied by a similar increase of women in the world of work which would in turn guarantee them independence from the family of origin and the chance to choose between traditional and alternative forms of union, or between marriage and divorce. Apart from the undoubted impact of morals and customs, we should not forget the economic bases of the existing agreements between cohorts and between men and women.

Another element which helps to modify these agreements is the system of taxation: in Italy two spouses who both work are taxed individually, whereas in many other countries it is the combined income of both spouses which is taxed. This places married couples at an enormous disadvantage with respect to *de facto* cohabitors in a system of sliding-scale taxation. This is probably another element which accounts for the differences observed in family models and about which we need to have more comparative information. The sudden increase of marriages in 1987 in Austria, following the proposal to withdraw the marriage allowance starting from 1988 (Council of Europe 1990), the recent spectacular increase in the number of marriage in Sweden after the introduction of a law assigning economic benefits (survivors' pensions) to spouses only, confirms how sensitive people are to such aspects, and how ready they are to change 'mentality' if it is rational to do so.

Finally, another aspect which has been important over the last fifteen years has been the state of the housing market. Rented accommodation has become gradually less available, especially in the big cities, caught between a law which—until very recently—granted too small an income to landlords and a parallel 'irregular' market where rents were, and still are, too high. Families therefore do their utmost to become home-owners, and, indeed, homes which are privately owned as a percentage of total homes have increased from 45.8

percent in 1961 to 58.9 percent in 1981 (Zajczyk 1988). But both the cost of renting accommodation and that of buying a house are prohibitive for young people, and it is in any case becoming increasingly difficult to find housing either to rent or to buy; in Milan, for example, the time necessary to find accommodation was four months in the period 1966–1971, eight months in the period 1971–1976, fourteen months in the period 1976–1981 and two years in the 1980s (Micheli 1988). The importance of the scarcity of low-priced rented housing is recognized as a constraint for couples who wish to marry.

Conclusion

The decline in fertility would appear to be almost exclusively linked to the decline in nuptiality and the delay of marriage, given that the results of the model relating to the probability of having a first child provide a cohort effect which is not statistically significant and the opinion surveys reveal a preference for a higher number of children than is presently the case.

The difficult situation faced by young people, and by women in particular, caused by existing problems in labor and housing markets have provoked a decline in nuptiality and the postponement of marriage, its stability and the scarcity of alternative forms of union, expecially as a conjunctural phenomenon. It is certainly true that there have been widespread changes in mentality and values especially amongst younger, more educated and less religious cohorts, but they have been prevented from having a more appreciable effect on the family system because of this period of difficulty. It is precisely under these circumstances that the family typically 'bolsters' the transition of young people to adulthood.

Appendix

Family Policy

In Italy there is no explicit family policy, with measure being introduced according to the general principles of social justice.

Tax Benefits. Tax allowances are provided for any economically dependent family members (that is, children under the age of twenty-six) and for the disabled. Tax deductions (income or benefits not subject to taxation) are extremely low. Spouses are taxed individually.

Family Benefits. These are granted to families living below the poverty line, which is very low; the self-employed are entitled to an allowance for any dependent children under the age of eighteen; salaried workers have been granted the 'family nucleus benefit,' which is higher.

Housing Benefits. Tax deduction for the family's first house purchase; state employees can borrow a large amount of money at a very low rate of interest, after the purchase of the first house; many banks grant convenient loans for the same purpose; there is a law—recently modified—which regulates the rent of apartments, but there is a flourishing 'irregular' market in which rents are very high.

Family Law

Minors. Introduced in 1975, the law rules that young people under the age of eighteen cannot marry irrespective of parental consent.

Unmarried Couples. Consensual unions are not recognized in law, but partners may register at municipality offices as two cohabiting persons. They can use the 'family advice service,' and are entitled to financial and social support for children, are entitled to succeed in a rented house after the death of a partner (this does not apply to owned property) and the right to alimony in case of the dissolution of the union.

Divorce Law. Introduced in 1970, and available after a compulsory three-year period of legal separation.

Legal Abortion. Introduced in 1978. Women are entitled to free legal abortion during the first three months of pregnancy on social, economic and psychological grounds.

Measures Directed at Working Parents

Maternity Protection. Employed mothers (both full and part-time) are protected against dismissal during pregnancy and the first year of the child's life; they are also protected against dangerous or unhealthy jobs and night work during pregnancy and up to seven months after childbirth.

Maternity Leave. Women are entitled to compulsory maternity leave two months prior to delivery and three months afterwards, enjoying full job security (maintenance of at least the 80 percent of the salary, the workplace, career promotion, etc.).

Parental Leave. Six months during the first year of age of the child. In case of serious illness of the mother, the father is entitled to same right. The state gives a provision equal to 30 percent of salary. During the first year of the child's life, the mother can rest for two hours per working day.

Unpaid Leave. During the first two years of a child's life both parents are entitled to unpaid leave; public sector employees are additionally entitled to a temporary suspension of work for general family reasons for a period of up to one year during which time their position and job security are guaranteed.

Part-time Work. In the public sector there is some flexibility in working schedules, but no explicit part-time arrangements. In the private sector, priority for part-time employment is given to workers (men or women) with children under the age of three, or for other family reasons. In any case, part-time work is very limited and mostly female (11 percent of working women as opposed to 3.1 percent of working men).

Services to Families

Public Day Nurseries. Available for children under three years of age and are run mainly by the municipalities; priority is given to children from low-income families, single-parent families, families where both parents work, immigrant families, and to handicapped children.

Nursery Schools. Public and private nursery schools are available for children from the ages of three to five years; some measure has been taken in order to modify the opening hours to accommodate the needs of working parents.

Home and Out-patient Services. Partial and part-time professional help is provided for the elderly, the handicapped, etc., in order to limit the numbers placed in residential institutions.

References

Becker, G. (1981). *A Treatise on the Family,* Cambridge (Mass.), Harvard University Press.

Blossfeld, H.-P. and U. Jaenichen (1992). "Educational Expansion and Changes in Women's Entry into Marriage and Motherhood in the Federal Republic of Germany," *Journal of Marriage and the Family,* 54, May, 302–15.

Blossfeld, H.-P. and A. De Rose (1992). "Aumento del livello d'istruzione e ritardo del primo matrimonio e della prima nascita: l'esperienza delle donne italiane," *Genus,* 3–4.

Council of Europe (1990a). "Household Structure in Europe," *Population Studies,* 22.

Council of Europe (1990b). "Evolution démographique récente dans les Etats membres du Conseil de l'Europe," Strasbourg.

Coward, J. (1987). "Conception Outside Marriage: Regional Differences," *Population Trends,* 49.

De Rose, A. (1988). "Mutamento della condizione femminile e andamento recente della fecondità," *Materiali di studi e ricerche,* 20, DSD, Rome.

De Sandre, P. (1988). "Quando i figli lasciano la famiglia," in Scabini and Donati (eds.) (1988). *La famiglia lunga del giovane adulto,* Studi interdisciplinari sulla famiglia 7, Milan, Vita e pensiero.

De Sandre, P. (1990). "Contributo delle generazioni ai cambiamenti recenti nei comportamenti e nelle forme familiari," in P. Donati (ed.), *Secondo rapporto sulla famiglia in Italia,* Rome, CISF.

ECE (1990). "The childcare services in ECE 1985–1990," *Women in Europe,* Brussels.

European Observatory on National Family Policies (1991). *Families and Policies,* Italian Report by Sgritta G.B. and Zanatta A.L., ECE.

Eurostat (1989). *Enquête sur les forces de travail résultat 1987.* Luxembourg.

Golini, A. and A. Nobile (1991). "Italy," in J.L. Rally and A. Blum (eds.), *European Population—Country Analysis,* Paris, John Libbey Eurotext—INED.

Gonnot, J.P. and G. Vukovich (1989). "Recent Trends in Living Arrangements in Selected Countries," background paper No. 1, presented at the UNECE/IIASA Task Force Meeting on "Social Security, Family and Household in Aging Societies," Laxenburg, Austria 9 October 1989.

Höpflinger, F. (1985). "Changing Marriage Behaviour: Some European Comparison," *Genus,* 3–4.

IRP (1988). *Secondo rapporto sulla situazione demografica italiana.* Rome.

ISTAT (1985). *Indagine sulle strutture e sui comportamenti familiari,* Rome.

ISTAT (1989). "Caratteristiche strutturali delle famiglie nel 1983 e nel 1988," *Notiziario,* S. 4, f. 41, No. 13.

Kaa, D.J. van de (1987). "Europe's Second Demographic Transition," *Population Bulletin,* 42, special issue 1.

Martini, M. (1988). "I giovani e il lavoro: la specificità del caso italiano," in Scabini and Donati (eds.) (1988). *La famiglia lunga del giovane adulto,* Studi interdisciplinari sulla famiglia 7, Milan, Vita e pensiero. Scabini et al. (1988).

Menniti, A. (1991). *Le famiglie italiane degli anni '80*, Rome, IRP.

Micheli, G. (1988). "Tendenze demografiche e strutture abitative," in IRP, *Secondo rapporto sulla situazione demografica in Italia*.

Monnier, A. (1990a). "La conjoucture démographique: l'Europe et les pays développés d'autre-mer, *Population*, 4–5.

Monnier, A. (1990b). "La situation démographique de l'Europe," paper presented at the conference "Popolazione, società e politiche demografiche per l'Europa," Fondazione Agnelli, Turin.

Muñoz-Pérez, F. (1987). "Le décline de la fécondité dans le Sud de l'Europe," *Population*, 6.

Palomba, R. (ed.) (1987). *Vita di coppia e figli*. Florence, La Nuova Italia.

Palomba, R. (1990). "Gli italiani e i loro figli. Opinioni, valori, ideali." IRP, Working Paper, No. 3, Rome.

Salvini, S. (1986). "L'approccio causale per lo studio delle determinanti della fecondità: il lavoro della donna e gli intervalli tra le nascite," *Atti della XXXIII Riunione Scientifica*, Bari, Sis.

Santini, A. (1986). "Recenti trasformazioni nella formazione della famiglia e della discendenza in Italia e in Europa," *Atti del Convegno "La Famiglia in Italia,"* Rome 29–30 October 1985.

Santini, A. (1988). "Natalità e fecondità" in IRP, *Secondo rapporto sulla situazione demografica in Italia*.

Scabini, E. and P. Donati (eds.) (1988). *La famiglia lunga del giovane adulto*, Studi interdisciplinari sulla famiglia 7, Milan, Vita e pensiero.

Zajczyk, F. (1988). "Abitazioni e famiglie," in Istat-Ais *Immagini della società italiana*, Rome, Istat.

Zanatta, A.L. (1988). "Donne e lavoro," in Istat-Ais *Immagini della Società Italiana,"* Rome, Istat.

9

Spain

MARGARITA DELGADO

Historically, the family is the institution which sustains, both materially and psychologically, an individual's development. It constitutes the primary locus of social reproduction and the basic unit of production and consumption. In modern capitalist society these functions have remained basically intact, except the production characteristic, which the family has to a great extent—if not completely—lost. Important changes have taken place in the process of family formation and in the appearance of new family-types. In the past the main route to family formation was marriage which constituted the preliminary step for cohabitation, sexual relations and reproduction. This sequence in the process of family formation has varied radically with regard to the first step: marriage is no longer necessarily a preliminary to the initiation of sexual relations, and on the contrary, sexual relations frequently precede non-marital cohabitation or marriage. This is due to the dissociation of sexual relations and procreation, which is in turn thanks to the developments in the methods and use of modern contraception in the second half of the twentieth century which allows young people to enjoy a fully affective relationship without the risk of an unwanted pregnancy. As a consequence, young couples may postpone marriage or choose not to marry, without having to forgo a stable sexual relationship and without the automatic risk of having to raise children irrespective of their desire to do so; frequently the only factor conditioning the initiation of cohabitation is that of having the necessary financial means to do so and not whether marriage and children will follow. Thus, on the one hand we find the traditional pattern where conventional marriage precedes sexual relations and the birth of children, and on the other the gradual appearance of new patterns, all of which have the common characteristics of initiating with sexual relations. In some cases, these unions will not be permanent, but others may lead to the formation of a family group living together. From the time these unions begin the family 'embryo' may evolve through different forms, either with marriage as the initial step to the formation of a union with or without children, or with marriage induced by the arrival of a child from a pre-marital conception. It may also lead to a childless family due to either biological or voluntary infertility, the latter being increasingly frequent, although

191

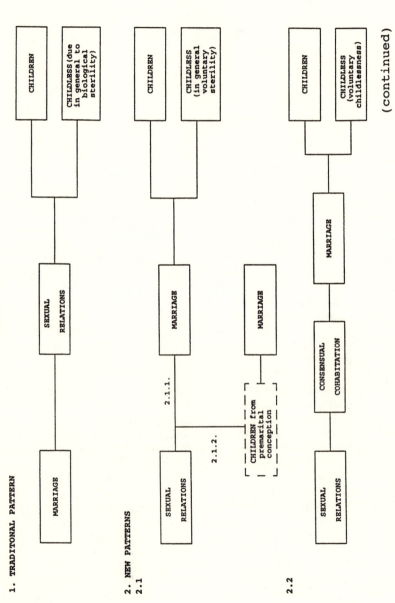

FIGURE 9.1

1. TRADITONAL PATTERN

MARRIAGE — SEXUAL RELATIONS — CHILDREN / CHILDLESS (due in general to biological sterility)

2. NEW PATTERNS
2.1

SEXUAL RELATIONS — 2.1.1. — MARRIAGE — CHILDREN / CHILDLESS (in general voluntary sterility)

2.1.2. — [CHILDREN from premarital conception] — MARRIAGE

2.2

SEXUAL RELATIONS — CONSENSUAL COHABITATION — MARRIAGE — CHILDREN / CHILDLESS (voluntary childlessness)

(continued)

FIGURE 9.1 (continued)

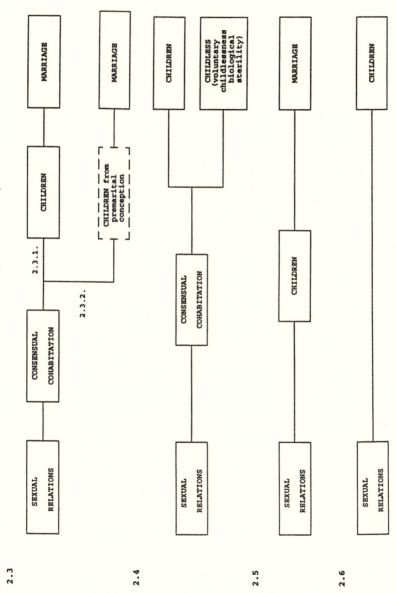

not in substantial percentages. In the traditional pattern of family formation, childlessness is usually due to biological infertility whilst in the new family and living-together patterns childlessness is frequently a deliberate choice. Figure 9.1 attempts to synthesize the different options for family formation.

All these forms of living together and variations of these forms, to which divorce or separation can be added, transforming them into single-parent families, generate new family situations which may lead to families containing children from different unions. This phenomenon has made the family spectrum more complex and has led to an exponential increase of possible family-types. This does not mean that divorce did not previously exist, or that there were no families with separated parents, but they were undoubtedly much less frequent than they are today. From the 1960s onwards, we have witnessed an increase in non-marital cohabitation, a decline in nuptiality and fertility, an increase in divorce and in the numbers of voluntary childless couples, and as a result, the proliferation of new forms of families and of new forms of relations between their members.

These changes do not occur with equal intensity across countries. There are still pronounced differences. For instance, the statistics of unmarried couples living together and of children born outside marriage registered in Southern Europe differ markedly from those for Northern Europe, and divorce rates in the greater part of Northern Europe are several times higher than those in the Mediterranean countries.[1] One of the reasons for the latter is that in Southern European countries legislation allowing divorce is relatively recent and there are cultural differences that are reflected in legislation and in the attitudes of people from different countries.

In Spain, the transformations involved in the processes of family formation have undergone some changes but marriage is still the preliminary step to procreation for the great majority of the population; the proportion of children born to unmarried mothers,[2] although on the increase, is still low in comparison with Northern Europe, and the incidence of non-marital unions is low with unmarried couples almost always being childless (Centro de Investigaciones Sociológicas 1991).

I will begin with a short review of the legislative measures related to family policy and the changes produced after the political transition in the second half of the 1970s. This marks the beginning of the period of analysis, although in some cases I will refer to previous periods.

After discussing the sources used, the changes produced in the processes of family formation will be analyzed through the evolution of age at first marriage and the observation of forms of living together. The variations in the intensity of fertility will be measured by cohort and period indicators and the transformations produced in the calendar and in the fertility structure will be studied through the evolution of mean age at childbearing and fertility rates by birth-order.

I will go on to look at the evolution of women's activity and education levels in Spain and try to relate these variables with the changes observed in the demographic indicators experienced by successive cohorts.

Spanish Legislation on Family Policy

In Spain the use of contraceptives was penalized up to 1978, however from 1975 onwards there was certain 'opening-up' of sexual freedoms, and it became less difficult to obtain them, and one can now buy both oral and some other forms of contraception without a prescription. As regards abortion, in 1985, the Organic Law made abortion legal if practised by qualified medical personnel in one of the following three circumstances: where there is a physical or mental health risk to the pregnant mother; where pregnancy is as a result of rape; or where there is a danger of the fetus being born with severe mental or physical defects.

Among the policies which benefit families are fiscal policy, housing policy and exemptions in educational and related matters. There is additionally direct aid, and related labor legislation. The *income-tax system* has undergone changes in recent years. In 1991, a law was introduced which has made it possible couples to be taxed either jointly or separately. For *child allowances*, in 1991, Law 26/1990 modifying the financial aid payable under the social security system for dependent children, retirement or disablement. An allowance of 3,000 pesetas per month (previously 250 pesetas) was fixed for each child under eighteen years of age or older if disabled by more than 65 percent, in which case the annual amount might be double or even reach 468,000 pesetas in certain cases. Other types of benefit cover large families and include, among other things, non-means-tested allowances to cover school fees and preferential allocation of housing.

Maternity provisions cover medical assistance during pregnancy, birth, and the immediate post-delivery period, and allowances payable to women workers (affiliated to the social security system) for paid leave of up to a maximum sixteen weeks at childbirth. Mothers who work—or the father—are also entitled to an hour taken off during the waking day for 'nursing time' during the three months following birth.

The Data

The total number of births was obtained from the vital statistics (M.N.P.) which allows us to calculate the age-specific fertility rate and the fertility rate by birth-order in order to observe the mean age at first birth and the mean age at childbearing. Only since 1975 (when data on births classified by rank first became available) has it been possible to calculate the mean age at first birth.

Two methods and two different sources have been used to estimate age-specific first marriage rates. The first uses the age-specific annual statistics of marriages and the previous marital status of the partners. The other method is to calculate the singulate mean age at marriage (SMAM), using Hajnal's method (1953), and is based on the population census. This indirect technique was used in order to take account of the subregistry observed in the number of marriages celebrated by Roman Catholic rite—which represent over 80 percent of all marriages—since 1979, when the agreement between the Catholic Church and the Spanish State became effective.[3]

TABLE 9.1   Mean Age at First Marriage, Spain, 1950-1987

Year	Males M.N.P.	Males SMAM	Females M.N.P.	Females SMAM
1950	-	28,97	-	26,43
1960	28,8	-	26,1	-
1970	27,4	27,53	24,7	23,66
1975	26,4	26,73	23,9	23,23
1980	25,8		23,5	
1981	-	26,01	23,6	23,11
1985	26,4		24,3	
1986	26,7	27,27	24,5	24,75
1987			24,6	
1988				
1989				

Source: EUROSTAT, Estadísticas Demográficas, 1990.
           SMAM 1950-70: B.Cachinero (1982); 1975-86:
           Own elaboration.

The data on forms of living together was taken from an unpublished survey of the Centro de Investigaciones Sociológicas carried out in 1991 for a sample of 7,531 men and women over the age of eighteen.

The rates of female labor activity were taken from homogenized series (Miguel and Agüero 1986), completed with more recent data from the "Encuesta de Poblacion Activa" (E.P.A.).[4]

The statistics relating to women's education level for different generations are based on the data from the 1981 population census.

Data from other studies and authors has also been used, such as completed fertility or the ratios of married women reached by different cohorts, with the purpose of complementing and enriching the analysis.

Existing data on the processes of family formation are not very rich in Spain and considerable efforts are currently being made to carry out a nationwide social-demographic survey of a retrospective character (on a sample of 160,000 people), which will allow much more in-depth studies on this and other demographic, economic, social and related aspects.

Marriage

The age at which women in Spain contracted their first marriage was slightly over twenty-six in both 1950 and 1960 (Table 9.1). The SMAM is not available in 1960 but the mean age at first marriage was calculated from vital statistics. This was the consequence of a rising trend in the age at marriage since the beginning of the century which changes course from the beginning of the second half of the century. The decline starts after 1950. The maximum reduction is registered in the period 1960–1970 with a drop of 1.4 years. This reduction persisted until the early 1980s when the mean age at first marriage rose to 24.6 years in 1987, the last date for which data is available.[5]

During the 1960s and 1970s, mean age at marriage in Spain was among the highest of all European countries, but when Spain started to recuperate, first marriage had already been postponed by almost ten years in other European countries, and this is why in 1987 Spain was among the countries with the earliest marriage age in Western Europe.

These changes in trend are closely related to the economic situation. The rise in the 1940s was due to the general economic crisis of the post-Civil War period, when the economy experienced a ruralization process. The conditions became more favorable in the 1950s with the beginning of industrialization, which peaked in the following decade. During this period there was an increase in marriage intensities and a rejuvenation in the marriage calendar, and as a result a pronounced decrease in mean age at first marriage. Between 1956 and 1975 the annual nuptiality indicator surpassed the unit in various occasions as the cohorts born 1931–1951 reached marriagable age. Taking a look at the marriage ratios reached by these cohorts, mainly those born between the 1930s and early 1940s, we can observe that these are the cohorts that would later experience the most intense marriage rate in the century, also due to the upturn in the economy.

The role played by nuptiality in Spain is very significant with respect to fertility levels,[6] mainly when marriage rates are measured longitudinally observing successive cohorts. As can be seen in Table 9.2, the cohorts that increased their completed fertility rate, coincide in part with those for which the final ratio of married women is higher. These factors, when added to the decline of mortality, made these cohorts the only ones in this century to reach a net reproduction rate above the unit. The up-turn in the decline of completed fertility observed until then is a consequence of the increase in the marriage rate given that marital fertility did not experience the same evolution—its course follows a declining pattern since the beginning of the century, whether it is observed through the Ig or through any other indicator.[7]

With the experienced increase between 1981 and 1986 (equal to an increase of 1.64 years, as measured by SMAM) Spain thus joins the same course as her European neighbors in the delay in age at marriage. It must be pointed out that such a delay is not compensated by an early initiation of non-marital cohabitation, at least according to the data available.

Table 9.3 shows the proportion of people over the age of eighteen who are either married or cohabiting (Centro de Investigaciones Sociológicas 1991). Only 1.27 percent of the population are living in non-marital unions, and if age is considered, the said percentage would be about 1 percent for those over thirty-five years of age, that is cohorts born before 1956. Those born after the second half of the 1950s show higher proportions (except the very young), but in no case reach 4 percent.

TABLE 9.2 Completed Fertility Rate and Proportion Married by Cohort

Cohort	CFR	NRR	Proportion Married	Cohort	CFR	NRR	Proportion Married
1901-02	3,28	0,94	0,80	1932-33	2,66	1,02	0,91
1902-03	3,22	0,94	0,80	1933-34	2,67	1,04	0,91
1903-04	3,16	0,93	0,80	1934-35	2,67	1,05	0,91
1904-05	3,11	0,93	0,80	1935-36	2,67	1,05	0,91
1905-06	3,07	0,92	0,80	1936-37	2,66	1,06	0,91
1906-07	3,02	0,92	0,80	1937-38	2,64	1,06	0,90
1907-08	2,97	0,91	0,80	1938-39	2,62	1,06	0,89
1908-09	2,93	0,91	0,80	1939-40	2,59	1,05	0,89
1909-10	2,89	0,90	0,80	1940-41	2,56	1,05	0,88
1910-11	2,84	0,90	0,80	1941-42	2,53	1,04	0,88
1911-12	2,80	0,90	0,80	1942-43	2,50	1,04	0,88
1912-13	2,76	0,89	0,80	1943-44	2,47	1,03	0,88
1913-14	2,72	0,89	0,80	1944-45	2,43	1,02	0,88
1914-15	2,68	0,88	0,81	1945-46	2,39	1,02	0,88
1915-16	2,65	0,88	0,83	1946-47	2,37	1,01	0,89
1916-17	2,62	0,88	0,84	1947-48	2,34	1,01	0,89
1917-18	2,60	0,88	0,85	1948-49	2,30	1,00	0,89
1918-19	2,58	0,88	0,85	1949-50	2,25	0,98	0,88
1919-20	2,56	0,88	0,85	1950-51	2,20	0,96	0,87
1920-21	2,55	0,89	0,85	1951-52	2,15	0,95	0,86
1921-22	2,53	0,89	0,85	1952-53	2,10	0,93	0,85
1922-23	2,52	0,89	0,85	1953-54	2,05	0,91	0,84
1923-24	2,51	0,90	0,85	1954-55	1,98	0,88	0,83
1924-25	2,51	0,91	0,85	1955-56	1,90	0,85	0,81
1925-26	2,52	0,91	0,86	1956-57	1,84	0,82	0,80
1926-27	2,53	0,93	0,86	1957-58	1,77	0,80	0,79
1927-28	2,54	0,94	0,87	1958-59	1,70	0,77	0,78
1928-29	2,56	0,96	0,87	1959-60	1,63	0,74	0,75
1929-30	2,59	0,97	0,88	1960-61	1,55	0,70	0,72
1930-31	2,61	0,99	0,89	1961-62	1,48	0,67	0,68
1931-32	2,64	1,01	0,90				

Source: J.A. Fernández Cordón, 1986.

TABLE 9.3   People in Marital and Non-marital Unions in 1991

Birth Cohort	Age Group	Married N	Married %	Non-marital Union N	Non-marital Union %	Total N	Total %
··· 1921	75 +	105	48,86	1	0,48	215	2,85
1916-1921	70-74	206	60,76	0	0,00	338	4,49
1921-1926	65-69	375	70,09	1	0,19	534	7,10
1926-1931	60-64	425	73,78	2	0,35	577	7,66
1931-1936	55-59	469	81,95	3	0,54	573	7,60
1936-1941	50-54	496	84,74	1	0,17	585	7,77
1941-1946	45-49	508	84,01	6	1,01	605	8,03
1946-1951	40-44	555	86,17	5	0,79	644	8,55
1951-1956	35-39	540	84,09	6	0,95	643	8,53
1956-1961	30-34	532	70,98	21	2,86	750	9,96
1961-1966	25-29	334	41,33	31	3,79	808	10,73
1966-1971	20-24	126	14,44	16	1,87	874	11,60
1971-1973	18-19	6	1,58	2	0,53	387	5,14
		4677	62,10	96	1,27	7533	100

Source: Centro de Investigaciones Sociológicas, 1991.

In some of the transformations produced in the marriage calendar, it is usual to point to the prolongation of the time dedicated to education and training, as well as to changing economic conditions. The decline in the intensity of nuptiality is usually accompanied by an increase of non-marital unions in the majority of the European countries. That this is not the case in Spain could be to some extent be attributed to the cost of housing—a factor of great importance in the decline of the marriage rates in Spain—and the difficulties that this creates for family formation. This also affects the formation of non-marital unions, which might explain why the decline in marriage is not compensated for by a rise in non-marital unions.[8]

The mean age at first marriage for men shows a similar course to that for women, both in its historical perspective and recently, with a reduction in the difference between age at first marriage between the two sexes in recent years; from 3.5 years in 1975 to a difference of only 2.57 years in 1986.

Completed Fertility by Cohort and Total Fertility Rates

Table 9.2 shows the progressive decline in the number of children per woman from cohorts at the beginning of the century to those of the early 1920s; that is, from more than three children to 2.5 (a reduction of 23 percent). However, if we observe the net reproduction rate we can see that even though the trend is parallel to that of completed fertility, the intensity of the decline represents only 5 percent, which indicates that the gains taken from mortality in that period compensate in great measure, in net terms, the decrease in fertility.

The cohorts born between 1926 and the mid-1930s increase their fertility in relation to both the preceding and successive generations. Likewise, they increase their net reproduction rate due to the persistent effect of the decrease in mortality and reach a net reproduction rate above replacement level in the co-

TABLE 9.4   Fertility Rates by Birth-Order, 1975-1987

Fertility	1975	1980	1985	1986	1987	Variation 1975-87 %
Order 1	1,007	0,897	0,725	0,661	0,687	-31,78
Order 2	0,837	0,693	0,529	0,548	0,499	-40,38
Order 3	0,481	0,343	0,227	0,209	0,188	-60,91
Order 4	0,228	0,148	0,089	0,078	0,067	-70,61
Order 5+	0,226	0,129	0,067	0,056	0,047	-79,20
TFR	2,781	2,210	1,637	1,552	1,487	-46,53

Source: Own elaboration from Encuesta de Población Activa (EPA).

horts born 1931–1949. Thus, this group of nineteen generations are the only ones so this century to register a net rate above one.

A steady decline in fertility, measured as completed fertility by cohort, starts with the 1936–1937 cohort and persists to the present day. However, the decreasing inversion in the net rate does not take place until the 1939–1940 cohort and the cohort born ten years later will be the first to once again have a fertility rate below zero and reach net reproduction rates of approximately two-thirds of replacement level.[9]

The influence of the described trends may be observed in the evolution of total fertility rate. The increase in total fertility that takes place from the mid-1950s and—mainly—1960s, reflects the arrival of prime reproductive age for what turned out to be the most fertile cohorts this century, and the rejuvenation of the calendar, detectable through the decline in the mean age at first birth.

Evolution of Fertility Rates by Birth-Order

Total fertility decreased almost 47 percent in the period 1975–1987, with rates for third-order and subsequent births dropping even more dramatically (see Table 9.4). If we split the period into two, we can see that in the second half of the 1970s the mean annual decrease was slightly smaller than in the 1980s, irrespective of birth-order.

The contribution made by each birth-order to total fertility rate has varied substantially. The most important variation is that for first-order births, which jumped from slightly over 36.24 percent total fertility in 1975 to just over 46 percent in 1987. The contribution of second-order births seems to be more stable, gaining three points. The most marked declines in terms of their relative importance are those for third and fifth-order births. In terms of magnitude

TABLE 9.5   Mean Age at Childbearing, 1950-1989

Year	TFR	Childbearing	First Birth
1950	2,508	30,60	
1960	2,789	30,00	
1970	2,849	29,30	
1975	2,781	28,82	25,27
1976	2,780	28,54	
1977	2,654	28,46	
1978	2,540	28,38	
1979	2,364	28,26	
1980	2,210	28,19	25,05
1981	2,035	28,23	
1982	1,938	28,33	
1983	1,797	28,37	
1984	1,726	28,43	
1985	1,637	28,46	25,79
1986	1,552	28,53	25,90
1987	1,474	28,57	26,14
1988	1,438		
1989	1,387		

Sources: TFR 1950-70: Fernández Cordón, 1986; Childbearing 1950-70: Agüero, I., 1986; rest: own elaboration.

the most remarkable change is the gain in first-order births, which reaches a value not far from half of total fertility. This leads to the evident decrease taking place in final family size. In Spain, average family size was 3.84 members according to the 1970 census, but by 1991 this had decreased to 3.28. These numbers include single-family households, but if we only looked at the decrease in the average size of the family with only a nucleus, it would be of a greater importance.

Mean Age at Childbearing

When contraceptive techniques were less effective and fertility was natural, marriage was postponed as a mechanism of birth control. Later, with controlled fertility, marriage was no longer conditioned by it and the birth of the first and successive children could be planned with relative exactitude, giving rise frequently to the 'empty-nest' phenomenon, that is the interval between marriage or non-marital cohabitation and first birth.

In Spain we can only calculate mean age at childbearing since 1922, and and information about birth-order by mother's age is only available since 1975. Therefore changes in age at first birth can only be analyzed for the most recent period (Table 9.5).

In 1950, mean age at childbearing in Spain was almost thirty-one. Since that date it has declined, dropping to 24.1 years in 1980. This variation is a consequence of a rejuvenation in the fertility calendar that has taken place throughout the century. This trend changes its course in the 1980s when mean age at childbearing starts to rise as a consequence of a delay. This is reflected in an increase of the relative importance of the groups between twenty-five and thirty-five years of age for total fertility; and not only in their relative importance, given that in 1985 for the first time the fertility rate for the thirty to thirty-four age group exceeds that for women aged twenty to twenty-four.

The same process is observed with respect to mean age at first birth. This registers a slight drop between 1975 and 1980, and a subsequent—more pronounced—increase due to the fact that when the percentage of first-order births increases, the influence of age at first birth over mean age at childbearing is greater. In the period considered the age at childbearing for women in Spain is high in comparison with other European countries where a concentration of fertility in the central fertile groups had occurred with quite some anticipation, while in Spain both in 1970 and in 1985—when total fertility had already dropped to a level below that of many other countries—the rates for women over thirty-five years of age continued to be comparatively higher (Delgado 1990:20–30).

Nonetheless, some changes may be detected in the process of family formation. From 1960 to 1980, both mean age at childbearing and at first marriage decreased but the *difference* between both indicators had increased as mean age at childbearing was quite high, influenced by relatively high rates at older ages, thus indicating that the childbearing period was quite dilated. After 1980, both indicators increase but the distance between them narrows as a consequence of a concentration of the fertility in the central ages and due to a very strong reduction in the rates of women over thirty-five years of age, thus indicating a shortening of the period dedicated to reproduction. This is corroborated by the reduction in the difference between mean age at first birth and mean age at childbearing.

With respect to the period between first marriage and first birth, this was of 1.37 years in 1975, increased in 1980 and dropped slightly to 1.54 years in 1987. It seems that the trend toward a delay in family consolidation by having children could be explained by various factors among which we can point to the increase in female activity rates. Such an increase is the product of the improvement in career and working opportunities experienced by women in recent decades due to an improvement in their education. Moreover, we must not forget the advances in contraceptive techniques which allow better family planning.

Table 9.6 shows the changes that have occurred between the different cohorts in the timing of first birth. As regards the fertility rate of women in Spain this century, the cohorts of the late 1940s and the first half of the 1950s were the most fertile at the youngest age as regards first birth, and have the lowest proportions of childlessness at the age of twenty of all cohorts examined, and also the lowest percentages of childless women at the age of twenty-five and thirty, which once again confirms that they have the highest com-

TABLE 9.6   Changes in the Timing of Entry into Motherhood as Measured by Proportions Childless at Specific Ages (percentages)

Birth Cohort	Age Group	Age							
		18	20	25	30	35	40	45	50
1971-1973	18-19	96,81							
1966-1971	20-24	90,10	83,82						
1961-1966	25-29	88,28	67,97	61,72					
1956-1961	30-34	83,56	50,96	27,40	21,37				
1951-1956	35-39	88,96	47,73	20,45	13,96	13,96			
1946-1951	40-44	90,06	42,86	14,29	11,80	10,56	10,25		
1941-1946	45-49	91,46	55,38	25,95	16,46	15,82	15,51	15,19	
1936-1941	50-54	93,26	52,13	19,50	12,06	10,28	9,93	9,93	9,57
1931-1936	55-59	96,47	72,12	29,49	16,35	13,46	12,82	12,50	12,50
1926-1931	60-64	93,84	67,03	36,96	23,55	19,20	18,48	18,12	17,75
1921-1926	65-69	94,44	70,83	38,19	23,96	19,44	18,75	18,40	18,40
1916-1921	70-74	91,19	72,02	37,31	27,46	22,80	22,80	22,80	22,80
- - - 1921	75 +	94,40	69,60	40,00	25,60	21,60	20,80	20,00	20,00

Source: CIS, Estudio 1965, 1991.

pleted fertility by cohort. These are the ones with the highest total fertility rate in the 1960s, due to a greater intensity in nuptiality. With the following group (born after 1956) there is a rise in the proportion of women of different ages without children, although not to the same extent as the previous cohort.

In Spain the trend towards earlier motherhood in cohorts born 1921–1926 was broken by the generations of the second half of the 1950s. A rupture in these cohorts can also be seen with regard to the number of births; these women had their children both in the early 1980s and later, but had fewer of them. We can note that in relation to other European countries, there is a certain delay in beginning these changes but that this is compensated by the speed at which they take place.

Female Activity Rates and Women's Educational Level

Taking the period 1970–1990 as a reference, we can see that the female activity rate has multiplied by 1.8. The figures show an irregular evolution, with an increase in 1970–1975 followed by a decrease in 1980 and a 'quasi' stabilization until 1985, after which the indicator experiences a leap of twelve points in a period of only five years (Table 9.7).

The course followed by female activity rates reflects the economic situation and the impact of the economic crisis that manifested itself most acutely in the early 1980s.[10] If we observe the evolution of the rates by age groups, we can see that between 1970 and 1990 the rates for women aged under twenty or over sixty decreased. The decrease in the younger group seems to be a consequence, in part, of a prolongation of the period dedicated to education and training. On the contrary, other age-groups increased their activity rates; the rate more than doubled for those aged twenty-five to twenty-nine, and almost trebled for those aged thirty-five to thirty-nine.

However, if we take a look at the evolution of each generational group and observe its course, even given the short time span considered, we can see that in 1970 women aged twenty to twenty-four reduce their activity rate when they reach twenty-five to twenty-nine and continue to do so from thirty to thirty-four. They then start increasing their rate again at thirty-five to thirty-nine and at forty to forty-four. These women belong to he 1946–1950 birth cohrots—one of the most fertile. Given the period in the life-course when these changes occur, it could be considered a temporary withdrawal from extra-domestic activities dedicated to reproduction and childrearing. The same occurs with the generations born 1951–1955; when they are between twenty-five to thirty-four years old they reduce their activity rate, which subsequently increases again. In neither case is there a total recuperation, and these women never reach the activity levels they had at twenty to twenty-four, however the loss is much less in the younger generation. It must be pointed out, however, that independent of activity levels, the age factor seems to play a more important role than the cohort effect, and is even more important than the economic one, given that in the first case the reduction takes place in 1975 and in the second case in 1980.

TABLE 9.7   Female Activity Rate by Age, 1970-1990

Year	16-19	20-24	25-29	30-34	35-39	40-44	45-49	50-54	55-59	60-64	65-69	70 y +	Total
1970	43,49	49,16	27,07	18,89	19,30	22,11	22,44	21,88	20,62	16,18	11,59	6,77	18,2
1975	41,69	56,43	35,82	26,03	25,88	27,46	29,84	27,06	25,23	21,40	13,86	5,03	27,8
1980	39,62	54,72	41,39	29,74	29,27	27,34	27,13	25,94	23,99	16,98	7,60	2,02	20,0
1985	32,01	54,24	52,82	39,95	32,39	30,61	25,95	23,92	22,73	15,63	4,44	1,16	21,2
1990	31,20	61,45	65,15	56,26	48,96	41,11	34,53	29,15	23,24	15,55	3,80	0,70	33,4

Sources: Agüero, I. y de Miguel, C., 1986; EUROSTAT; INE, Encuesta de Población Activa (EPA) and own elaboration.

The behavior of the following cohorts (born 1956–1960) is quite different: they start at the age of twenty to twenty-four with a relatively high activity rate—albeit slightly lower than that of the immediately preceding cohort. They hardly show a decrease at twenty-five to twenty-nine, and at thirty to thirty-four they have already recovered or even slightly increased the rate they had at twenty to twenty-four. If we take a look at the 1961–1965 cohorts, in spite of the short period for which they are observed, we can see that the decrease does not continue on reaching twenty-five years of age. On the contrary, there is a gradual increase. Therefore, we can point to some kind of rupture between the women born before 1956, who withdraw to a greater degree from the labor force when they reach their most intense fertility age, and those born after that date, who seem to be more successful in combining work and motherhood, although this takes place in a more concentrated time and with less intense fertility.

The Evolution of Women's Education Level

In 1981, the surviving women from pre-1916 birth cohorts had an illiteracy rate of almost 28 percent. This percentage is reduced by half approximately in the ten following cohorts and continues to fall, dropping to below 1 percent for women born after 1960. The category with no education—which includes those who can read and write but have not completed primary schooling—shows a similar evolution and the improvements are equally remarkable for younger generations. A change may be observed in the group of generations born 1946–1956, the ones that belong to the twenty-five to thirty-four age group in Table 9.8. It is with these cohorts born in the second half of the 1940s that an improvement in the education level achieved starts to take place, consolidated by the cohorts from the second half of the 1950s. There is a relation between this phenomenon and the observation previously made that women born after 1956 withdraw to a lesser extent from the labor force when they reach their most intense reproductive age. The higher the level of qualification the more professionally satisfying and better paid the employment, the less likely women are to want to abandon it. This is corroborated by the data on female activity by level of education; almost without exception, the higher the level of education, the higher the activity rate.[11]

On the other hand this coincides closely enough with what we observed when analyzing the completed fertility reached by the successive cohorts, since it is these cohorts born around 1954–1955 that are the first to reach a quota below replacement level when observed longitudinally. They are also those who play the most important role in a transversal perspective of the sharp fall in fertility initiated in the second half of the 1970s when these women are between twenty-five and thirty-five years of age.

In Spain, the advances experienced in the educational level of the population in general are much more pronounced when we observe what has happened with respect to women (Centro Nacional de Investigacion y Documentacion Educativa 1988:155–61). The advances in education levels, however depart from a clearly unequal situation. According to the 1900 cen-

TABLE 9.8   Female Education, 1981 Census

Age Group	Illiterate	No Educat.	First Grade C	First Grade I	Second Grade First Cycle C	First Cycle I	Second Cycle C	Second Cycle I	University First Cycle C	First Cycle I	Second Cycle C	Second Cycle I	No Classif.	Total
10-14	0,59	0,92	2,08	30,59	1,92	56,86	0,00	7,03	0,00	0,00	0,00	0,00	0,00	100
15-19	0,82	3,93	5,40	2,54	28,38	9,54	4,61	39,00	0,05	2,23	0,01	3,16	0,32	100
20-24	1,19	7,35	12,49	4,88	33,38	5,12	9,29	7,89	5,13	3,49	1,79	7,79	0,21	100
25-34	2,17	15,52	37,35	8,35	13,74	2,01	5,55	3,57	5,90	0,52	3,58	1,56	0,18	100
35-44	6,14	25,23	37,07	11,72	8,09	0,96	2,76	1,77	3,82	0,20	1,64	0,43	0,17	100
45-54	10,79	29,87	34,28	13,04	4,63	0,51	1,86	1,21	2,48	0,09	0,88	0,17	0,17	100
55-64	13,72	32,37	31,07	13,92	3,28	0,39	1,26	1,01	2,03	0,04	0,67	0,09	0,14	100
65 +	27,67	31,32	23,03	12,36	1,75	0,15	0,60	0,40	1,93	0,06	0,53	0,05	0,13	100

Notes:

C = Complete.
I = Not complete.

Source: Spanish census of 1981 and own elaboration.

sus the global rate of illiteracy for women over ten years of age was 66 percent whilst that for men was 46 percent. Forty years later the respective illiteracy rates were 23.22 and 13.76 percent. The improvements are already noticeable in the 1970 census.

Summary

In recent decades the process of family formation in Spain has experienced important changes similar to those experienced in other European countries but with a delay. There has been a decline in nuptiality rates since 1975, accompanied by a slight decrease in mean age at marriage until the early 1980s. This slight decrease starts to rise again in the following years, becomes rather significant, and persists to the present. This means a decline in the number of women married in the prime fertility ages and hence a reduction in reproductive potential. Such a decline in the marriage rates is perceived not only in a transversal perspective, but also throughout successive cohorts. A decline in the final proportion of married women was initiated with women born after 1950.

The increase in mean age at first marriage and the decline in marriage rates are not counterbalanced by an increase in non-marital cohabitation. This is one of the characteristics which differentiates Spain from other European countries, where similar transformations have occurred. In Spain, as in other Southern European countries, non-marital cohabitation is a phenomenon of little relevance. The proportion of children born to unmarried women is among the lowest in Europe, which indicates that even if there are a certain number of unmarried couples living together, the union is not normally consolidated by the presence of children. Divorce is a phenomenon of the 1980s and, in the context of declining marriage rates, is the only component to show a rising trend.

The decline in fertility in the second half of the 1970s is another of the great transformations in the process of family formation. The total fertility rate period decreased almost 50 percent between 1975 and 1989. This is not only due to timing effect given that the completed fertility of the cohorts shows very important reductions and the estimated net fertility rate for the cohorts born in the early 1960s shows values near 67 percent of the necessary values for replacement. The greatest reductions have occurred in third-order and subsequent births, which dropped from 34 percent of total births in 1975 to 20 percent in 1987. This means a reduction in family size, with families with more than two children becoming infrequent.

Mean age at first birth has also experienced a delay in recent years, partly as a consequence of a delay in age at first marriage, but also due to a postponement of first birth. The delay in the initiation of family formation may also be influenced by the prolongation—for both men and women—of the period spent in education. For women this has meant significant increases in educational levels attained by the most recent cohorts—mainly those born after 1950. This in turn lead to better labor-market opportunities, greater activity rates, and a greater unwillingness to abandon the labor force on childbirth, as expressed by the evolution of female activity rates by age for successive cohorts.

Parallel to the delay in the initiation of family formation is a shortening of the childbearing period, which is consistent with a narrowing of the gap between women's age at first marriage and their mean age at childbearing, as well as of the difference between the mean age at childbearing and mean age at first birth.

In Spain the second half of the 1970s marks the beginning of a series of transformations regarding the family, which had already started taking place before in other European countries. It is the age of legalized birth control and selective abortion, followed by legislation allowing divorce in the 1980s. Spain thus joins the new trends which had been in an embryonic stage but had not been able to materialize due to the country's particular sociopolitical situation. On the other hand the impact of the consequences of the economic crisis was felt most strongly during the 1980s. This is why labor activity rates did not experience significant increases until the late 1980s. However, the phenomenon of a retarded chronology in Southern European countries in respect to changes in family patterns is a relatively recurrent characteristic. Furthermore, the changes experienced at the turn of the century with respect to fertility transition and other demographic variables in the Southern countries, became visible a few years later than in Northern European countries. The chronological delay is counterbalanced in some cases by other factors. An example is the delay in the fertility decline, which is compensated by a sharp decline in a more concentrated period. This does not happen with other phenomena such as divorce, non-marital cohabitation and children born outside marriage.

Notes

1. The divorce rates in Italy and Spain were 0.5 per thousand population in 1987. In the same year the figure was 2.8 in Denmark, 1.9 in the Netherlands and 2.9 in the United Kingdom (*Eurostat*: 1989).

2. This does not specifically refer to young or uneducated women. The highest non-marital fertility rate is *not* for young women.

3. As regards the problem of subregister in the number of marriages, see Delgado and Fernández Cordón (1989).

4. For a discussion on the sources related to activity, its evolution and levels, see Espina (1991).

5. The mean age at first marriage for women (see Table 9.1 under M.N.P.) has been calculated from age-specific marriages rates for single women aged from fifteen to forty-nine.

6. See Delgado and Livi Bacci (1992).

7. For the Ig values see Coale and Watkins (1986: 144–48).

8. Between 1985 and 1990 the price of newly-built housing per square metre multiplied by an average of 2.5 throughout Spain, and by as much as 3.3 in some areas, such as Madrid. On the problem of housing see, Checa Morán, Valcárecel and Martín García (1986), Instituto de la Juventud (1988), Centro Investigaciones Sociológicas (1990), and Zamora López (1990).

9. The last generation's rates are partly extrapolated; see Fernández Cordón (1989: 60).

10. One of the most attractive and stressed promises in the PSOE's successful campaign in the 1982 national elections was the creation of 800,000 new jobs. This gives the idea of the extent to which unemployment was one of the greatest, if not *the* greatest social problem in Spain at the time.

11. See the Instituto Nacional de Estadística, Encuesta de Poblaciíon Activa (E.P.A.) for recent years.

References

Cachinero Sánchez, B. (1982). "La evolución de la nupcialidad en España (1887–1975)," *R.E.I.S.,* 20, 81–99.

Centro de Investigaciones Sociológicas (1990). *Estudio 1863. Problemática de las Grandes Ciudades: Madrid, Barcelona, Valencia, Bilbao,* Banco de Datos (unpublished).

Centro de Investigaciones Sociológicas (1991). *Estudio 1965. Familia y formas de convivencia,* Banco de Datos (unpublished).

Centro Nacional de Investigación y Documentación Educativa (C.I.D.E.) (1988). *La presencia de las mujeres en el sitema educativo,* Madrid, Instituto de la Mujer.

Coale, A.J. and S.C. Watkins (eds.) (1986). *The Decline of Fertility in Europe,* Princeton, Princeton University Press.

Checa Morán, N., R.E. Valcárecel and J.J. Martín García (1986). *La demanda de viviendas ligada al matrimonio,* Comunidad de Madrid, Consejería de Ordenación Territorial, Medio Ambiente y Vivienda, Madrid.

Delgado, M. (1990). "La fecundidad en España por grupos de edad. 1975–1985," *Documentos de Trabajo,* 3, Instituto de Demografía, Madrid, C.S.I.C.

Delgado, M. and J.A. Fernández Cordón (1989). "Análisis de las cifras de matrimonios en España desde 1975," *Estadística Española,* Vol. 31, 121, 281–95.

Delgado, M. and M. Livi Bacci (1992). "Fertility in Italy and Spain: The Lowest in the World," *Family Planning Perspectives,* Vol. 24, 4: 162–71.

Espina, A. (1990). *Empleo, democracia y relaciones industriales en España,* Ministerio de Trabajo y Seguridad Social, Madrid.

Eurostat (1989). *Estadísticas Demográficas,* Luxembourg.

Fernández Cordón, J.A. (1986). "Análisis longitudinal de la fecundidad en España," *Actas del Simposio Internacional sobre Tendencias demográficas y planificaci ó económica,* Ministerio de Econom a y Hacienda, Madrid.

Hajnal, J. (1953). "Age at Marriage and Proportions Marrying," *Population Studies,* 7, 2: 111–36.

Instituto de la Juventud (1988). *Informe Juventud en España 1988,* Madrid.

Miguel, C. de and I. Agüero (1986). "Evolución demográfica y oferta de fuerza de trabajo," *Actas del Simposio Internacional sobre Tendencias demográficas y planificación económica,* Madrid, Ministerio de Econom a y Hacienda.

Zamora López, F. (1990). "Le dépeuplement de Madrid: 1970–1986," Seminar AIDELF "Croissance demographique et urbanisation," Rabat, May 1990.

10

Hungary

PETER ROBERT AND HANS-PETER BLOSSFELD

Historical Trends and Family Policy

Family formation, entry into marriage and motherhood, and the incidence of consensual unions are all influenced by the historical traditions and family policy of a given country. As Andorka (1978) points out, there is a strong historical connection between marriage customs and fertility. In this respect Hajnal (1965) distinguishes between a 'European' and a 'non-European' type of marriage, which in turn affects the respective birth control solutions. In Western societies, on the one hand, late entry into marriage, higher rates of unmarried men and women, and the widespread use of modern birth control techniques generally function to keep the fertility rate relatively low, while in Eastern European peasant societies, early entry into marriage, lower rates of unmarried men and women, and the use of traditional methods of family planning (*coitus interruptus* or 'folk forms' of abortion) generally lead to higher fertility (Andorka and Balázs-Kovács 1986).

In Hungary, at the end of the nineteenth century, the age at entry into marriage was twenty to twenty-four for men and seventeen to nineteen for women with only 4–5 percent remaining unmarried at the age of fifty (Tárkány-Szúucs 1981). In the twentieth century, due to economic improvements and an increasing level of urbanization, age at marriage began to increase and stood at twenty-five to twenty-nine for men and twenty to twenty-four for women in the interwar period (Csernák 1976). The so-called 'marriage boom' had its consequences in Hungary too, but due to the low fertility during World War II, and emigration in 1956 (Klinger 1958), the proportions of men and women entering marriageable age declined in the 1960s. In addition, the 'inclination to marriage' started to drop from the beginning of the 1970s (Klinger and Monigl 1981). In comparison to these trends, age at marriage has picked up slightly since the mid–1970s (Csernák 1982).

As regards fertility in the twentieth century, the traditionally high Hungarian fertility rates have been declining permanently since the end of the nineteenth century and, disregarding some temporary fluctuations, this is still the trend today. After World War II there was a period in the 1950s (1953–1956), when abortion was strongly regulated and practically prohibited which led to a peak in the natality rates, followed by a strong decrease in the 1960s when the abortion law was liberalized.

Policy measures were taken in Hungary, first of all, to influence the fertility rates in a situation characterized by a high proportion of female employment. One of them being the so-called 'childcare leave,' which enabled working women to stay at home until a child reached the age of three whilst maintaining their place of work and receiving a monthly allowance from the state. The childcare allowance law was introduced in 1967 and was changed and extended in 1973 and again in 1985. On the other hand, considering the demographic peak of the 1960s, it is obvious that the ratio of 'potential mothers' has also increased in this period. This demographic effect and the impact of population policy measures generated a second demographic peak in the 1970s in Hungary. However, analyses make it clear that the population policy did not achieve its original goal. Women did not bear more children but instead gave birth to their first child earlier than they would have done without the law on childcare allowance. Thus the real consequence of the law was a decrease of age at entry into motherhood (Miltényi 1971). Due to policy measures, on the other hand, positive changes can be mentioned such as a drop in the number of miscarriages, infant mortality and premature births, and an increase in the widespread and accepted use of oral contraceptives (begun in 1967) (Klinger 1980).

In the 1980s, as the signs of economic crisis in the socialist system became more visible, the former measures of population policy became even less effective, the childcare allowance has decreased in value, meaning that women could hardly afford to stay at home on childcare leave. Modification and expansion of the childcare allowance system in 1985—increasing the amount of benefit to around 75 percent of the mother's previous income—did not bring about any significant change in the tendencies towards lower fertility. The economic difficulties (due to inflation the cost of living for families with children rose much faster than the financial support given to them by the state; and despite promises made by the government, the housing shortage did not improve) led to further drop in the inclination to marriage. Low fertility gave rise to another demographic consequence, namely that Hungary's population started to decrease in the late 1980s.

Changes in the Social Role of Women:
Women's Changing Educational Attainment

According to Becker's economic theory of family formation (1981), unmarried men and women act as potential trading partners who decide to marry if they gain more by marrying than by remaining single. Traditionally, women have been less educated and less likely to be employed than their male counterparts and there has been a much stronger cleavage between men's and women's roles in the household. As women's educational attainment, labor force participation and money-making capabilities have increased, however,

TABLE 10.1   Educational Attainment of Women from Selected Cohorts (%)[a]

Educational Attainment	Birth Cohort						
	1929-1933	1934-1938	1939-1943	1944-1948	1949-1953	1954-1958	1959-1963
Up to 8 grades of primary	85.8	74.9	64.3	47.0	38.4	36.2	26.8
Vocational training	.6	2.1	4.2	8.9	15.0	18.3	23.3
Vocational secondary	5.5	12.1	10.2	12.9	14.5	16.3	20.7
Secondary gymnasium	3.3	6.1	12.5	18.7	22.0	17.3	20.7
College	2.4	2.5	5.7	7.2	6.4	9.0	7.7
University	2.3	2.4	3.1	5.3	3.6	2.8	.8
Total	100.0	100.0	100.0	100.0	100.0	100.0	100.0
N	1341	1293	1342	1477	1538	1521	1044

[a]Weighted data, not controlling for censoring variables or father's occupation.

Source: Hungarian Social Mobility Survey, 1983.

women have begun to consider marriage as one of several alternatives open to them. The same applies to the decision to have children, given that entry into motherhood may jeopardize a woman's career goals.

Traditionally in Hungary—as elsewhere—women's level of educational attainment has always been below that of men. Significant changes took place in this respect after World War II, when the entire educational system was reorganized and expanded, and the age for compulsory education was raised. One of the results of this process was that the level of educational attainment for women increased faster than that of men (Simkus and Andorka 1982).

Table 10.1 presents the clear improvement of women's educational chances across cohorts. Educational expansion led to a strong decrease in the proportion of those with only primary education. This level was typical for around 86 percent of women of the oldest cohort and this proportion decreased to less than 30 percent for the youngest cohorts. The strongest increase in educational attainment can be seen for those cohorts which benefitted in particular from the postwar changes in the Hungarian educational system. In the 1950s, marked educational expansion had an impact on the population which in turn generated an increase in educational enrollment and educational attainment; the proportion of women with secondary (academic) education doubled from the second to the third cohort, as did the figures for tertiary (college only) education (see Table 10.1). For the next decades, in the 1940s and 1950s, the intensity of educational expansion began to decrease and the improvement in educational chances of the younger cohorts levelled off.[1]

Women's increasing educational attainment also led to an increase of their participation in the labor force. This process started in Hungary at the end of nineteenth century, but women's employment only began to increase more dynamically after 1990. However, between the two World Wars female employment mainly consisted of young unmarried females as women tended to leave the labor market immediately after marriage and particularly after the first child (Koncz 1983). A big increase in women's employment can be observed in Hungary after World War II. This process was supported by the increasing demand for labor in developing socialist industry and by the ideological goal of equality between sexes in socialism. As a result, in 1960 about 50 percent of women of working age were already economically active, and in 1970 this rose to around 60 percent with the proportion of women in the labor force becoming stable (70–75 percent) in the 1980s. Another typical feature of the Hungarian context is that given the low level of wages, most families need two full breadwinners, with a full income also supplied by the woman. Many women would prefer the option of part-time employment, despite the fact that it is economically unviable and that the supply of such employment for women is low.

Consensual Unions

Entry into marriage and motherhood are strongly influenced by consensual unions in many Western European countries. Cohabitation, however, is quite rare in Hungary. According to the 1970 census, the proportion of cohabiting couples was below 3 percent and this percentage was still below 5 percent in the 1990 census. The low proportion of cohabitation can be explained partly by housing shortages and partly by cultural traditions. The former means that it is very difficult for young couples to rent apartments and establish consensual unions, while the latter implies that parents usually do not allow young people to live together in the parental home without being married. Although there has been a slight increase in cohabitation in Hungary in recent years, this mostly applies in the poorest and least educated families whereas cohabitational unions are formed when the partners are relatively young.[2]

Accordingly, in Hungary the alternative to marriage is not cohabitation but for young couples who are sexually active to live separately. Since this type of relationship is not a consensual union, the ratio of extra-marital childbirths is also low (approximately 7 percent) by Western European standards, although there has been a slight, but permanently increasing, trend since the mid–1970s. At the same time the proportion of women who are pregnant at the time of marriage is estimated at about one-fifth of all women entering marriage (Mészáros and Monigl 1982). Another analysis from 1983, however, estimates this proportion to be higher, based on the fact that 29 percent of married women under the age of thirty-five give birth to their first child within seven months of marriage (Central Statistical Office 1986).

Entry into Marriage and Motherhood:
Theoretical Perspectives

There is a vast literature on analyses of determinants of timing of entry into marriage and/or motherhood in general (for example Elder and Rockwell 1976, Hogan 1978, Rindfuss and St.John 1983, Marini 1978, 1984, 1985, Michael and Tuma 1985, Huinink 1987, Oppenheimer 1988). A basic approach is to analyze the timing of transition to other adult roles. The answer to the question, who is 'ready or not ready for marriage' is, of course, influenced by cultural and historical traditions. Moreover, completing education and entering the labor force are usually considered signs of 'readiness' for adult roles such as marriage or parenthood. An additional element which is particularly important in the Hungarian context is residential autonomy (Goldscheider and DaVanzo 1985), with those, who left their parental home and live with a partner (cohabitee or spouse) being considered residentially independent. Considering the housing shortage in Hungary, this part of transition to adulthood can be realized only with longer or shorter delay, resulting that pre-adulthood is likely to last longer in this respect than is normally the case in Western European countries. Married couples usually start their 'independent' life in one room of the parental home, whereas the proportion of young married couples who start life together in the household of their own, varies between 22–31 percent, depending on the region (Central Statistical Office 1986).[3]

The approach discussed above combined with women's extended educational enrollment, may generate a delaying effect in family formation. Indeed, being in full-time education usually implies economic dependence on the parental family and, therefore, tends to be inconsistent with adult family roles.

On the other hand, there are factors, such as low parental income, a low level of parental education, a large number of siblings, and bad housing conditions which tend to increase the advantages of marriage, especially for young girls who choose marriage as a way to escape from such parental families. A good measure of the class-specific orientation is socioeconomic background which has a strong effect on age at entry into marriage or motherhood (Michael and Tuma 1985, Marini 1985, Huinink 1987). Theoretically it is considered a measurement for cultural resources, material position and consumption style of the parental family as well as attitudes and value orientations in respect of marriage.

Data and Methods

The data used in this analysis are from the 1983 Hungarian Mobility and Life History Survey carried out by the Central Statistical Office.[4] The data is based on oral interviews using a standardized questionnaire. The sample consists of a disproportionately stratified selection of households out of a total of 32,301 respondents (weighted scores have been used in the analysis), and the survey provides data on individuals, families and households. In the analysis, timing of first marriage and first birth are the dependent variables specified as the instantaneous rate of entry into marriage and motherhood. These probability rates are defined as functions of time-constant and time-dependent covariates. Observation begins at the age of fourteen and ends with the event of first marriage or first birth or—for right censored cases—with the date of interview or age forty-six, whichever occurs first. For the time-dependent measures, the method of episode-splitting was used and a separate data record was created for half-yearly intervals. In order to present the probability of a woman remaining unmarried or childless until a certain age, survival functions were estimated separately for the different cohorts.[5]

The independent variables in the study are measures of age-dependence, education, father's occupational class and cohort. The non-monotonic age-dependence is measured by a combination of two variables: $\log(Di) = \log$(current age - 14); and $\log(Ri) = \log$ (46 - current age); assuming that timing of first marriage and first birth is between the ages of fourteen and forty-six.

An additional dynamic measure used in our causal models consists of two dummy variables: 'being pregnant' for models of entry into marriage and 'being married' for models of entry into motherhood. These measures are based on the observed ages at these two events and express the mutual causal relationship between entry into marriage and motherhood.[6]

Educational investments were measured by the average number of years required to obtain them in the Hungarian educational system, according to the following six levels: completed primary education (eight years); vocational training (eleven years); completed secondary school diploma (twelve years); secondary school diploma plus vocational certificate (fourteen years); college diploma (fifteen years); and university degree (seventeen years). This variable was transformed to the age when women should be/are expected to obtain each higher level in the educational hierarchy in order to model the changing accumulation of qualifications over the life course.

In addition, a time-dependent dummy variable was computed, indicating whether or not a woman was attending the educational system at any specific age, in accordance with our former theoretical statement, that educational enrollment influences the timing of family formation.

Social origin is measured by father's occupational position, according to the following categories: professionals, skilled white-collars, unskilled white-collars, skilled manual workers, unskilled manual workers, and farmers, with the last being used as a reference category for regression estimates.

In examining historical changes, we distinguished between seven five-year birth cohorts (with about 1200–1500 cases for each). The oldest age group was born in 1929–1933 and the youngest in 1959–1963. Thus our analysis studies the changes in the process of entry into marriage and motherhood over a period of three and a half decades. The oldest cohort entered the marriage market after World War II, and the youngest cohort reached a similar age about the end of the 1970s. In order to control for the effects of historical changes during this period, dummy variables were computed for each cohorts and taking the oldest cohort as the reference group.

TABLE 10.2   Changes in the Timing of Entry into
             Marriage, Measured by Proportions
             Unmarried at Specific Ages (%)

Birth Cohort	Proportion of Unmarried Women at Age						
	20	24	28	32	36	40	44
1959-63	51						
1954-58	48	18					
1949-53	48	15	7				
1944-48	52	17	8	6			
1939-43	52	18	7	5	4		
1934-38	51	17	8	5	4	3	
1929-33	55	21	10	7	5	4	4

Source: Hungarian Social Mobility Survey, 1983
        (weighted data).

Results

Tables 10.2 and 10.3 show the percentages of women remaining unmarried and childless at specific ages by birth cohort. These percentages are based on estimates of survival functions for the events investigated for each cohort.

Table 10.2 presents the changing proportion of unmarried women from the oldest to the youngest cohorts. According to our data, the age at first marriage fell and reached its lowest point for the 1949–1953 and 1954–1958 cohorts. Figures in this table display the effect of postwar 'marriage boom,' but the decrease of ages at entry into marriage continued after the 1950s until about the beginning of 1970s. The so-called 'sexual revolution,' a more widespread use of contraceptives and changes in partnership norms during these twenty years did not lead to an increase of age at first marriage in Hungary.

This trend began to change for the last two cohorts (born 1954–1958 and 1959–1963). Our data indicates that the most important changes in age at entry into marriage occur amongst women aged twenty to twenty-four. Moreover the first two columns of Table 10.2 shows that the age pattern of first marriage is more or less similar for the oldest and youngest cohorts. It means the age at entry into marriage began to increase again in the 1970s.

Table 10.3 displays age pattern for entry into motherhood. The biggest variation across cohorts can again be seen amongst women aged twenty to twenty-four. Age at first birth decreased after World War II as a consequence of the 'baby boom' and the prohibition of legal abortion in the 1950s. The data then indicate a small increase for the 1939–1943 cohort, probably due to the

TABLE 10.3   Changes in the Timing of Entry into
              Motherhood, Measured by Proportions
              Childless at Specific Ages (%)

Birth Cohort	Proportion of Childless Women at Age						
	20	24	28	32	36	40	44
1959-63	67						
1954-58	68	30					
1949-53	70	28	13				
1944-48	74	33	16	11			
1939-43	77	38	17	10	9		
1934-38	74	35	18	12	9	8	
1929-33	76	37	20	15	13	12	11

Source: Hungarian Social Mobility Survey, 1983
        (weighted data).

liberalization of the abortion law at the end of the 1950s. For the subsequent cohorts age at first birth fell continuously, probably due to the pro-natalist population policy measures mentioned earlier. Other statistical sources also show that age at entry into motherhood began to increase slightly after the end of the 1970s, and our data reflect this change of trends: for example the figure at the 1954–1958 cohort at the age of twenty-four may be considered the start of this increase.

Event history models were then applied to find out how the improvement of women's educational attainment had affected timing of entry into marriage and motherhood across cohorts. In these models we also controlled for other important determinants such as dynamic measures of age-dependence, social origin, and birth cohort. The models use metric coefficients, which cannot be compared within models because of the different scales of measurement. Instead, a significance level of variables is applied to evaluate the importance of the variables' influence. In addition, we also compared our models to a baseline using a likelihood ratio test which provides Chi-square values.

Model 1 in Table 10.4 is the baseline model including only the constant rate. In the second step, Model 2 adds the two measures of non-monotonic age-dependence, log (current age - 14) and log (46 - current age). Both estimates are significant proving the presence of a non-monotonic pattern of the observed marriage rate. Since the coefficient of log (46 - current age) is greater than that of log (current age - 14), we have a right-skewed 'bell-shaped' curve for entry into marriage.

TABLE 10.4 Estimates for Models of Women's Rate of Entry into Marriage, Hungary 1983

Variables	Models					
	1	2	3	4	5	6
Intercept	-4.62***	-42.58***	-42.78***	-42.81***	-44.97***	-40.82***
Log(current age-16)		2.15***	2.17***	2.17***	2.14***	1.85***
Log(46-current age)		5.09***	5.13***	5.13***	5.50***	5.02***
Professionals			-0.58***	-0.61***	-0.55***	-0.30*
Skilled white collars			-0.42***	-0.45***	-0.36***	-0.16
Unskilled white collars			-0.35**	-0.38**	-0.33*	-0.13
Self-employed			-0.05	-0.05	-0.09	-0.01
Skilled manual workers			-0.08	-0.10	-0.05	0.07
Unskilled manual workers			-0.03	-0.05	-0.04	-0.01
Cohort 1959-63				-0.01	-0.02	0.15
Cohort 1954-58				0.09	0.08	0.16*
Cohort 1949-53				0.18*	0.18*	0.26***
Cohort 1944-48				0.06	0.05	0.13
Cohort 1939-43				0.04	0.09	0.11
Cohort 1934-38				0.03	0.04	0.05
Is pregnant (dynamic measure)					1.24***	1.18***
In training (dynamic measure)						-1.55***
Level of education (dynamic measure)						-0.01
Number of events	2512	2512	2512	2512	2512	2512
Number of episodes	42854	42854	42854	42854	42854	42854
Log-Likelihood	-9843.3	-8905.4	-8877.9	-8873.8	-8711.6	-8577.1
Chi-Square		1875.8	1930.8	1939.0	2263.4	2532.4
df		2	8	14	15	17

Notes:
*** = significant at level .001; ** = significant at level .01; * = significant at level .05.
Source: Hungarian Social Mobility Survey, 1983 (weighted data).

In the third step, Model 3 introduces dummy variables for father's social position. The estimates show that daughters of professionals, and skilled and unskilled white-collars marry significantly later than the daughters of farmers. However, ages at entry into marriage for women from self-employed, skilled and unskilled manual-worker families do not show any difference. This indicates that the most important cleavage in timing of entry into marriage is between the non-manual and manual families in Hungary.

Model 4 includes historical changes measured by cohort dummy variables. The reference category is the oldest birth cohort (1929–1933). The only significant estimate is the coefficient for the 1949–1953 cohort and this variable has the strongest positive effect which means that women born in this cohort married youngest. This result can be judged as a confirmation of our earlier descriptive finding about a non-monotonic relationship across cohorts (see Table 10.2).

In Model 5 we controlled for the relationship between marriage and motherhood. The time-dependent covariate for being pregnant had a significant positive effect indicating that becoming pregnant leads to an increase in the rate of entry into marriage.

Finally, Model 6 includes the last two variables, measuring educational improvement. Two measurements were used here in order to separate the influence of the level of educational attainment from that of educational enrollment in the family formation process. Our results show that educational enrollment has a strong and significant negative effect and thus generates a delay in timing of entry into marriage. However, level of educational attainment does not significantly affect entry into marriage. It means that women who attend school are 'not ready' for marriage and that the longer participation in the educational system leads to a delay in the entry into marriage. However, the investment made in a higher level of educational attainment does not influence the timing of marriage; educated women marry later because they postpone the transition from youth to adulthood and *not* because they prefer to choose an alternative (personal and economic independence, starting a career of their own) to marriage. This also means that increasing educational attainment only modifies women's transition to adult roles but does not influence their entire adult life in respect of marriage.

As far as effects on entry into motherhood are concerned, we performed a similar type of causal model building as for entry into marriage. (See Table 10.5.) Model 2 displays the pattern of unobserved heterogeneity and the coefficients indicate the same left-skewed 'bell-shaped' curve for entry into motherhood. Model 3 shows that coming from a professional or skilled or unskilled white-collar family leads to a significant delay in the timing of first birth. Model 4 reveals the non-monotonic cohort effects, with the 1949–1953 and 1954–1958 cohorts having the strongest positive effect on rate of entry into motherhood, indicating that these women gave birth to their first child at the youngest age compared to the other cohorts. The significant positive effect of dynamic measurement for being married in Model 5 is the equivalent of the effect of being pregnant in the former model for entry into marriage. Controlling for the interaction of the two demographic events also leads to a change

TABLE 10.5 Estimates for Models of Women's Rate of Entry into Motherhood, Hungary 1983

Variables	Models					
	1	2	3	4	5	6
Intercept	-4.93***	-53.29***	-53.46***	-52.87***	-39.36***	-36.64***
Log(current age-16)		2.98***	3.00***	2.99***	1.47***	1.33***
Log(46-current age)		6.25***	6.28***	6.17***	4.68***	4.38***
Professionals			-0.65***	-0.74***	-0.34*	-0.14
Skilled white collars			-0.33***	-0.41***	-0.06	0.08
Unskilled white collars			-0.46***	-0.55***	-0.37**	-0.23
Self-employed			-0.06	-0.06	-0.05	0.01
Skilled manual workers			-0.12	-0.17**	-0.14*	-0.07
Unskilled manual workers			0.00	-0.05	-0.03	-0.01
Cohort 1959-63				0.20	0.28**	0.40***
Cohort 1954-58				0.25**	0.31***	0.40***
Cohort 1949-53				0.31***	0.26***	0.35***
Cohort 1944-48				0.15*	0.14	0.21**
Cohort 1939-43				0.09	0.06	0.08
Cohort 1934-38				0.05	0.03	0.03
Is married (dynamic measure)					2.71***	2.61***
In training (dynamic measure)						-1.55***
Level of education (dynamic measure)						-0.04***
Number of events	2337	2337	2337	2337	2337	2337
Number of episodes	54105	54105	54105	54105	54105	54105
Log-Likelihood	-9679.9	-8617.4	-8590.6	-8578.6	-7232.6	-7183.7
Chi-Square		2125.0	2178.6	2202.6	4894.6	4992.4
df		2	8	14	15	17

Notes:
***= significant at level .001; **= significant at level .01; *= significant at level .05.
Source: Hungarian Social Mobility Survey, 1983 (weighted data).

in the cohort effects, the non-monotonic pattern almost disappears. It means, that this age pattern is practically mediated by the marriage process.

The most essential model, Model 6 now produces a different result, in this case both educational enrollment and level of educational attainment have a significant effect on the timing of first birth. Thus, educational enrollment produces a delay in the transition to adulthood, and educational investments lead to a delay in entry into motherhood. Contrary to our former finding regarding the timing of marriage, the effect of educational expansion on motherhood does not appear to be limited to the phase of transition from youth to adulthood but influences the birth of child over the whole life course.

Conclusion

This chapter has focused on the social and demographic determinants of family formation in Hungary, paying special attention to the consequences of women's educational expansion, namely the overall increase in educational enrollment and educational attainment in the timing of two essential demographic events. Using retrospective data from the Hungarian Social Mobility and Life History Survey (1983), we described long-term changes in women's educational attainment and women's ages at entry into marriage and motherhood. We then modelled the process of family formation, using educational enrollment and the level of educational attainment as predictor variables and controlling for age-dependent factors, social origin and cohort effects to obtain their estimated effects on rate of entry into marriage and motherhood.

According to our data, educational expansion led to a long-term improvement in women's educational career over the three-and-a-half decades investigated. Changes show a linear trend in the increase of both women's level of educational attainment and their educational enrollment rates, from the oldest to the youngest birth cohort.

Descriptive analysis of timing of marriage and first birth, however, did not show any linear trend but a non-monotonic pattern for the timing of these events. According to the Western European results on this topic presented by the other chapters in this volume, ages at entry into marriage and motherhood fell starting from the pre-war cohorts until the cohorts which entered into the marriage and reproductive age at the end of 1960s, and have been rising again since then. The Hungarian pattern seems to be somewhat different. First, Hungarian women generally enter marriage and motherhood earlier than women in Western societies. Second, the period of 'marriage boom' and 'baby boom' lasted about ten years longer than elsewhere for two reasons: the population policy measures taken to support marriage and especially childbirth; and because of housing problems and—hence—the low proportion of cohabiting couples, meant that—despite improvements—there is still no feasible alternative to marriage for young people in Hungary. Third, the timing of marriage and motherhood also displays certain differences; age at entry into marriage began to increase at the end of 1970s, but age at first birth remained low, despite the decreasing tendency in natality.

An analysis of the causal relationship between these events and the socio-economic determinants revealed differences in effects on entry into marriage and motherhood. The essential point of this analysis has been to present the delaying effect caused by changes in women's educational career due to educational expansion, on the timing of marriage and first birth. In the case of marriage, our model showed that this effect is limited to the period of transition to adulthood. For first birth, however, both educational enrollment and level of educational attainment exert a significant influence on the timing of this event, which means that educational expansion also has a persistent effect on entry into motherhood.

This is probably due to the poor housing conditions in Hungary. That is, after getting married, it takes some years for a couple to obtain residential autonomy. Thus, young couples have two options: to have a child after getting married even if housing conditions are inadequate (for example, they have only one room to live in); or to wait until their housing conditions have improved. This decision is clearly influenced by norms, traditions and cultural level in a certain sense by educational attainment.

Traditionally, less educated people, especially in rural areas, lived in very cramped housing, with an entire family sharing a single room. However, aspirations and perceived needs of the younger generations in respect of modernization and housing conditions have increased markedly in the 1970s and 1980s, due, among other things, to the consequences of educational expansion. There is thus good reason to suppose that this fact contributes to the postponement of marriage, or even more, to that of first birth. Indeed, higher educated women tend to postpone first birth under these circumstances and thus level of educational attainment has a significant delaying effect on timing of first birth in addition to educational enrollment.

We can conclude that the Hungarian case indicates both dissimilarities and similarities with Western European societies in respect of timing of marriage and first birth. Based on a comparative analysis of different countries including Hungary, Coale (1971) concluded that in different populations, under widely different social conditions there is a common curve which describes first marriage frequencies as a function of age for different cohorts of women. On the other hand, according to historical and cultural traditions entry into marriage and motherhood are demographic events which occur to women earlier on in life in Hungary compared to more developed societies. Both developments in the process of modernization and urbanization and women's increasing educational attainment have led to significant changes in family formation in Hungary, but—considering the changes in Western European countries in this respect—Hungary is not much closer to these countries today. That is, despite the improvements, the demographic gap is almost the same. Two main reasons must be mentioned here. First, although the changes in sexual and partnership norms which led to a decrease of marriage and fertility and an increase of cohabitation in the Western countries, can also be observed in Hungary, these changes did not lead to a similar delay in entry into marriage and motherhood because of the lower level of industrialization and modernization. Second, we should mention the so-called 'second economy'—

not to be confused with a black or shadow economy—as an important feature of former Hungarian society, which provided a legal opportunity for about 70–80 percent of families to earn money by taking a second (or even a third) paid job or by producing agricultural products for sale. Since it is especially the men who have these second jobs in the family, while women have one paid job and take care of the household, this 'division of labor' generates special differences in money-making and labor market opportunities for men and women and leads to a continuation of traditional customs and values in family formation despite modernization processes.

As far as future perspectives for patterns of family formation in Hungary are concerned, the direction of the trend is similar to that in Western European societies. The pace of this process, however, depends on the continuation of political, and especially economic, change. Currently, the pullback effect of former state socialism together with that of a 'more traditional' society, can clearly be seen. Nevertheless, it is also clear that the transformation to a modern market economy will ease, for example, the problems caused by housing shortages, and can help to generate higher levels of income which will in turn render the special money-making activities in 'second economy' unnecessary. Hence the modernization process in Hungary means the realization of certain 'technical' conditions of everyday life (such as housing supply), on the one hand, and—partly in consequence—the change of historical and cultural traditions, on the other. The more rapidly Hungarian society continues to develop towards a modern market economy, the more rapidly the patterns of family formation will resemble those found in post-industrial societies, albeit with an initial lag of several cohorts.

Notes

The empirical analysis for this study was carried out in October–November 1990 during the professional visit of the first author to the European University Institute. We are grateful to Johannes Huinink for helpful comments on an earlier version of this text.

1. In particular, the pattern of women's enrollment in university is interesting because it drops far more sharply, indicating that colleges (the lower form of tertiary education) are much more typical form of education for women in Hungary. For more gender-specific differences see, Róbert 1991).

2. The increase of cohabitation has a formal reason as well, namely that the age limit of legal marriages was raised from sixteen to eighteen years in 1987. The 1990 Census found a large increase of cohabitation for those aged fifteen to nineteen years. We have good reason to assume that the majority of these consensual unions are young gypsy couples.

3. On conflicts of transition into adulthood, and the coexistence of dependence and independence of young adults in Hungary, see for example, Róbert and Tóth 1984.

4. Data are available in machine-readable form from the TÁRKI Data Archive Catalogue, No. A39.

5. For techniques of event history analysis see Tuma and Hannan 1984 or Blossfeld, Hamerle and Mayer 1989.

6. If the difference between the ages at first marriage and first birth was not over twelve months, a causal component of 'being pregnant' was included in the model for

marriage and a similar causal component of 'being married' was included in the model for motherhood.

References

Andorka, R. (1978). *Determinants of Fertility in Advanced Societies*, London: Methuen.

Andorka, R. and S. Balázs-Kovács (1986). "The Social Demography of Hungarian Villages in the Eighteenth and Nineteenth Centuries (With Special Attention to Sárpilis, 1792–1804)," *Journal of Family History*, 11:169–92.

Becker, G. (1981). *A Treatise on the Family*, Cambridge (Mass): Harvard University Press.

Blossfeld H.-P., A. Hamerle and K.-U. Mayer (1989). *Event History Analysis*, Hillsdale, New Jersey: Erlbaum.

Central Statistical Office (1983). *Social Mobility and Life History Survey*. Machine-readable data file, distributed by TÁRKI, study number A39 in the TÁRKI Data Archive Catalogue, Budapest: TÁRKI.

Central Statistical Office (1986). *Establishing a Family 1983*, Budapest: Central Statistical Office.

Coale, A.J. (1971). "Age Patterns of Marriage," *Population Studies*, 25:2:193–214.

Csernák, J. (1976). "A nőtlen és hajadon népesség házasságkötési életkorának vizsgálata házassági táblák alapján" (Investigation of Age at Marriage of Single Male and Female Population on the Basis of Nuptiality Tables), *Demográfia*, XIX:2–3: 131–83.

Csernák, J. (1982). "Születési kohorszok elsó házasságkötéseinek alakulása Magyarországon a II," világháború után: (Development of First Marriages of Birth Cohorts after World War II) *Demográfia*, XXV:4:429–64.

Elder, G.H. Jr. and R.C. Rockwell (1976). "Marital Timing in Women's Life Patterns," *Journal of Family History*, 1:34–53.

Goldscheider, F.K. and J. DaVanzo (1985). "Living Arrangements and the Transition to Adulthood," *Demography*, 22:4:545–64.

Hajnal, J. (1965). "European Marriage Patterns in Perspective," in D.V. Glass and D.E.C. Eversley (eds), *Population in History*, London: Edward Arnold.

Hogan, D.P. (1978). "The Effects of Demographic Actors, Family Background, and Early Job Achievement on Age at Marriage," *Demography*, 15:139–60.

Huinink, J. (1987). "Soziale Herkunft, Bildung und das Alter bei der Geburt des ersten Kindes," *Zeitschrift für Soziologie*, Vol.16, No. 5, 367–84.

Klinger, A. (1958). "Magyarország népmozgalma a legutolsó években" (Hungary's Vital Statistics in Recent Years) *Demográfia*, I:1:95–108.

Klinger, A. (1980). "A népesedéspolitikai határozat eredményei, 1973–1979. I–II" (Population Policy Decision and its Results I–II) *Statisztikai Szemle*, Vol.58, No.6, 453–69 and No.7, 565–74.

Klinger, A. and I. Monigl (1981). "Népesedés és népesedéspolitika Magyarországon az 1970-as és 1980-as évtizedben" (Demographic Situation and Population Policy in Hungary in the 1970s and 1980s) *Demográfia*, XXIV:4:395–433.

Koncz, K. (1983). "A núok foglalkoztatásának alakulása és a feminizálódás tendenciája Magyarországon 1890 és 1980 között" (The Employment of Women and the Tendency for Feminization in Hungary between 1890 and 1980), *Demográfia*, XXVI:1: 140–54.

Marini, M.M. (1978). "The Transition to Adulthood: Sex Differences in Educational Attainment and Age at Marriage," *American Sociological Review*, 43:483–507.

Marini, M.M. (1984). "Women's Educational Attainment and the Timing of Entry into Parenthood," *American Sociological Review*, 49:491–511.

Marini, M.M. (1985). "Determinants of the Timing of Adult Role Entry," *Social Science Research,* 14:309–50.

Mészáros, á. and I. Monigl. (1982). "A házasságon kívüli születések és ezek demográfiai összefüggései" (Extra-marital Births and their Interdependence with Various Demographic Factors), *Demográfia,* XXV:2–3:209–24.

Michael, R.T. and N.B. Tuma (1985). "Entry into Marriage and Parenthood by Young Men and Women: The Influence of Family Background," *Demography,* 22:4:515–43.

Miltényi, K. (1971). "A gyermekgondozási segély népesedési és gazdasági hatásai" (The Demographic and Economic Effects of the Childcare Allowance) *Statisztikai Szemle,* Vol.49, Nos. 8–9, 816–26.

Oppenheimer, V. K. (1988). "A Theory of Marriage Timing," *American Journal of Sociology,* Vol. 94, No.3, 563–91.

Rindfuss R. R. and C. St.John (1983). "Social Determinants of Age at First Birth," *Journal of Marriage and the Family,* Vol.45, 553–65.

Róbert, P. and O. Tóth (1984). "Die Institutionalisierung einer neuen Lebensphase durch verz gerten Berufseintritt. überlegung zur aktuellen Situation der Jungerwachsenen in Ungarn," *Angewandte Sozialforschung,* Vol.12, No.4, 311–20.

Róbert, P. (1991). "Educational Transition on Hungary from the Postwar Period to the End of the 1980s," *European Sociological Review,* Vol.7, No.3, 213–36.

Simkus, A. and R. Andorka (1982). "Inequalities in Education in Hungary 1923–1973," *American Sociological Review,* 47:740–51.

Tárkány-Szúucs, E. (1981). *Magyar jogi népszokások* (Hungarian Legal Customs), Budapest: Gondolat.

Tuma, N.B. and M.T. Hannan (1984). *Social Dynamics: Models and Methods.* New York: Academic Press.

PART THREE

Discussion of Results and Conclusions

11

Women's Education and the Costs and Benefits of Marriage

ANNEMETTE SØRENSEN

The collection of studies that make up this book is a good example of how fruitful comparative research can be when it is well planned and well thought out. It also demonstrates that meaningful comparisons between countries can be made even in the absence of strict comparability in terms of the nature and structure of the data and the models estimated. These nine studies take as their central question whether the recent increase in women's age at first marriage and the delay in first births can be seen as a result of the economic independence women are presumed to gain when their educational attainment increases. The studies make several important contributions to existing research on this topic. Two of these are of particular significance because they provide the foundation for the authors to reject the hypothesis that women's independence delays family formation and thus reject the economic theory of marriage, while at the same time maintaining that increases in women's education have contributed to the delay in family formation in recent birth cohorts of women.

First, each study provides highly interesting and hard-to-find data on trends in education and family formation, including trends in non-marital cohabitation. These data show the complexity of the changes that have occurred during this century and they provide clear evidence that there is no simple linear relationship between trends in women's educational attainment and trends in family formation. This raises the question, whether women's education, and the independence that is presumed to come with it, can be seen as a major reason for the recent increases in women's age at marriage and in the postponement of the transition to parenthood.

The second major contribution of these studies is that they, in the pursuit of the answers to this question, estimate the effect of education as two separate effects, namely that of school enrollment and that of educational attainment, net of enrollment. The results of these analyses are first, that school enrollment delays the transition to marriage and parenthood in all of the nine countries studied (with the exception of Italy, where enrollment has no effect on the timing of first births after marital status has been taken into account). Women enrolled in school have significantly lower rates of marriage and first childbirth than women not enrolled. The second result is that the effect of educational attainment, net of enrollment, is not the same in all countries. The net effect of women's educational attainment is strongly negative in Italy, and weakly negative in France and the Netherlands, whereas it is positive in the United States and there is no effect in Hungary, Sweden and West Germany. It is largely this pattern of effects which is taken as evidence against the economic theory of marriage which expects a negative effect of educational attainment, regardless of institutional context. In the following I shall discuss this issue in greater detail.

Does Education Lower Women's Gain from Marriage?

As pointed out throughout this volume, education can affect the timing of marriage in two different ways; marriage may be delayed due to increasing time spent enrolled in school, and the gains from marriage may be reduced by an increase in women's earnings capacity due to higher levels of education. Longitudinal data are needed to distinguish between these two types of effects, and it is the availability of longitudinal data for several countries which makes the analyses presented in this volume unique. The working hypothesis guiding the comparative analysis is that an increase in education will have a delaying effect on the rate of marriage in all countries, but once school enrollment has been taken into account, educational attainment will lower the rate of marriage only in countries where the family is traditional in the sense of having a division of labor that assigns men to market work and women to domestic work. In these societies, it is argued, higher education for women will lower the gains from marriage, as suggested by the economic theory. In societies with more 'modern' family systems, however, the observed negative relationship between age at marriage and education is solely a delaying effect due to longer time spent enrolled in the educational system: education delays the transition to adulthood, but there is no long term effect of educational attainment on the rate of marriage. Empirical support for this hypothesis is found if the effect of women's educational attainment on the rate of entry into marriage is *not* negative once enrollment status has been taken into account.[1]

As already noted, this is indeed what is found in some countries. In Sweden, West Germany and Hungary, no significant effect, and in France and the Netherlands only a small, negative effect of educational attainment is found.

How should we interpret this pattern of effects? It may be tempting to see it as evidence of the failure of economic theory to explain marriage patterns except in countries with a traditional family system with a strict sexual division of labor in the family (Italy). In such countries, an increase in women's education will affect the timing of marriage in two ways: it will have a delaying effect due to school enrollment, and it will lower the gains from marriage so that women with higher education are less likely to marry than others. Exactly as expected by the economic theory.

The question is whether the evidence for other societies really provides a challenge to the insights generated by the economic theory. I would argue that this is not the case, that indeed the pattern of effects reported for the other countries (with the possible exception of the US) is perfectly consistent with the economic theory, and that an interpretation of the data based on that, tells us more about the ways in which more education for women have affected the relations between women and men, than the proposed sociological alternative does.[2]

Let me try to interpret the results of these country comparisons within the framework of Becker's theory.

The theory assumes that marriage between two partners only takes place if they both gain from getting married, and in Becker's formulation the gain is strongly dependent on what is to be gained from a sexual division of labor within marriage. The fact that highly educated women in some societies are as likely to marry as other women (once they are out of school) then suggests that their gains from marriage are no different from other women's. How can that be?

I would argue that there are two factors at work here: men continue to have higher wages and better opportunities in the labor market, and family systems change partly in response to changes in men's and women's educational attainment. The independence argument presented by the economic theory is an argument about wage rates, not about educational attainment as such. Education is used as a proxy for wages, but there is substantial evidence that educational attainment is a far from perfect indicator of a woman's wage rate and career opportunities. This should not be a surprise to sociologists. The implication is, of course, that an increase in women's educational attainment and a closing of the gap in men's and women's education are not synonymous with a closing of the gender gap in wages. Women and men may under these conditions still have something to gain from a sexual division of labor in marriage.

Becker's own arguments about the nature of the sexual division of labor are helpful here. It is *comparative advantage* that drives the process.[3] The spouse with the higher wage rate will be the one to specialize in market work, while the other spouse *either* specializes in house work *or* becomes the one member of the household that will work both in the market and at home (Becker 1981). This is, of course, exactly the new division of labor that has emerged in recent decades.

The closing of the gender gap in education is, as noted above, perfectly consistent with the continuation of men's comparative advantage with respect to wage rates. Therefore, even highly educated women still have something to gain from marriage. But the gain may be smaller than if they had less education, and therefore it becomes crucial to examine what the *costs* are for women to get married. If they turn out to be too high, then they might exceed the benefits, and no marriage will take place.

This is, of course, where changes in the family system, or the modern and traditional family, comes into the picture. In a society, such as Italy, with a traditional division of labor in the family, and with fairly strong negative views of divorce, it seems likely that the costs of marriage may outweigh the benefits for a substantial number of well-educated women. In other societies, where the family division of labor may be more flexible, the costs of marriage are lower for women, because their role in the family and in marriage is more flexible and may be more compatible with employment and pursuit of a work career.

In sum, the extension of education for both women and men, as well as the narrowing of the gender gap in education, have had profound impacts on the early adult lifecourse. It also has had some influence on the timing of marriage, especially for women. The results presented earlier in this volume suggest that this is largely due to a delay resulting from an extended enrollment in the educational system, while the level of education has little or no effect in most countries on the timing of marriage. I have tried to argue that this pattern of effects can be understood perfectly well within the economic theory of marriage. Precisely by using economic theory to understand why there does not seem to be a difference by educational level in the propensity to marry in some countries leads to the conclusion that the increase in women's educational attainment and the closing of the gap between women's and men's educational qualifications, important as they are, have not resulted in fundamental changes in gender relations, because women continue to be at a comparative disadvantage to men with respect to wages and career opportunities in the labor market. In other words, the lack of an education effect on the rate of marriage tells us that the education revolution in Europe and North America during the latter half of the 20th century improved women's educational level tremendously, but did not make them equals with men in the labor market. Similarly, education has improved women's earnings capacity significantly but did not remove their economic dependence on men, and thus reduced the gains from marriage enough to make remaining single more attractive in societies where the costs of marriage remained high.

Women's education has, however, contributed significantly to changing the family from traditional to modern: Women's higher education and better qualifications clearly are important reasons for the increase in married women's employment and thus significant for a change in the sexual division of labor in marriage. Increase in divorce rates can also to some extent be attributed to women's greater economic independence.

Education and the Transformation of Marriage

The next question which these studies can help us to understand better is how the role of the marriage institution as women's only acceptable way to independence of the parental household was changed.

I shall take as my starting point the lack of similarity between the trend in educational attainment for women and the trend in the timing of marriage. As pointed out by Blossfeld, the trend in age at marriage is U-shaped while the trend in education is linear in all countries. If the effect of education at the individual level remains constant over time, then other factors must have worked in the opposite direction of the delaying effect of education on marriage, so that we in fact in some countries see a drop in the age at marriage for cohorts with a relatively high proportion of women with higher education. Alternatively, the effect of education might have been smaller for these cohorts, that is the difference in marriage timing between women with varying levels of schooling was smaller than it had been previously. The data presented earlier in this volume do not allow us to distinguish between these two possibilities, that is we do not have data that will tell us whether very early marriage in some cohorts was the result of a narrowing of education differentials or of a general movement towards early marriage, in which women of all educational levels were equally likely to participate. Data for West-Germany show that the effects of school enrollment and education attainment do not vary by cohort (Blossfeld and Jaenichen 1992). This suggests that the latter explanation is the correct one.

The key to understanding the pattern of early marriage for the first cohorts benefitting from educational expansion is young people's desire to move away from home. When young people have the economic resources to marry, they will do so unless there are other ways for them to become independent of their parents. The move towards very early marriage began at a time when economic conditions made it feasible for young people to marry earlier than their parents had, and it began at a time when cohabitation outside marriage was morally frowned upon and institutionally controlled, for example by policies allocating scarce housing according to marital status (in many European countries) or by laws making sexual relations between unmarried people illegal (in the United States).

The fact that early marriage began first in the United States, then was observed in Northern Europe and last in Southern Europe suggests that economic development is one of the sources of the early transition to marriage.[4] It seems likely, however, that if emancipation from the parental household would have been possible without marriage, that other routes would have been chosen. The cohorts who married very early despite relatively high levels of education were characterized by two things: (1) they had very few alternatives to marriage as a route to independence of one's parents, and (2) young people, especially young men, but increasingly also young women, had the economic resources to establish an independent household. Eventual doubts that well-educated women might have had about the blessings of marriage and its costs for them were overridden by the wish to move away from home as soon as possible. Again, if we use the economic language, the gains from marriage were positive, also for women with more education, not because the costs to women were low, but because the *perceived* benefits were high; the benefits were not high because of gains from the sexual division of labor, but because the marriage contract made independence of the parents possible.

Once marriage lost its functions as the main avenue to independence, the delaying effects of school enrollment came into force and we see an increase in the age at marriage, possibly in part due to an increase in the negative effects of education on marriage.

The question is, of course, why cohabitation outside marriage becomes morally acceptable and quite common in most of the countries we compare here over a fairly short period of time. It is likely that women's education played a major role, but a number of other factors also contributed. Most important among these was the availability of effective contraceptive techniques, which made it easy to have perfect control over fertility, and thus considerably reduced the costs of being sexually active before getting married, at least in countries where the influence of the Catholic church was small. The importance of women's education for the emergence of rather rapid changes in the living arrangements for young adults probably largely reflects a change in the centrality of marriage in the life plans of young women (Buchman 1987). Getting married continued to be important, but completing education and entering the labor market was becoming important as well, and more important than it had been for earlier cohorts of women. Women's *interests* were changed by education, and this in turn meant that if it was possible economically as well as normatively to become independent of one's parents in other ways than by marrying, then many women would prefer that.

In the Nordic countries, where the cohabitation trend began earlier than in other countries (in the mid-to-late 1960's), religious resistance to non-married cohabitation was relatively small, and the economic conditions were quite favorable for young people to establish their own households, even though they were enrolled in higher education. Economic support for students was quite generous, it was relatively easy to get part-time jobs, and the housing market was less tight than it had been since the Second World War. In other countries, education also no doubt changed women's interests in early marriage, but other factors were not nearly as supportive of new living arrangements for young people, and it thus took longer for the cultural diffusion of the nonmarital cohabitation as an acceptable living arrangement to take place.

In conclusion, I would argue that the increase in women's education only begins to delay marriage when cohabitation becomes an alternative route to emancipation from the parental household. Women's education did contribute to the emergence and to the cultural acceptance of non-marital cohabitation largely because women lost interest in early marriage. In societies where economic and cultural constraints did not prevent young women from realizing both their interest in independence from their parents and in pursuing education and work and not just a marriage partner, cohabitation then emerged as the new living arrangement for young people. In societies where the constraints were stronger, the process of change took longer, but it nonetheless has been an important demographic trend in most societies where women receive as much education as men do.

Notes

1. It might indeed be zero or positive. In the latter case the observed association between educational attainment and the rate of marriage would approach zero.
2. I shall here assume that the estimates of the effects of educational attainment are unbiased and thus assume, with the authors, that small or insignificant effects are in-

deed small or nil. This is not necessarily a reasonable assumption. In the statistical models a number of variables are introduced as control variables before the effects of enrollment and educational attainment are estimated. There are two control variables that present potential problems. One of them, pre-marital pregnancy, may capture the effect of educational attainment, or, put differently, there may in fact be a negative effect of education on the rate of marriage, but it is all accounted for by differences in pre-marital pregnancy. Highly educated women may be less likely to marry, because they are less likely to become pregnant. If this is the case, then it would seem that the model specification in fact controls away the effect that we are interested in. Fortunately, results reported by Huinink and Blossfeld (1991) for West Germany suggest that this is not the case; nonetheless the model ought not include pre-marital pregnancy as a control variable.

A potentially more serious problem stems from the inclusion of both age and enrollment status in the models estimating the effect of educational attainment. The control for enrollment status is crucial for the theoretical argument, of course, but the question is whether the control for age in fact truncates the education distribution, possibly resulting in a downward bias in the estimate. The co-variation between age, enrollment status and educational attainment makes the following situation likely: Among young women not enrolled in school, there will be few, if any with a high educational level; conversely among older women enrolled in school, there will be few if any with a low educational level. This should be the case, especially in countries where the educational system is structured so that it is difficult to re-enter the system at older ages (such as Germany's).

3. The comparative advantage perspective also has been applied to the sexual division of labor in a very interesting way by Amartya Sen (1990).

4. Public policy may have a similar effect, as the experience in the Soviet Union and Eastern European countries before 1989 testifies to. In these countries marriage took place very early in women's lives in part because being married and having a child made it more likely that one would get independent housing (Bodrova and Anker 1985).

References

Becker, Gary (1981). *A Treatise on the Family,* Cambridge, MA: Harvard University Press.

Blossfeld, Hans-Peter and Ursula Jaenichen (1992). "Educational Expansion and Changes in Women's Entry into Marriage and Motherhood in the Federal Republic of Germany." *Journal of Marriage and the Family,* 54:333.

Bodrova, Valentina and Richard Anker (Eds.). (1985). "Working Women in Socialist Countries: The Fertility Connection." Geneva: International Labour Office.

Buchman, Marlis. (1987). *The Script of Life in Modern Society,* Chicago: University of Chicago Press.

Huinink, Johannes and Peter Blossfeld. (1991). "Human Capital Investments or Norms of Role Transition? How Women's Schooling and Career Affect the Process of Family Formation." *American Journal of Sociology,* 97:143-68.

Sen, Amartya. (1990). "Gender and Cooperative Conflicts." in Irene Tinker (ed.) *Persistent Inequalities,* New York: Oxford University Press.

12

The Role of Women's Economic Independence in Marriage Formation: A Skeptic's Response to Annemette Sørensen's Remarks

VALERIE KINCADE OPPENHEIMER

In the previous chapter Annemette Sørensen takes issue with some of the major findings in this volume which indicated that women's rising economic independence of men has not been a major factor in the international trend toward more delayed marriage. Sørensen appears quite supportive of the independence argument, particularly as reflected in Becker's specialization and trading model of marriage. Hence, the main thrust of her comments are to explain why we should not trust this apparently negative evidence. My task, as a skeptic of the independence hypothesis, is to comment on Sørensen's critique but, in part, I will do this by questioning the whole conceptualization of the "gain" to marriage as expounded by Becker as well as many others.

Sørensen bases her critique on two major arguments. Since greater economic independence is measured in terms of educational attainment by these studies, the first critique questions the adequacy of *educational* equality as a measure of *earnings* equality which is presumably the critical issue in the declining-gains-to-marriage argument. The second suggests that the reason the trend in the age at marriage has followed a U-shaped pattern over time while educational attainment has been increasingly monotonically is that schooling only starts to have an impact on marriage formation once nonmarital cohabitation provides an alternate route to emancipation from parents but this is a relatively recent phenomenon and hence the effects have not yet been adequately observed. I think there are serious problems with both arguments and will address them in turn. In the process, I will also raise some additional questions about the limitations of the specialization and trading model of marriage.

Education as a Poor Proxy for Earnings

Sørensen argues that the reason why most of the studies in this volume failed to find any substantial negative effect of a woman's greater economic independence on marriage formation is that educational attainment is a poor proxy for earnings and it is really the effect of earnings that the economic theory is making predictions about. Thus while women's educational attainment has risen considerably over time, it is well known that they still remain at an earnings disadvantage compared to men at a similar educational level; hence the gains to a marriage based on the division of labor have persisted, even for more educated women. In essence, then, Sørensen is saying that the independence hypothesis has not really been put to the test yet because of persisting sex differentials in earnings—i.e., women are still economically dependent.[1] However, although the relevance of the education variable is an important concern, a supporter of the economic theory pays a steep price in making this argument. The problem is that there are actually two hypotheses at stake and "saving" one sacrifices the other. The first is whether or not there is such a thing as an independence effect; the second is, if there is, whether it can account for recent trends in marriage formation. By suggesting that the economic theory has not really been tested yet because women's earnings are still well below those of comparable men and hence there has not been any major increase in economic equality, the independence hypothesis may possibly be granted a reprieve but at the price of undermining the whole argument of Becker and others that women's rising employment is *the* major factor behind the dramatic declines in the rate of marriage formation in many European populations as well as in the United States. As a result, we are left without an explanation of these trends. In short, "saving" the hypothesis in this manner also robs it of its explanatory power and makes it empirically uninteresting.

We might also go on to consider the effect of earnings themselves on marriage formation. The articles in this volume used educational attainment as an indicator of potential current and long-term earnings—a strategy commonly employed by economists–because the goal was to analyze whether there were intercohort changes in the effect of women's potential labor-market position on marriage and first birth behavior. Retrospective earnings data were typically unavailable and would probably be of questionable value if they could be obtained. However, recent work in the U.S. on the NLSY cohorts aged 14–21 at their first interview in 1979 and followed annually thereafter[2] indicates that women's earnings (net of their educational attainment and other work-related factors) do not, in fact, have a *negative* impact on marriage formation. On the contrary, the effect of earnings is *positive*, indicating that women who can make a greater economic contribution to a marriage are in a more favorable marriage-market position and/or are more desirous of marrying (Lichter 1993; Oppenheimer and Lew forthcoming). Hence these data, historically and geographically limited though they may be, do not provide any support for the argument that the failure of tests of the independence argument is just because of the inappropriateness of the education variable.

Since the declining-gains-to-marriage argument is largely a product of how the nature of the marriage relationship is conceptualized, it is also important to examine the conceptualization itself rather than just to limit the discussion to empirical tests of the theory. There are two aspects I want to critically examine. The first is the issue of the economic benefits of marriage per se—to both men and women—while the second goes beyond this to question the narrow basis of the marriage relationship envisioned by the theory.

A basic tenet of the independence hypothesis is that as women's earnings approach those of men they will achieve an economic independence of men, thereby reducing their gains to marriage. For men the argument is that as women become less specialized in child-rearing and home production, their gains to marriage are also declining. The possibility of any gains from having an earning wife is not generally considered. I have always found this relative earnings argument and its relationship to the economic gain to marriage generally unpersuasive. First of all, it implicitly assumes there are no economies of scale in sharing a household. However, only if it costs twice as much for two equal earners to live together at the same level of living will there be no mutual economic advantage to combining households. But this is manifestly untrue; there are considerable economies of scale in living as a couple.[3]

The argument seems particularly specious in the case of low earners, each of whose incomes might be too low to bring an individual above the poverty line but could, when combined, support the couple at a moderate level of living. Any lower gains to marriage for such couples may lie more in the uncertainties surrounding the stability of the earnings of either spouse rather than the lowness of the earnings per se. And a relatively high earnings couple may achieve an even more comfortable life style by pooling resources. Even when earnings are *not* equal, strong interdependencies may still exist which may be quite important to the husband as well as the wife if he has relatively few alternative sources of income enhancement—via career advancement, for example—that are on the same scale as his wife's contribution. What is also being overlooked is the fact that people's life styles are increasingly based on a two-earner household. Hence, whether or not a woman can achieve an income equal to an educationally similar man is becoming less and less meaningful since she will rarely be able to achieve a life style comparable to that of the increasingly relevant reference group: the *two*-earner married couple with other similar characteristics (Oppenheimer 1982).

Wives' earnings may also provide an important backup or supplement to husbands' earnings which may suffer due to periodic unemployment or involuntary part-time or part-year employment, ill health, etc. In fact, I would argue that a specialization model such as Becker's is a risky family strategy in societies characterized by a small independent nuclear family system since it makes the family's welfare vulnerable to the temporary or permanent loss of one of the two major specialists—the husband or the wife. Role flexibility and a certain amount of role redundancy seems to be a much more viable strategy for maintaining a family's socioeconomic stability over time in a modern industrialized society.[4]

Examining the problem from a somewhat broader perspective, one should recognize that the notion that the gains to marriage decline for women as their earnings approach that of men is primarily a function of the very narrow (if not impoverished) conceptualization of the nature of the marriage relationship and one which is extremely asymmetric. Women are viewed as the providers of an extremely broad but ill-defined range of home-produced goods and services while men have the much more narrowly defined role of the providers of income and status. As such, provided one assumes that the *economic* advantages to marriage decline as women's employment rises, it inevitably follows that the gains to marriage *in general* will decline because the function of husbands are limited to their economic contribution. But marriage can more reasonably be viewed as a much more complex package of mutual interdependencies than envisioned by Becker's specialization and trading model and one which involves contributions by the husband to the marriage that extend well beyond his income, critical though that may be. For example, it can provide companionship that extends over a long period of time and hence also provides the rewards of a shared past that are not possible with more ephemeral relationships; it involves mutual love and affection as well as sexual gratification and the cohesiveness all these can bring to a marriage; it provides a readily available companion for leisure activities that are often not very pleasurable when done alone; then there are the rewards and mutual support provided by raising children tied to each parent by blood as well as the affection parenting itself instills; finally there are the economic interdependencies derived from the pooling of the market as well as the non-market produced resources contributed by both spouses. This does not exhaust the possibilities nor do all these components characterize all marriages or remain in force throughout the history of any particular marriage but such examples should be enough to indicate that marriages can involve a very varied and large set of mutual rewards (as well as obligations) for both women and men. Hence focusing only on a very narrow set of components, especially in the case of males, provides a very incomplete view of the nature of the relationship and the gains to be achieved in marriage by both spouses. One of the increasing sources of the fragility of marriage, however, may be that it has become too complex a package of interdependencies so that failures of spouses or potential spouses in one arena is more threatening to the marriage than when more is invested in other social relationships that can compensate for imperfections in one area of the marital relationship.

Discussions of the declining-gains-to-marriage arguments also tend to be curiously vague about the alternatives to marriage which remain largely implicit. For example, instead of marriage, will people engage in repeated short-term casual liaisons or are they more likely to involve themselves in longer-term cohabiting relationships but which nevertheless involve very limited commitments and are also periodically subject to breakups? Whatever the nature of the implicit alternatives envisioned, however, there are also fundamental aspects of the process of forming relationships that are being ignored and which should provide insights into what types of unions result. These are the search and transaction costs involved. Searching for a partner is costly:

there are often substantial time costs involved and the necessity of participating in activities that one might otherwise not be particularly interested in doing; there is the constant need to present oneself in a favorable light for new people as well as the psychic costs involved in rejection; there are also the direct money costs involved in searching.[5]

In general, there are at least two aspects of the situation that seem to point toward the continued importance of marriage as a partnership characterized by strong as well as public commitments. One is that since marriage typically involves a multi-dimensional package of mutual interdependencies, this makes it a relatively "efficient" type of social relationship, especially in modern industrial societies characterized by high social and geographical mobility and a very truncated kinship system. And while this package could be broken up into a number of separate relationships, each fulfilling some of its individual functions, this tends to multiply the search and transaction costs involved if these relationships are unstable as may be the case with siblings and friends or may be broken by death as is the case with parents. Second, the number of eligible and desirable partners tends to decrease over time if *other* people wish to make the commitment of marriage even though any given individual may not. And, since search is costly, desirable partners are also likely to demand greater commitments than a more limited contract would involve. In sum, the dynamics of establishing relationships should lead people to form more permanent and institutionalized unions rather than ephemeral relationships characterized by low-level and narrowly defined commitments: scarcities in the availability of desirable partners and the increase in these scarcities over time, the considerable search and transaction costs that finding attractive partners and establishing a relationship often entails, and the resulting bargaining behavior involved in forming such relationships.

Education and Cohabitation

The second part of Sørensen's critique addresses the finding that age at marriage first declined and then increased, all against the backdrop of a monotonic rise in educational attainment—a finding that is also inconsistent with the hypothesized negative effect of completed schooling on marriage formation. Here Sørensen attempts to counter these results by arguing that rising educational attainment will only start to have an effect once marriage is no longer the major means of achieving independence from parents and this has only occurred very recently with the rapid rise in nonmarital cohabitation which Sørensen also partly attributes to women's increasing education. While this might be the case, the arguments presented are not supported by any accompanying strong empirical evidence. First, there is the assertion that "once marriage lost its functions as the main avenue to independence, the delaying effects of school enrollment came into force and we see an increase in the age at marriage, possibly in part due to an increase in the negative effects of education on marriage" (pp. 6–7). However, we have already seen that no such negative effect has emerged so far, despite the strong upward trend in nonmarital cohabitation, and the lack of a significant negative cohort/education interaction also does not support this argument. Moreover, once again, Sørensen has defended the theory by arguing that conditions have not yet been ripe for it to come into effect, thus once more leaving us without an explanation of the substantial changes that have already occurred. Furthermore, as the article on the U.S. in this volume indicated, rising school-leaving ages per se did not have a major impact on delaying marriage much less the effect of higher levels of schooling themselves. A second assumption is that the main reason young people married at an early age in the postwar period was to obtain independence from their parents. This may be the case but, once again, Sørensen cites no empirical evidence to support this contention. Nor are marital or nonmarital cohabitation the only ways of leaving one's parental household. It is certainly possible for young people to cut expenses by sharing apartments and other living expenses with others of the *same* sex. This would be particularly feasible for those with greater educational attainments since their market earnings would be greater and this kind of educational effect would not depend on achieving earnings comparable to that of potentially eligible males and hence should show up as an absolute education effect. However, in the United States, at least, we were unable to observe any real educational differences in the proportions married for those recently out of school and this pattern has remained relatively unchanged over time. Moreover, a considerable amount of independence of parents can be achieved by college and university students through living in dormitories or other student living arrangements, suggesting that more extended schooling can provide a substitute for marriage in achieving a greater independence of parents.

Finally, Sørensen also argues that education was an important (though not the only) factor in the increase in nonmarital cohabitation, thus apparently subscribing to the commonly held view that cohabitation was pioneered by the more educated. However, Bumpass and Sweet (1989) have shown, for the U.S., that cohabitation has been historically most prevalent among the *less* educated and continues to be so to this day (as discussed by Oppenheimer, Blossfeld and Wackerow in this volume). Moreover, the U.S. does not appear to be alone in this pattern (Hoem 1986; Villeneuve-Golkap 1991). Sørensen's argument also implies that cohabitation is largely serving as a substitute for marriage. However, the evidence in the U.S. and several of the countries examined in this volume is that a substantial proportion of cohabitations end in marriage and hence operate as part of the courtship process rather than as a substitute for marriage. All in all, the hypothesized interaction between rising educational attainment and increasing cohabitation does not appear to be a highly plausible explanation for the lack of a strong negative effect of education for the studies included in this volume.

Conclusion

In her chapter commenting on the implications of the research reported in this volume Sørensen has argued that the lack of evidence in support of the economic independence hypothesis is largely because the negative impact of women's improving economic position has not yet really been observed.

Women are not actually as economically independent of marriage as their rising educational attainment might suggest; moreover the delaying effects of education only really come into play as nonmarital cohabitation becomes a viable alternative to achieving independence from one's parents. The basis of my critique of these positions is that, although I believe they have intrinsic empirical and theoretical problems, more importantly they "save" the independence argument by making it incapable of explaining the enormous changes in marriage behavior already observed. Hence such a defense, in effect, tries to win the battle at the expense of losing the war.

Going beyond these issues, I have also argued that basing the economic independence hypothesis on the notion of a very narrow specialization and trading model, such as Becker proposes, has severe problems. Contrary to the hypothesis, the economic gains to marriage for women should persist even if they achieve earnings equality with educationally similar males and the earnings of wives can also increase the gains to marriage for men as well as increase the economic stability of the family unit over time. Furthermore, marriages involve a bundle of interdependencies and hence if a woman achieves earnings equality this will not, *ipso facto*, reduce the gains to marriage, even if one assumes no economies of scale in living as a couple. Finally, I have argued that the dynamics of forming heterosexual relationships in a modern society plus the multifaceted nature of such relationships greatly raises the search and transaction costs of substituting casual or even more long-term partnerships of very limited commitment. This too should help support marriage as a major institutional form in our society.

Notes

1. Nevertheless, if there has been some increase in the relative earnings position of women, which is implied by the long-term decline in sex-differentials in completed schooling, we should observe an appropriate interaction effect of educational attainment with cohort. However, this was not found in these studies. In the U.S., the reverse is actually the case: the positive effect of completed schooling on marriage formation was significantly greater for younger cohorts.

2. The NLSY refers to the National Longitudinal Survey of Labor Market Experience, Youth Cohorts (Center for Human Resource Research 1992).

3. For an interesting discussion along these lines which makes a similar argument, see Lam (1988).

4. For a more extensive discussion of this issue, see Oppenheimer 1994.

5. Becker (1981) does bring in the notion of search and search costs but mainly in his discussion of divorce rather than marriage formation. For a more extensive discussion of the application of search models to marriage timing, see Oppenheimer 1988. See also the lengthy discussion of marriage market searches, transaction costs and implicit contracts in England and Farkas (1986) which is along the lines of the argument made here.

References

Becker, G. (1981). *A Treatise on the Family,* Harvard University Press, Cambridge, MA.
Bumpass, Larry L. and J. Sweet. (1989). "National Estimates of Cohabitation," *Demography,* 26, 615–625.

Center for Human Resource Research. (1992). *NLS Handbook: 1992. Center for Human Resource Research,* Ohio State University.

England, P. and G. Farkas. (1986). *Household, Employment, and Gender,* Aldine, New York.

Hoem, J. (1985). "The Impact of Education on Modern Family-Union Initiation." *European Journal of Population,* 2, 113–133.

Lam, D. (1988). "Marriage Markets and Assortative Mating with Household Public Goods: Theoretical Results and Empirical Implications," *The Journal of Human Resources,* 23, 462–487.

Oppenheimer, V. (1994). "Women's Rising Employment and the Fate of the Family in Modern Industrial Societies," *Population and Development Review,* 20 (June).

_____. (1988). "A Theory of Marriage Timing: Assortative Mating Under Varying Degrees of Uncertainty," *American Journal of Sociology,* 94, 563–591.

_____. 1982. *Work and the Family: A Study in Social Demography,* Academic Press, New York.

Oppenheimer, V. and V. Lew. (Forthcoming). "American Marriage Formation in the Eighties: How Important Was Women's Economic Independence?" In *Gender and Family Change in Industrialized Countries,* Edited by Karen Oppenheim Mason and An-Magritt Jensen, Oxford University Press.

Villeneuve-Gokalp, C. (1991). "From Marriage to Informal Union: Recent Changes in the Behaviour of French Couples," *Population* 3, 81–111.

PART FOUR

How the Other Half Lives

13

Education, Work, and Family Patterns of Men: The Case of West Germany

JOHANNES HUININK

Despite the existence of relatively recent studies which present findings for both women and men (Marini 1985, Rindfuss, Morgan and Swicegood 1988, Huinink 1987, Bumpass and Call 1989, Diekmann 1990, Witte 1990, 1991), investigations of family formation have tended to concentrate on women. This is also true for the previous chapters of this volume. Detailed theoretical discussions and empirical analyses of the family formation patterns of men are rare (Marini 1978, Oppenheimer 1988), so we do not know much about them. However, in this last chapter for the case of West Germany, we have studied the determinants of men's marriage and fertility behavior in greater detail. The central question of this analysis then is whether the impact of particular life conditions and life events in the process of transition to adulthood, such as the likelihood to marry and to have children, are different for men, and to what extent this depends on patterns of sex-role segregation.

The main thesis is the following: As it is shown in the previous chapters of this volume, the pattern of family formation for women (timing and events) are regulated to a large extent by women's educational participation, educational inequality, and prospects in the labor market. For men, we propose, their placement and career in the occupatinal structure is also decisive. However, for them, good prospects in the labor market, a good occupational position and good income are prerequisites for family formation activities, and are positively correlated with the prevalence of marriage and childbirth. The arguments, we assume, are such that one could expect a similar pattern of men's family formation patterns in most of the countries analyzed in previous chapters.

The first part of the chapter is devoted to theoretical considerations and applies Oppenheimer's approach for the explanation of 'trends and differentials in marriage timing' (Oppenheimer 1988) in order to develop a hypotheses on the changing structure of the family formation process of men in contrast with women. The data and variables used in the multivariate models of the timing of marriage and the entry into parenthood of men in the former Federal Republic of West Germany are presented in the second part of the chapter. This is followed by a presentation of the findings of the descriptive analyses and a discussion of the estimated effects of various factors applied in these models for the three-year birth cohorts 1929–1931, 1939–1941, and 1949–1951.

Determinants of Men's Family Formation

A theoretical approach, based on the impact of social norms on individual life plans and opportunities, would argue that people expect partners to marry and have children only when they can afford to do so (Rindfuss, Morgan and Swicegood 1988). The affordability of a family with children depends on the economic situation and the income of the partners. This means, above all, that at least one of the partners must guarantee a stable income for the family, and in the case of strong sex-role segregation this is the male partner (Parsons 1959). Men are consequently expected to have stable employment with good prospects of advancement before they are regarded as eligible for marriage and ready for fatherhood.

Thus, in line with the findings for women (Galler 1979, Blossfeld and Huinink 1991, Witte 1991), the first hypothesis is that *marriage should be very rare for men during phases of education and unemployment*. Secondly, in contrast to the findings for women, *there should be a positive impact of education and, in particular, of vocational training, on the transition to marriage*. Thirdly, *it is expected that the level of the socio-economic status and income works in the same direction*.

In a recent contribution to the theoretical framework on the timing of entry into marriage by men and women, Oppenheimer (1988) proposes an approach borrowed from economic job-search theory. When people start the mate-selection process, Oppenheimer argues, they try to minimize uncertainty regarding the choice of a suitable partner. Thus, in early adulthood they enter into a more or less 'costly' search process. The uncertainty surrounding the 'matching' of the attributes of potential partners increases the likelihood of making an unsuccessful match. A young person's opinion as to what constitutes a suitable partner may be ambiguous in the early phases of the transition to adulthood and will change over the life course, and young people are often uncertain about their own future plans and life options. Moreover, the future attributes of potential partners are more or less uncertain or unknown. Thus, the avoidance of early marriage and fatherhood means avoiding early restrictions on future opportunities. During the early phase of transition to adulthood young people may not consider themselves 'at risk' of marriage except in the event of an unexpected pregnancy for the female partner.

Oppenheimer differentiates between a regime of traditional sex-role segregation and a regime of egalitarian gender-relationships. Her point of departure is Becker's economic theory of the family which supports a strong sex-specific division of labor between the partners in a household (Becker 1981), with a match being considered optimal when the partners fulfill the requirements of an optimal division of labor, organized in the following way: the man is assumed to take responsibility for the welfare production of the household exclusively by non-household work. This does not mean that the woman cannot also engage in non-familial work, but that she will spend more of—or even all—her time in the household and rearing children. The man as the breadwinner (Davis 1984) has to provide sufficient financial support for the family. Even today, in a phase of changing sex-role norms in the former Federal Republic of West Germany, women must still take into account that they face serious disadvantages in their work-lives when a child is born (Huinink 1989a). Consequently, it should still be the case that only those men who are able to guarantee a stable economic situation for a family are attractive to women as potential partners and fathers. Therefore, assuming a traditional pattern of modern family formation, as long as there is little prospect for young men to establish stable employment, they will tend to delay marriage. Additionally, men with a lower level of qualifications and lower occupational status will tend to be disadvantaged in the mating process. They will marry later and a higher proportion will never marry at all. At the other end of the skill scale, men with high level of education have to delay marriage while they are enrolled in the educational system. Considering the changing conditions in the marriage market one would expect to find a higher proportion of unmarried (and childless) men not only in the low qualification group, but also in the high qualification group).[1] However, after completing education and training, and after starting their work-life one would expect them to marry at a high rate.

Assumptions as to the impact of the change in sex-role patterns lead to hypotheses about the overall change in the transition rates to marriage. First, an overall delay of marriage is expected for men and women in more recent cohorts. One reason is that the change in sexual norms and in cohabitational patterns has reduced the pressure for early marriage. Another reason is that, as we know, an increasing proportion of women in the younger cohorts finished school and entered their first employment at a later age than their counterparts in older birth cohorts. In this case women try to avoid an early transition to marriage for the same reasons as men: they are uncertain about their individual life plans. Additionally, for men the period of uncertainty as regards their future life status of their potential partners has been prolonged.

Second, hypotheses on the change in the impact of the social status of men on their prospects of marriage can differ greatly. On the one hand, one can assume that the aspirations regarding the occupational achievement of the male partner remain high, and that family formation without a solid basis in terms of work and income will lead to social deprivation. At the same time the individual and social pretension connected with parenting have risen (Kaufmann 1988): parents' claims and current societal expectations regarding the quality of the care and upbringing of children are now preconditioned by the need for a well-established economic base. Furthermore, when women try to continue working after the birth of a child they incur relatively high childcare costs. Is there any reason why a woman should not continue to search for a man with a good occupational position and higher income for marriage and family formation? That is, by "setting higher standards for the minimally acceptable match" (Oppenheimer 1988, 587). Such a partner may be able to guarantee that his spouse does not have to interrupt her employment because of childbirth and can provide the resources needed for childcare arrangements (Schütze 1992). This would mean that one has to expect little change in the effects of the male work-life on the transition rates to marriage over cohorts.

On the other hand, higher education and occupational positions and the higher level of economic independence of women, as well as a more egalitarian relationship between men and women could help reduce the effects of the past and current socio-economic conditions of men. Compared to the traditional regime, the criteria for a successful match appear to have been reshaped. The search process is no longer governed to the same extent by the trnasition rate to marriage and the birth of the first child (Huinink 1987, Blossfeld and Huinink 1991).

Level of Education

The level of education is included as a time-dependent variable. Each level of education, depending on the actual status in the educational career, is measured by the required number of years to obtain it.

Activity Status

Current activity is measured by two time-dependent covariates. I differentiate between phases of education or training and being in the labor force, with being out of the labor force as the reference category. In the case of employment, I also observed the socio-economic status of the respondent using the same socio-economic scale as for the father. In addition, I included the mean income of the respondents in each employment episode.[2]

Partner Attributes

In the model estimating the rate of entry into marriage one very important time-dependent variable was included, indicating whether the female partner of the respondent was pregnant or not. In the case of pregnancy, I expect a strong increase of the marriage rates. In the model for the transition rate to fatherhood for married men I included two variables measuring other important attributes of the spouse of the respondent; the educational attainment of the spouse measured by the required years to obtain the reported level, and the time-dependent indicator of whether the spouse is employed or not. From studies on family formation among women we know that the labor force participation of women in Western countries plays a decisive role in the process of family formation (Huinink 1989a). A strong negative effect of this indicator is expected.

Male Unemployment Rate

Finally I included an indicator for an aspect of the macro-economic conditions in the model: the unemployment rate of men. It is assumed that high unemployment rates indicate unfavorable labor market conditions. This may indicate a higher probability for the emergence of an unstable work situation or insecure prospects in future work-life. Therefore high unemployment rates are expected to correspond with lower transition rates to criteria of a partner's social status, and love and personal compatibility now come into play far more than before. As a result, indicators of men's socio-economic status may become less relevant.

With respect to entry into fatherhood, most of the arguments mentioned in this section hold true (Rindfuss, Morgan and Swicegood 1988, Falaris 1987). For men, we can assume that the positive impact of a potentially promising work-life on the likelihood of marriage will be even stronger with respect to the birth of the first child. One of the preconditions of fatherhood is a stable economic family situation and *not only* an emotionally stable partnership or marriage. After the birth of a child, it is still normal for the man to be the sole guarantor of the household income, particularly given that even today in the former Federal Republic of West Germany the entry into motherhood forces many women out of employment.

Data and Operationalization of Variables

Data from the German Life History Study (GLHS) (Mayer and Brückner 1989) were used for the empirical test of the hypotheses. The life histories of 2,171 West German respondents born 1929–1931, 1939–1941, and 1949–1951 were collected retrospectively, of which 1,089 males respondents made up the sample. This was reduced to 1,067 after excluding cases with missing values. I observed the family and occupational career of men aged seventeen to fifty-five; even though men could marry or become fathers either before or after these ages, this interval covers these events for the great majority.

The multivariate models include five classes of covariates (background variables, level of education, activity status, partner attributes and as macro-indicator, the male unemployment rate.

Background Variables

Using indicators of cohort membership I have attempted to test overall trends in the timing of marriage and the birth of the first child. I also included an indicator for the size of the city where the respondents lived when they were fifteen years old. It is assumed that growing up in a large city has a delaying effect on both marriage and the birth of the first child. The indicator is coded 1 when the city has more than 100,000 inhabitants and 0 otherwise (Huinink 1987). Another assumption is that the number of siblings is negatively correlated with the proportion of never-married and childless men respectively. The same is assumed with respect to a variable measuring the importance of

TABLE 13.1   Percentage of Unmarried Men at Specific Ages by Cohort and Level of Education

	Proportion of Unmarried Men at Age					
	20	24	28	32	36	40
Cohorts:						
1949-51	97	62	35	24		
1939-41	98	65	26	13	10	9
1929-31	98	71	31	13	7	5
Level of education:						
Low	98	69	35	21	16	
Middle	98	61	24	11	6	
High	100	87	60	38	20	

Source: German Life History Study.

religion in the everyday life of their parental household. Finally, I used a measure of the socio-economic status of the father as an indicator for the social status of the parental family (see Mayer 1979), expecting it to have a negative, partial effect on marriage and the birth of the first child (de Cooman, Ermisch and Joshi 1987).

Empirical Analyses

Descriptive Results

Vital statistics and other previous demographic research indicate that in the former Federal Republic of West Germany the mean age for marriage of single males was about twenty-six in the 1930 cohort, declined to just over twenty-five years in the 1945 cohort, and will probably rise again to over twenty-six years for the 1955 cohort. In the 1930 cohort, about 95 percent of the men married at least once. The figure for the 1947 cohort is about 83 percent, and will probably be about 75 percent for the 1955 cohort (Schwarz 1988). It is well known that married men in the former Federal Republic—as elsewhere—are on average two to three years older than their spouses. Men also leave the parental household later than young women, regardless of whether they marry at the same time or not (Wagner and Huinink 1991). On average, the educational attainment of husbands was higher than that of their spouses; Ziegler (1985) found that for about 50 percent of all marriages in older birth cohorts (people born between 1900 and 1935) the educational level of the husband is higher than that of his spouse. For younger cohorts the percentage has declined to about 40 percent in the 1946–1956 cohort.

Tables 13.1 and 13.2 present the specific patterns of the timing of family formation events among men of different cohorts and educational attainment for the sample. I have distinguished between three levels of educational attain-

TABLE 13.2   Percentage of Childless Men at Specific
              Ages by Cohort and Level of Education

	Proportion of Childless Men at Age					
	20	24	28	32	36	40
Cohorts:						
1949-51	98	84	61	40		
1939-41	99	78	44	24	18	15
1929-31	97	80	51	28	17	13
Level of education:						
Low	97	79	50	30	23	
Middle	98	79	47	24	17	
High	99	96	81	57	27	

Source: German Life History Study.

ment: lower secondary school qualification and intermediate school qualification without any vocational training (Low); lower secondary school qualification and intermediate school qualification with vocational training (Middle); and upper secondary school qualification with or without training or a university degree (High).

It is clear from Table 13.1 that there has been an overall trend towards earlier entry into marriage (Table 13.1) and fatherhood (Table 13.2) from the 1929–1931 cohort to the 1939–1941 cohort in the former Federal Republic and that this overall trend reverted for the successive cohorts, despite a considerable proportion of men who married fairly young in the 1949–1951 cohort. The figures for respondents with different educational attainment are in line with expectations: the members of the 'Middle' group start family formation first, followed by the 'Low' group; men with upper secondary school education (High) marry and have the first child latest; and the proportion of never-married and childless men is also the highest in the 'Low' and the 'High' groups.

Table 13.3 gives a descriptive analysis on the propensity to marriage and fatherhood of men in different activity statuses. By counting the events and relating them to the 'at-risk' person-months in these activity statuses one can estimate transition rates depending on the respective activity status. We see that for all cohorts nearly all marriages and first-order births occurred when the respondents were employed. There is no major difference between marriage and entry into fatherhood.[3] The difference between the number of respondents who were enrolled in school or training when their partner became pregnant and who were enrolled at the time of the birth of the first child shows that few of them interrupted their educational career because of entry into fatherhood.

Multivariate Analyses

The different models estimating the effects of covariates on the transition rate to marriage and entry into fatherhood have been constructed on the basis of a

TABLE 13.3   Descriptive Analysis of Entry into Marriage and
Fatherhood during Various Activity Statuses

		Cohort		
		1929-31	1939-41	1949-51
Event: Marriage[a]				
In school/				
in training	# events	10	11	21
	# months at risk	8310	11032	17985
Employed	# events	193	201	159
	# months at risk	25187	25192	18355
Not employed	# events	0	7	12
	# months at risk	1454	1730	3429
Event: Birth of the first child				
In school/				
in training	# events	9	12	17
	# months at risk	13229	15986	22759
Employed	# events	286	297	179
	# months at risk	49159	44218	30978
Not employed	# events	6	8	15
	# months at risk	3022	2582	4525
Event: "Pregnancy"				
(8 months before the birth of the first child)				
In school/				
in training	# events	16	17	25
	# months at risk	13134	15867	22582
Employed	# events	277	292	170
	# months at risk	46909	41856	29582
Not employed	# events	8	8	16
	# months at risk	2956	2518	4410

Note:
[a]Only those marriages which started at least 8 months before a
childhool were included.
Source: German Life History Survey.

stepwise procedure of log-rate regressions. The life course of respondents was split into one-month episodes ti starting at seventeen and ending at fifty-five, until the date of the analyzed event or the interview, whichever occurred first. Assuming the rate is constant in each month estimated then:[4]

$$r(t_i) = \exp[\beta_1 X_1 + \beta_2 X_2(t_i) + \beta_3 X_3(t_i)].$$

X_1 is a vector of time-constant covariates; $X_2(t_i)$ is a vector of time-dependent covariates, measured at the beginning of each time interval ti, and X_3 is a vector of age-specific covariates. They generate a continuous approximation of the baseline age pattern of the transition rates by a logistic approach (Huinink 1989b, Blossfeld and Huinink 1991).
That is, $X_3 = [\beta_1 A_1(t_i) + \beta_2 A_2(t_i)]$ and:

$A_1(t_i) = \log(\text{current age at } t_i - 17)$
$A_2(t_i) = \log(55 - \text{current age at } t_i)$

If $\beta_1 < \beta_2$ the estimated curve is left-skewed which is expected to be the case in the models for entry into marriage and fatherhood.[5]

Entry into Marriage

Table 13.4 shows the estimates of the β-coefficients of the covariates in several models of transition rates to marriage giving the t-values in parentheses.[6] How can these findings be interpreted?

Age, Cohort, and Background Variables. In each model the comparison of the coefficients of the age variables points to a left-skewed bell-shaped pattern of the age-specific baseline rate as expected and requires no further comment. In Models 1 to 5 the contrast between the cohorts reported in Table 13.1 proved to be insufficiently strong to generate significant cohort effects.

Only one of the four background variables—the socio-economic status of the father—plays a major role in the models. In almost all of them the effect of this variable is significantly negative. This means that coming from a higher status family of origin corresponds with a delay of marriage. One can argue that a higher social status of the parents leads to greater economic and social opportunities for the offspring and to more individual non-traditional beliefs and value orientations so that they can afford to wait longer to marry. They may also have to wait longer because, assuming that they aim to marry a partner from a suitable social background, a higher proportion of their eligible female counterparts will avoid early marriage (Blossfeld and Huinink 1991).

Level of Education. All models show a positive effect for the level of education, but in no model it is significant.[7] Only when activity status is not controlled for is the effect significant and positive. Therefore, it is the activity status and the socio-economic condition which are the decisive factors and not the level of education.

Activity Status, Socio-economic Status, and Income. As can be seen from the positive β-coefficient in Model 2, being employed is an essential prerequisite for men in order to marry.[8] Being in training means avoiding marriage; even compared non-employed men, men who are in training have significantly lower transition rates to marriage.

The inclusion of socio-economic status and mean income (Model 3) leads to a further substantial improvement of the model fit. The higher the socio-economic status of the job, the higher the transition rate to marriage, as expected from earlier theoretical discussion. In Model 3 the effect of employment status drops. The significant improvement of fit shows that socio-economic status itself plays a substantial role in addition to labor force participation whereas income is not as decisive. Although positive, the effect of the mean income is not significant in any model of Table 13.4.

Pregnancy of Partner. After the occurrence of a pregnancy for the respondent's female partner, the transition rate to marriage increases dramatically. This probably happens relatively frequently during training as the inclusion of the pregnancy indicator reduces the training effect considerably.

Cohort Interactions and Period Effects. The last models include cohort interactions with education and socio-economic status as well as the annual unem-

TABLE 13.4 Estimates for Models of the Rate of Entry into Marriage for Men (T-values in parentheses)

Variables	1	2	3	4	5	6
Intercept	0.292 (0.70)	-0.624 (1.26)	-0.271 (-0.54)	-0.991 (-1.93)	-0.986 (-1.92)	-0.542 (-1.02)
Log (current age - 17)	2.021* (13.13)	1.937 (12.36)	1.724 (12.14)	1.719 (11.04)	1.719 (11.01)	1.710 (10.85)
Log (55 - current age)	5.374* (9.58)	5.407* (9.50)	5.488* (9.55)	4.666* (8.26)	4.637* (8.19)	4.854* (8.34)
Cohort 1929-31	Reference Category					
Cohort 1939-41	0.030 (0.34)	0.027 (0.31)	-0.187 (-0.21)	0.015 (0.17)	-0.003 (-0.02)	-0.464 (-2.60)
Cohort 1949-51	-1.176 (-1.27)	-0.058 (-0.61)	-0.151 (-1.44)	-0.057 (-0.54)	-0.121 (-0.80)	-0.470 (-2.77)
Socio-economic status father/100	-0.187 (-2.82)	-0.119 (-1.63)	-0.171 (-2.30)	-0.151 (-2.03)	-0.146 (-1.95)	-0.143 (-1.92)
Urban residence at age 15	-0.017 (-0.57)	-0.011 (-0.35)	-0.009 (-0.30)	-0.008 (-0.25)	-0.007 (-0.23)	-0.004 (-0.12)
Number of siblings	0.006 (0.31)	-0.003 (0.18)	0.005 (0.30)	-0.014 (-0.78)	-0.014 (-0.76)	-0.012 (-0.69)
Role of religion	0.015 (1.05)	0.020 (1.35)	0.017 (1.16)	0.018 (1.22)	0.019 (1.26)	0.019 (1.24)
Level of education (time dependent)		0.038 (1.75)	0.013 (0.58)	0.014 (0.59)	0.014 (0.60)	0.022 (0.91)
Non-employed		Reference Category				
In training (time dependent)		-0.378 (-2.54)	-0.334 (-2.25)	-0.264 (-1.77)	-0.263 (-1.77)	-0.251 (-1.70)
Employed (time dependent)		0.369 (3.07)	0.037 (0.24)	-0.173 (-1.01)	-0.173 (-1.11)	-0.131 (-0.84)
Socio-economic status respondent/100 (time dependent)			0.204 (2.51)	0.332 (4.10)	0.298 (2.61)	0.202 (1.74)
Mean income/100 (time dependent)			0.013 (1.77)	0.006 (0.82)	0.050 (0.67)	0.051 (0.70)
8 months before first birth (time dependent)				3.269* (38.40)	3.270* (38.30)	3.257 (38.20)
Socio-econ. Status * Cohort 1939-41					0.026 (0.19)	0.122 (0.88)
Socio-econ. Status * Cohort 1949-51					0.081 (0.60)	0.219 (1.58)
Unemployment rate						-0.067 (-4.47)
Number of events	789	789	789	789	789	789
Number of episodes	89682	89682	89682	89682	89682	89682
CHI-SQUARE	387.24	430.34	441.75	1271.43	1271.43	1291.63
Degrees of freedom	8	11	13	13	18	19

Note:
* Significant at the 0.05 level

Source: German Life History Survey.

ployment rate for men. Even though there seems to be an increasing positive impact of socio-economic status on the transition rate to marriage over cohorts, particularly in Model 6, none of the coefficients is significant. One can conclude that there is at least no weakening of the relevance of the social status of male respondents from cohort 1929–1931 to cohort 1949–1951. The question of what will happen for more recent cohorts will certainly merit further investigation.

The unemployment rate shows a strong negative effect, but one has to be very cautious when interpreting it. The strong change in the coefficients of the cohort indicators shows that there is a considerable correlation between these variables and the unemployment rate. However, introducing this macro-indicator leads to a significant increase of the overall model fit. Indeed, it points to the expected fact that a deterioration of the economic prospects of men leads to a delay or an avoidance of family formation. However, this finding needs to be confirmed on the basis of an analysis with a larger range of cohorts and periods. Let us compare these findings for men with those for women (compare Chapter 3, Blossfeld and Huinink 1991). The logic of action differs between men and women at the point of completed occupational training and successful entry into an occupational career. Men and women at this point are ready to marry, especially if their training has taken a long time. For men, the transition rate to marriage increases significantly with the level of the occupational position achieved. A good qualification is an important prerequisite for this task. For women of the same cohorts, we also find the shift in the marriage rates after leaving the educational system. However, there is no substantial effect of the occupational position (Blossfeld and Huinink 1991).

Entry into Fatherhood

Table 13.5 presents the results for models of the transition to fatherhood. Models 1 to 4 of Table 13.4 are based on all men irrespective of their marital status. Most variables from the marriage model are also included here and—with the exception of the income variable—Model 1 in Table 13.5 is similar to Model 3 in Table 13.4. In my discussion of the models in Table 13.5 I have concentrated on those findings which differ from the marriage model.

Age, Cohort, Background Variables, and Level of Education. In these models the transition rate to fatherhood in the 1949–1951 cohort is significantly lower than in the older cohorts. This reflects a stronger decline in the birth rates than in marriage rates. From analyses of the family formation of women we know that the trend of delaying the birth of the first child starts earlier than the trend of delaying marriage (Huinink 1989a). On the one hand, social norms and—until the early 1970s—even law, urged young couples to marry if they wished to live together. On the other hand, the rise in the proportion of women who stayed employed after marriage has in particular led to a considerable delay in entry into parenthood. Moreover, growing up in a large city leads to a significant delay of the entry into fatherhood for married men (Huinink 1987), while the social status of the father has no further effect on the timing of this event.

TABLE 13.5 Estimates for Models of the Rate of Entry into Fatherhood (T-values in parentheses)

Variables	1	2	3	4	5
Intercept	0.094 (0.16)	-5.476* (-8.96)	-5.327* (-7.80)	-5.408* (-7.80)	-1.281 (-1.68)
Log (current age - 17)	2.415* (12.29)	0.556 (3.17)	0.540 (3.06)	0.450 (2.79)	0.397 (11.01)
Log (55 - current age)	5.807* (10.37)	4.008* (8.14)	4.127* (8.31)	4.053* (8.16)	3.997* (6.19)
Cohort 1929-31	Reference Category				
Cohort 1939-41	-0.036 (0.38)	0.061 (0.65)	0.002 (0.03)	0.139 (0.22)	-0.114 (-0.63)
Cohort 1949-51	-0.251 (-2.38)	-0.469 (-4.37)	-0.576 (-5.22)	-0.682 (-1.08)	-0.887 (-3.95)
Socio-economic status father/100	-0.095 (-1.17)	0.073 (0.86)	0.006 (0.74)	0.073 (0.86)	0.021 (0.22)
Urban residence at age 15	-0.046 (-1.35)	-0.094 (-2.74)	-0.096 (-2.80)	-0.103 (-2.91)	-0.087 (-2.28)
Number of siblings	0.026 (1.37)	0.025 (1.26)	0.023 (1.16)	-0.022 (1.11)	-0.009 (0.44)
Role of religion in parental household	0.037 (2.35)	0.025 (1.67)	0.021 (1.40)	0.017 (1.08)	0.026 (1.58)
Level of education (time dependent)	0.012 (0.52)	0.014 (0.56)	0.015 (0.55)	0.038 (0.93)	0.041 (1.28)
Non-employed	Reference Category				
In training (time dependent)	-0.517 (-3.28)	-0.365 (-2.00)	-0.336 (-1.82)	-0.317 (-1.72)	-0.102 (0.46)
Employed (time dependent)	0.158 (0.32)	0.077 (0.43)	-0.038 (-0.19)	-0.096 (-0.52)	0.271 (1.25)
Socio-economic status respondent/100 (time dependent)	0.187 (2.30)	0.025 (0.29)	-0.060 (-0.67)	-0.104 (-1.21)	-0.134 (-1.36)
Married (time dependent)		3.725* (25.46)	3.718* (25.39)	3.713* (25.27)	
Mean income/100 (time dependent)			0.017 (3.64)	0.015 (1.76)	0.012 (1.84)
Education of the spouse					-0.064 (-2.17)
Spouse employed (time dependent)					-0.428 (-4.19)
Income * Cohort 1939-41				0.007 (0.70)	0.007 (0.51)
Income * Cohort 1949-51				0.026 (2.24)	0.026 (2.08)
Unemployment rate				-0.029 (-1.68)	-0.053 (-2.75)
Number of events	658	658	658	658	573
Number of episodes	119624	119624	119624	119624	22776
CHI-SQUARE	484.19	1711.43	1722.49	1729.61	297.55
Degrees of freedom	12	13	14	19	19

Note:
* Significant at the 0.05 level

Source: German Life History Survey.

Activity Status, Socio-Economic Status, and Income. If marriage status is not controlled for, the socio-economic status of the respondent has a similar impact on the transition rate to fatherhood as on marriage (Model 1 in Table 13.5). However, this effect diminishes after controlling for marriage status. A higher socio-economic status supports the entry into marriage and only leads indirectly to a higher propensity to fatherhood. At this point, the financial indicator of the quality of men's work life, which reflects the economic condition of the family, becomes increasingly important (Model 3). A higher mean income favors an entry into fatherhood net of the effect of social status. As the estimates of Model 4 show, this effect differs significantly over cohorts, with income becoming more important for the younger cohorts. These results again confirm the general hypothesis that for men the prospect of stable employment is a necessary precondition for parenthood, since men are still regarded as the primary breadwinner in the family (Davis 1984). The better the economic conditions of the partners, the more confident partners are with respect to future plans for family formation and raising children. We see from Chapter 3 in this volume and Blossfeld and Huinink (1991) that this is, as expected, contrary to the findings for women.

Partner Attributes. If education and the activity status of the female partner are controlled for, no major changes in the coefficients of the other covariates can be observed (Model 5 in Table 13.5). As expected, strong negative effects of the level of education and the labor force participation of the spouse are found.

Summary

In this analysis I have investigated the determinants of the timing and incidence of marriage and fatherhood for West German men. In contrast to the findings for women, the analyses of the hypotheses on the relevance of a stable work life, higher social status and a favorable economic situation for men starting a family 'career' have been confirmed. Moreover, in accordance with the theoretical discussion, and in line with the findings for women, there is a long delay for entry into fatherhood in the youngest cohort. We know that this is also true for marriage in cohorts born after 1950 (Schwarz 1988). However, what was found for the male members of the 1929–1931, 1939–1941, and 1949–1951 cohorts does not support an expectation of substantial change in the impact of completed training, skilled employment and financial stability on family formation. There is no indication of a decreasing relevance of the economic position of men for family formation in the cohorts examined.

This pattern appears to fit precisely with the assumption of an enduring traditional form of family formation in West German society, irrespective of changes in the societal position of women. However, I already presented an alternative explanation for the continuing relevance of men's socio-economic conditions on their opportunities and intentions with respect to marriage and fatherhood. First, assuming a more egalitarian relationship between partners, good economic prospects of the male partner need not be a source of destabilization of the occupational career of the woman, and could even support their stability in the case of motherhood; second, the economic and financial burden of a family is strong and has increased in recent times, and raising children needs a solid economic basis (Kaufmann 1988). One could then ask whether parenthood will become the privilege of members of upper level social status groups. Indeed, aspects of social inequality could once again become highly important for union formation and parenthood, in spite of, or even because the development of the family is not governed by traditional norms, but is more the result of a decision process where aspects of social and ⸗conomic status of—primarily—men and women (Huinink 1989b) will play a major role in the future.

Notes

1. Aspects of the marriage market situation—although they do not contribute as much to an explanation of the timing of marriage—do play an important role as they help to explain the quality of the match and why a rising proportion of the never-married continue a long-term search or phases of moratorium with respect to family formation (Goldman, Westoff and Hammerslough (1984).

2. It would be interesting to look at the effects of major changes in the income of respondents. One could assume that notable shifts in income increase the propensity for marriage and the birth of the first child.

3. Only those marriages which began at least eight months before a childbirth have been included here.

4. For the expression of likelihood, see for example Blossfeld, Hamerle and Mayer (1989).

5. The reasons for modelling the baseline age pattern in this way are discussed in Blossfeld and Jaenichen (1990).

6. Estimates which are differ significantly from 0 (on the level of 0.05) are printed in italics.

7. There is no linear effect of education on the transition rate to marriage. In particular vocational training has a strong positive impact on transition rates to marriage, in spite of the attained level of education. It is only for untrained men with an upper secondary school education that we find a fairly strong negative effect on the transition rate to marriage.

8. I also estimated models including discrete indicators for different periods of duration of employment. These variables did not contribute any significant improvement to the model fit (Witte 1991).

References

Becker, G. (1981): *A Treatise on the Family,* Cambridge (Mass.): Harvard University Press.

Blossfeld, H.-P., A. Hamerle, and K.-U. Mayer (1989): *Event History Analysis. Statistical Theory and Application in the Social Sciences.* Hillsdale: Erlbaum.

Blossfeld, H.-P. and J. Huinink (1991): "Human Capital Investments or Norms of Role Transition? How Women's Schooling and Career Affect the Process of Family Formation." *American Journal of Sociology* 97(1):143–68.

Blossfeld, H.-P. and U. Jaenichen (1990): "Bildungsexpansion und Familienbildung. Wie wirkt sich die Höherqualifikation der Frauen auf die Neigung zu heiraten und Kinder zu bekommen aus?" *Soziale Welt* 41(4):454–76.

Bumpass, L.L. and V.R.A. Call (1989): *The Timing of Marriage and Education.* University of Wisconsin-Madison: Center for Demography and Ecology.

de Cooman, E., J. Ermisch, and H. Joshi (1987): "The Next Birth and the Labour Market: A Dynamic Model of Births in England and Wales." *Population Studies* 41:237–68.

Davis, K. (1984): "Wives and Work: The Sex-role Revolution and Its Consequences." *Population and Development Review* 10:397–417.

Diekmann, A. (1990): "Der Einflu;ds schulischer Bildung und die Auswirkungen der Bildungsexpansion auf das Heiratsverhalten." *Zeitschrift für Soziologie* 19(4):265–77.

Falaris, E.M. (1987): "An Empirical Study of the Timing and Spacing of Childbearing." *Southern Economic Journal* 54(2):287–300.

Galler, H.P. (1979): "Schulische Bildung und Heiratsverhalten." *Zeitschrift für Bevölkerungswissenschaft* 5:199–213.

Goldman, N., C.F. Westhoff, and C. Hammerslough (1984): "Demography of the Marriage Market in the United States." *Population Index* 50(1):5–25.

Huinink, J. (1987): "Soziale Herkunft, Bildung und das Alter bei der Geburt des ersten Kindes." *Zeitschrift für Soziologie* 16(5):367–84.

Huinink, J. (1989a): "Ausbildung, Erwerbsbeteiligung von Frauen und Familienbildung im Kohortenvergleich," in G. Wagner, N. Ott, J.-J. Hoffman-Nowotny (eds.), *Familienbildung und Erwerbstätigkeit im demographischen Wandel,* proceedings from the 23rd Arbeitstagung der Deutschen Gesellschaft für Bevölkerungswissenschaft, 28 February–3 March 1989, Bad Homburg v.d.H., Berlin: Springer, 136–58.

Huinink, J. (1989b): "Das zweite Kind. Sind wir auf dem Weg zur Ein-Kind-Familie?" *Zeitschrift für Soziologie* 18(3):192–207.

Kaufmann, F.-X. (1988): "Familie und Modernität," in K. Lüscher, F. Schultheis, M. Wehrspaun (eds.), *Die "post-moderne" Familie—Familiale Strategien und Familienpolitik in einer übergangszeit.* Konstanz: Universitätsverlag, 391–416.

Marini, M. M. (1978): "The Transition to Adulthood: Sex Differences in Educational Attainment and Age at Marriage." *American Sociological Review* 43:483–507.

Marini, M.M. (1985): "Determinants of the Timing of Adult Role Entry." *Social Science Research* 14:309–50.

Mayer, K.-U. (1989): "Berufliche Tätigkeit, berufliche Stellung und beruflicher Status— empirische Vergleiche zum Klassifikationsproblem," in F. U. Pappi (ed.), *Sozialstrukturanalysen mit Umfragedaten. Probleme der standardisierten Erfassung von Hintergrundsmerkmalen in allgemeinen Bevölkerungsumfragen.* Königstein: Athenäum, 79–123.

Mayer, K.-U. and E. Brückner (1989): "Lebensverläufe und Wohlfahrtsentwicklung. Konzeption, Design und Methodik der Erhebung von Lebensverläufen der Geburtsjahrgänge 1929–1931, 1939–1941, 1949–1951" (Materialien aus der Bildungsforschung Nr. 35). Berlin: Max-Planck-Institut für Bildungsforschung.

Oppenheimer, V. K. (1988): "A Theory of Marriage Timing." *American Journal of Sociology* 94:563–91.

Parsons, T. (1959): "The Social Structure of the Family," in R.N. Anshen (ed.), *The Family: Its Function and Destiny.* New York: Harper.

Rindfuss, R.R., S.P. Morgan, and G. Swicegood (1988): *First Births in America: Changes in the Timing of Parenthood.* Berkeley: University of California Press.

Scheller, G. (1985): "Erklärungsversuche des Wandels im Heirats-und Familiengründungsalter seit 1950." *Zeitschrift für Bevölkerungswissenschaft,* 11(4):549–76.

Schütze, Y. (1992): "Geburtenrückgang und Kinderwunsch," in E. Voland (ed.), *Fortpflanzung: Natur und Kultur im Wechselspiel. Versuch eines Dialogs zwischen Biologen und Sozialwissenschaftlern.* Frankfurt: Suhrkamp, 170–88.

Schwarz, K. (1988): "Familienpolitik und demographische Entwicklung in den Bundesländern nach dem Zweiten Weltkrieg. Ein Beitrag zur Abschützung der demographischen Wirkungen familienpolitischer Ma;dsnahmen" (Materialien zur Bevölkerungswissenschaft, Heft 57, Band 1+2). Wiesbaden: Bundesinstitut für Bevölkerungsforschung.

Wagner, M. and J. Huinink (1991): "Neuere Trends beim Auszug aus dem Elternhaus," in G. Buttler, H.-J. Hoffmann-Nowotny, G. Schmitt-Rink (eds.). *Acta Demographica 1991*. Heidelberg: Physica, 39–62.

Witte, J.C. (1990): "Entry into Marriage and the Transition to Adulthood Among Recent Birth Cohorts of Young Adults in the United States and the Federal Republic of Germany" (DIW Discussion Paper No. 17). Deutsches Institut für Wirtschaftsforschung, Berlin.

Witte, J.C. (1991): "Discrete Time Models of Entry into Marriage Based on Retrospective Marital Histories of Young Adults in the United States and the Federal Republic of Germany" (DIW Discussion Paper No. 23). Deutsches Institut für Wirtschaftsforschung, Berlin.

Ziegler, R. (1985): "Bildungsexpansion und Partnerwahl," in S. Hradil (ed.), *Sozialstruktur im Umbruch. Karl Martin Bolte zum 60. Geburtstag*. Opladen: Leske und Budrich, 85–106.

About the Book

This is the first book to systematically track postwar changes in family formation in Western Europe and the United States. Cohabitation and motherhood outside of marriage have become more widespread at the same time that women's social roles are evolving. Women are attaining higher levels of education, marrying at an older age, more frequently working outside the home, and have more reproductive freedom due to new advances in contraception.

In this original collection of essays, sociologists and demographers from eight Western European countries and the United States use longitudinal data to compare national variations and explain the connection between the new role of women and family formation in postwar society. The contributors provide a thorough review of the social demographic literature to advance a variety of hypotheses about the relationships between changing women's education and family formation outcomes, which are empirically examined and compared across countries.

About the Editor
and Contributors

Hans-Peter Blossfeld is professor of sociology at the University of Bremen and External Professor of Sociology at the European University Institute in Florence. He has published in the fields of social stratification, educational sociology, life course research, demography and statistical methods.

Jenny de Jong Gierveld is director of the Netherlands Interdisciplinary Demographic Institute in the Hague and professor of social research methodology at the Vrije Universiteit, Amsterdam. She has published on numerous topics including transitions in the lives of young adults, the living arrangements and social networks of the elderly, and loneliness.

Margarita Delgado is a sociologist specialized in population and human ecology. She is a demography researcher in the High Council of Scientific Research and databank director at the Centre of Sociological Research in Madrid. She has published on fertility, marriage and family formation and is currently working on adolescent fertility in Spain.

Alessandra De Rose is a statistician at the Italian Ministry of Health and temporary professor of demography at the University of Salveno Benevento. She has published on fertility, marriage and divorce in relation to the female condition.

Britta Hoem is senior statistician in the Forecasting Institute of Statistics Sweden, Stockholm. Previously she was a research associate in the Demography Unit of Stockhom University. She is a demographer who has published on gender equality and on family dynamics and its interaction with women's labor force participation.

Johannes Huinink is scientific researcher at the Max Planck Institute for Human Development in Berlin, Germany. He is a sociologist and has published on a range of topics relating to family development, female labor force participation, methods and concepts of analyzing life course data, and multilevel modelling in the social sciences.

Kathleen E. Kiernan is senior research fellow in demography at the London School of Economics. She has published widely on a range of topics relating to the family, including leaving home, cohabitation, marriage, divorce, fertility and singlehood.

Éva Lelièvre holds a joint research post as Chargé de recherche at the Institut National d'Etudes Démographiques in Paris and Research Officer at the London School of Economics. She is a demographer who has published in the field of life event history analysis and co-organized in 1991 a European Survey on Family and Employment.

266 About the Editor and Contributors

Henri Leridon is Directeur de recherche at the Institut National d'Etudes Démographiques in Paris. His main research work is on fertility and the family; he has published several books in the INED series and authored *Human Fertility: The Basic Components*.

Aart C. Liefbroer is a researcher at the Netherlands Interdisciplinary Demographic Institute in The Hague. He is a sociologist and has published mainly on union formation processes. His current research focusses on living arrangements of the elderly and life-course related changes in household composition.

Valerie Kincade Oppenheimer has been professor of sociology at the University of California–Los Angeles since 1969. She is a social demographer who has published extensively on the relationship between work and family behavior over the life cycle. Currently she is engaged in research on marriage formation and how it is affected by the ease or difficulty of the transition to a stable work career.

Antonella Pinnelli is professor of social demography at the University 'La Sapienza,' Rome. She was previously director of the Department of Demography. She has published on a range of topics including the female condition and fertility, the family, infant health and aging.

Peter Robert is associate professor at the Institute for Sociology of the Eotvos Lorand University, Budapest and is head of the research department at the Social Science Information Center (TÁRKI). He was previously senior research fellow at the Institute for Political Sciences of the Hungarian Academy of Sciences. He is a sociologist who has published on a range of topics relating to social stratification, social mobility and reproduction of social inequalities.

Götz Rohwer is assistant at the University of Bremen and was previously research fellow at the European University Institute in Florence. His current research interests are in methodological and empirical studies using event history and panel data.

Annemette Sørensen is a sociologist and demographer working as a senior scientist at the Max Planck Institute for Human Development and Education in Berlin. She has published in the fields of gender relations, sociology of the life course, and comparative studies of economic well-being.

Laurent Toulemon is Chargé de recherche at the Institut National d'Etudes Démographiques in Paris. Together with Henri Leridon, he conducted the INED 1988 Fertility Survey (retrospective studies on contraceptive behavior, pregnancies, fecundity and *de facto* marital situations). He is currently working on fertility intentions.

Achim Wackerow is research associate at ZUMA in Mannheim in the department of microdata, specializing in social science program development and applications. He has published on high-speed algorithms and program utilities to store and process very large data sets. He also works as a research consultant dealing with the efficient application of statistical program packages.